Social Cognition

Social Cognition

Studies of the
Development of Understanding

Edited by

George Butterworth

Lecturer in Psychology,
University of Southampton

and

Paul Light

Lecturer in Psychology,
University of Southampton

THE HARVESTER PRESS

First published in Great Britain in 1982 by
THE HARVESTER PRESS LIMITED
Publisher: John Spiers
16 Ship Street, Brighton, Sussex

© 1982, The Harvester Press Ltd

British Library Cataloguing in Publication Data

Social Cognition—(The Developing
Body and Mind; 2)
1. Cognition in children
2. Social psychology
I. Butterworth, George
II. Light, Paul   III. Series
155.4'13   BF723.C5

ISBN 0 7108 0095 9

Typeset by The Wessell Press, Hagworthingham, Spilsby, Lincs
Printed in Great Britain by Mansell (Bookbinders) Ltd, Witham, Essex

Contents

Contributors

George Butterworth
Department of Psychology
University of Southampton
England

John Churcher
Department of Psychology
University of Manchester
England

Donald Clementson-Mohr
Department of Psychology
Denison University
Ohio
U.S.A.

Julie Dockrell
Department of Psychology
University of Stirling
Scotland

Martin Glachan
Department of Psychology
University of Southampton
England

David Hamlyn
Department of Philosophy
Birkbeck College
University of London
England

Paul Harris
Department of Experimental Psychology
University of Oxford
England

Paul Light
Department of Psychology
University of Southampton
England

Irene Neilson
Department of Psychology
Glasgow College of Technology
Scotland

John Newson
Department of Psychology
University of Nottingham
England

Tjeert Olthof
Department of Developmental Psychology
The Free University
Amsterdam
Holland

Michael Scaife
Department of Social Psychology
University of Sussex
England

John Shotter
Department of Psychology
University of Nottingham
England

Chris Sinha
Hester Adrian Research Centre
University of Manchester
England

Peter Smith
Department of Psychology
University of Sheffield
England

Colwyn Trevarthen
Department of Psychology
University of Edinburgh
Scotland

Preface

'Social cognition' is presently amongst the liveliest research topics in the psychology of child development, yet it remains one of the most difficult areas to define. Rather than being characterised by any one identifiable common factor of content or theory, a complex network of relationships links a variety of researches under the same umbrella.

At one level social cognition can be seen in terms of a demarcation dispute between two areas of study which have historically been quite separate: that of individual cognitive development on the one hand and social and affective development on the other. Topics traditionally within the preserve of the latter, such as shared reference, attachment and emotional development are now being approached from a cognitive standpoint, with the focus being on the child's developing understanding. At the same time, issues once firmly within the domain of 'cold blooded cognition', such as concept formation, conservation and equilibration are now being approached from a social standpoint, and cognitive tasks are being considered in terms of their social-interactional aspects. If nothing else, it is clear that the traditional demarcations are no longer supportable.

At another level of analysis, some of the recent research in social cognition can be seen as readdressing a fundamental conceptual issue that has long lurked behind the scenes. This concerns the social nature of knowledge. In what sense, if any, is human understanding necessarily social? To what extent do basic terms in cognitive psychology, such as intentionality or judgement, presuppose a social process? These questions are, of course, as much philosophical as psychological.

This volume will, we hope, offer a valid picture of current thinking on these topics. The chapters have been organised into four sections, although there is considerable overlap. Section one focusses on conceptual issues. The first chapter, by Butterworth serves an introductory function and offers a closer analysis of the concept of 'social cognition' than we have attempted in these prefactory remarks. He notes the tendency to draw dichotomous distinctions in this field, as for example between the physical and the social, or the individual and the social, and he suggests that these might more profitably be regarded as elements within dialectical relationships. More generally, he emphasises the need for a clearer conceptual analysis of individual and social aspects of knowing. The chapters which follow contribute to such an analysis.

Hamlyn's chapter tackles the problem of knowledge in its philosophical aspect. Knowledge is, and must be, social, he argues, since it depends upon criteria for the truth and falsity of judgements which are necessarily socially derived. Hamlyn also stresses the sense in which knowing one thing always involves knowing a great deal more. This 'embeddedness' of knowing is re-emphasised by Shotter and Newson in the chapter which follows. They attempt to shift the focus of attention in the study of cognitive development away from processes developing independently within the child, towards changes in the child's effective environment. Taking Gibson's approach to visual perception as their model, they offer a 'social-ecological' view of cognitive development, in which they argue for a directly perceptible ecology of the social world. Their notion of direct perception is reiterated by Clementson-Mohr in the final chapter of this section. He examines the social learning theory approach to imitation and its development and finds it unsatisfactory. While social learning theorists have been forced to postulate cognitive mechanisms as responsible for the 'matching' behaviours observed in imitation, they have not been able to offer a convincing account of *what* the underlying cognitive mechanisms are. The basic problem is *how* imitation is possible and this is, at one and the same time, a problem in social and cognitive psychology. The 'direct perception' of equivalence of self and others offers a solution to this problem in social-cognitive terms.

The second section 'Origins of Social Cognition in Infancy' contains three chapters which may throw further light on the origins of social cognition in universal processes of perception and action observable in infancy and early childhood. Trevarthen makes a powerful case for the fundamental role of human social motives in laying the foundations for cognitive growth. A wealth of research on the human infant shows that from the neonatal period onward the baby is 'competent', being in possession of psychological processes that enable him or her to engage with objects and events in the world. Trevarthen argues that the function of much of this competence is to allow the infant to relate to other human beings, and that this has often been overlooked in the search for simple, 'parsimonious' explanations. He argues that it is time to return to a more holistic analysis, in which the study of psychological processes is made from the perspective of the functional systems that psychological mechanisms serve. In particular he emphasises mechanisms allowing reciprocity in interpersonal relations basic to symbolism and language. In their chapter, Churcher and Scaife extend this analysis in considering the origins of referential communication in process of joint visual attention to objects and environment by the mother and her infant. From a purely structural point of view, such interactions have no obvious connection with language but from a functional analysis it soon becomes apparent that looking and pointing can play a basic role in the acquisition of language. Gesture has its roots in early cooperative action. In the final chapter of this section, Sinha extends the argument to the social negotiation of concepts in early childhood. Again, he takes a functional approach to the problem of concept formation and argues that humans in interaction display qualitative features of cognitive processes not apparent at the individual level. In particular, aspects of meaning may emerge from socially constituted functional descriptions of objects which then become interiorised by the developing child as a part of the cognitive system. He describes a series of investigations which examine the child's concept of a cup. Containment, the 'canonical' function of a cup, comes to be understood both in terms of the perceptual attributes of the cup and in terms of the set of social and functional relations into which it enters in joint activity. The case is made that cognitive development is *both* an individual and a social process.

Part three, 'Social Cognition and Affect' contains two chapters which address the relationship between cognitive and emotional development. The universality of emotional experience and expression has been recognised since Darwin's time and the importance of affect as the 'cement' of social relations is apparent from the earliest age. Indeed, as Smith points out in his chapter, the literature on attachment and caretaking presupposes an important link between affective and social development. He reconsiders Bowlby's thesis on monotropism in the light of recent experimental evidence and concludes that infants are not harmed by the experience of a limited number of caretakers. It is clearly the case that the constraints that exist on the formation of attachment bonds have their roots in cognitive processes but the precise nature of these processes has not yet been established. This should be a matter for urgent consideration in future research. The next chapter by Harris and Olthof is on children's cognitive appraisal of their own emotions; the metacognition of emotional development. This is a topic that readily fits into a burgeoning literature on children's capacity to reflect upon psychological processes, and Harris' results are readily understandable in terms of Piaget's stages. Here the emphasis is on the process of understanding emotion as an 'object' of experience. The social cognition of affective development still awaits a holistic analysis of the role of affect in establishing and maintaining social relations, which in turn feed into elaboration of the cognitive system itself.

The final section 'Social Cognition and Intellect' deals with the evaluation of cognitive tasks as social interactions. Neilson and Dockrell review recent studies of Piagetian tests of operational thinking which have shown how social factors can have a dramatic bearing on outcome. These studies suggest that the test situation must be considered as an interaction between tester and child, in which the child is drawing on a wide range of cues to interpret the adult's requests and instructions. Neilson and Dockrell argue that this issue is of more than methodological significance. While defending Piaget against what they see as unjustified criticism, they acknowledge that developments in this field may eventually necessitate a major reappraisal of the nature of cognitive and linguistic development.

Glachan and Light concern themselves with social interactions not in a testing but a learning situation. The importance of peer interaction in learning, hinted at by Piaget in the 1930s, has only recently become a focus of sustained empirical evaluation. Glachan and Light review this work and present new evidence of the powerful impact which joint engagement on a task can have upon subsequent individual performance. Under certain conditions it would appear that interaction between two unsuccessful strategies can produce a successful one. It is argued that such 'symmetrical' social interactions may provide an important impetus to the cognitive growth of the individual.

It is apparent that 'social cognition' is a polymorphous topic, certainly it encompasses a variety of aspects of behaviour and experience that have not previously been juxtaposed. It remains to be seen whether the underlying concern with the criteria for objective knowledge, which links such diverse issues, will serve as the unifying force for lasting changes in cognitive and social developmental psychology. We hope that this book will increase the likelihood of such an outcome.

George Butterworth
Paul Light
Department of Psychology, University of Southampton
July, 1981

Acknowledgements

This book has its origin in a number of papers, now extended and revised, originally presented at the Annual Conference of the Developmental Section of the British Psychological Society, at the University of Southampton, England, in September 1979. For reasons of space and balance we were not able to include all the papers we would have wished, but we gratefully acknowledge the contributions of all the conference participants to the issues discussed and elaborated here. Thanks are also due to the committee of the Developmental Section, particularly Mr Peter Barnes, for help in organising the meeting. The full abstracts are available in *The Bulletin of the British Psychological Society*, 1980, *33*, 93-9.

PART I

CONCEPTUAL ISSUES

1 A brief account of the conflict between the individual and the social in models of cognitive growth
George Butterworth

> The active sense of living, which we all enjoy before reflection shatters our instinctive world for us, is self luminous and suggests no paradoxes. When the reflective intellect gets to work however, it discovers incomprehensibilities in the flowing process. Distinguishing its elements and parts it gives them separate names and what it thus disjoins it cannot easily put together.

William James. The thing and its relations. 1912. Reprinted 1947, p.92.

Introduction

It has often been claimed that scientific progress occurs when different conceptual frameworks come into conflict at the boundaries between disciplines and that attempts to reconcile differences between points of view will generate a new and more harmonious understanding of the phenomena under investigation. The developmental study of 'social cognition', at the border between cognitive and social developmental psychology, exemplifies the principle of creative conflict in a variety of ways. In this brief introduction, some of the sources of conflict which will be addressed in the chapters that follow, will be reviewed.

In its most general sense, social cognition can be defined as 'knowledge of others'. Its study consists both in the investigation of the social content of children's minds and in a variety of theories of the acquisition of objective knowledge itself. Since influences come from so many directions, various conflicts arise between explanatory constructs. For example conflicts occur between those who advocate 'individual' as opposed to 'social' approaches to knowledge; between accounts of knowledge in terms of the properties of 'physical' as opposed to 'social' objects, or even between biological, psychological and sociological levels of discourse. This brief discussion may lead us further towards a work-

3

able explanation of the role of social factors in cognitive growth.

Perhaps the first pre-requisite is to establish a more precise definition of social cognition. Barker & Newson (1979) define it as 'how children of different ages construct a relation between themselves and the social objects of knowledge'. It is immediately clear that such a definition goes beyond the question of the social content of children's minds and pre-supposes a dialectical theory of cognitive growth; that knowledge of others necessarily involves parallel forms of self knowledge. This approach has several advantages, the individual and the social are not considered mutually exclusive but as mutually complementary objects of knowledge. Another advantage is that the study of metacognitive processes can be brought under the umbrella of 'social cognition', whereby the child comes to reflect upon the workings of its own mind (and the minds of others) as if from the viewpoint of another (see for example the chapter by Harris and Olthof). A disadvantage however may lie in Barker and Newson's emphasis on *the construction* of social knowledge, since this might be taken to imply that social objects may not be directly accessible to immediate experience.

The question whether it is necessary to construct social objects in development will be addressed in the following pages, as will the problem of disentangling the interacting effects of the child's own cognitive structures with structures in the physical and social environment. How do individual and social factors enter into the process of thinking about the emotions, perceptions and thoughts of others? The approach adopted is firstly to outline the recent history of the topic of social cognition. Then, two apparently diametrically opposed theories within the tradition of cognitive developmental psychology will be briefly compared. These are the 'individualistic' approach of Piaget and the 'social' approach of Vygotsky. Throughout this introduction, comments will be made on the implicit assumptions of various theories that have given rise to false dichotomies and consequently needless conflict in the explanation of social reasoning.

The recent rise of 'social cognitive' psychology.

The major influences in the recent rise of a cognitive psychology of social development can be gleaned from the various reviews of the area published in the later 1970's (e.g. Shantz 1975, Chandler 1977, Kuhn 1978, Damon 1979, Barker & Newson 1979) as well as two recent texts (Doise 1978, Perret-Clermont 1980). The reader is referred to these articles for an extensive overview since the intention here is simply to raise the major issues.

Perhaps the greatest impetus in the rise of 'social cognition' was a certain disaffection within two kinds of mainstream psychology, the behaviourist social learning theories on the one hand and the Piagetian structuralist approach to cognitive development on the other. Kuhn (1978) contrasts these as the 'mechanistic' and 'organismic' approaches; the former focussing on overt behaviour, conceptualised as discreet behavioural elements under environmental control, the latter focussing on cognitive structures internal to the organism. The problem with each type of theory is that the mechanistic approach leaves unanalysed the role of the individual's cognitive processes in social learning, while the cognitive approach leaves unanalysed the specific role of the environment in generating cognitive structures (except perhaps as touched upon in the Piagetian concept of horizontal décalage, which is specifically concerned with the 'resistance' of various environments to assimilation by various cognitive structures). Kuhn maintains that, in a sense, Piagetian cognitive developmental psychology has characterised the social environment in a relatively passive or unstructured fashion, while social learning theory has made the same mistake with respect to the child.

Leaving aside the question of whether this is a fair description of either approach, the prospect of a reconciliation between the cognitive developmental and behaviourist frameworks seems somewhat distant. At the very least, this would require a clear account of the cognitive structures that are prerequisites for social learning to supplement learning theory and a description of the social ecology to supplement cognitive theory (see chapters by Clementson-Mohr and by Shotter and Newson for further elaboration of these points). However, a basic incompatibility between the cognitive and behaviourist traditions may preclude any such rapprochement. Certainly, a dissatisfaction with 'cold-blooded' cognition on the one hand and social learning theory on the other may have contributed to the rise in studies of 'social cognition' but it has not led to a new theoretical synthesis.

As yet, neither a social psychology of cognitive development nor a cognitive psychology of social development has emerged from the study of social cognition. Instead, theories have been imported from cognitive development on the one hand and social psychology on the other, to lie in an uneasy relationship. This is sad because the topic has the potential to unify the two levels of discourse. In the next sections, a few of the basic conflicts in the study of social cognition will be discussed.

The dichotomy between the physical and the social world

Perhaps the most basic dichotomy that has been invoked in the study of social cognition is between the cognitive processes necessary for cognition about physical and social objects. Do the cognitive processes that serve for physical reality also serve for social reality? This dichotomy arises through various attempts to characterise Piaget's theory as concerned solely with logico-mathematical knowledge. Piaget is said to present the child as a 'social isolate', for example acquiring the rudiments of number by solitary play with pebbles. Of course Piaget's reply is that logico-mathematical structures are perfectly general, they serve both the physical and social universe and that neglect of social objects in his theory is an omission but not a basic error.

However, a quite different solution has been to argue that cognitive processes do not differ for physical and social objects because all cognition is *intrinsically* social. Damon (1979) for example, maintains that concept formation never occurs in social isolation and that all knowledge is therefore 'co-authored'. This would appear to be a social determinist approach to the problem of knowledge, requiring merely a subsidiary distinction between physical and social objects. These can be differentiated in terms of intentionality; only social objects have the property of 'mutual intentionality' and this is sufficient to distinguish people from things. Frye (1980) also insists upon the criterion of mutual intentionality in the development of social cognition, arguing that the infant will not perceive people as social objects until intentionality has developed, although he would not insist that all knowledge is socially determined.

As a criterion for distinguishing between the physical and the social, the concept of intentionality has several drawbacks, not the least being the definition of intentionality itself. In Piaget's theory (1953, 1954) mutual intentionality would not occur before eight or nine months, with the co-ordination of secondary circular reactions. Bruner (1968) or Bower Broughton and Moore (1970), on the other hand, might argue that human action is intentional from the outset, even though they would probably be using the word in a different sense from Piaget. Hence, the definition of the social hangs upon the definition of intention and this is not a satisfactory solution to the problem of distinguishing the physical from the social.

A third approach would be to argue that the physical and social worlds do differ and consequently, they may require different, or at least additional, hierarchically structured, cognitive processes. However, the physical and social worlds also interpenetrate and any satisfactory account should neither render them mutually exclusive nor totally inclusive. As Broughton (1978) has clearly stated, social objects are at the same time physical objects and some physical objects are treated as social objects. What is required is a basis for *categorising* people and things (as well as intermediate categories of animate objects which may or may not be social).

Instead of the criterion of mutual intentionality, it may be fruitful to concentrate on the phenomenon of *reciprocity* as a defining criterion of social action. Certain relations between humans may then be considered *intrinsically* social, even though the young infant for example, may lack the concepts or self-conscious knowledge to define them as such. Mutual intentionality, defined in the Piagetian fashion, may rest upon an earlier form of mutuality, which Trevarthen (this volume) considers to be 'built in' to the behavioural repertoire of the neonate. He discusses these behaviours as 'basic human motives'. These are ways in which people are alike by virtue of species-typical structures upon which intersubjective processes are built. One advantage of this formulation is that the ability to engage in social behaviour does not *depend upon* cognitive development. Instead, a level of social participation is built into the system and this is not derivative of the capacity for reflection, although it may contribute to it.

Another advantage of this approach is that it allows a clearer basis for a distinction between physical, organic and social objects. MacMurray argued that consciousness of mutual relationship, the meeting of like with like, distinguishes what is personal from what is sub-personal. He said:

> Complete objectivity depends upon our being objectively related,
> in action as well as reflection, to that in the world which is
> capable of calling into play all the capacities of consciousness at
> once. It is only the personal aspect of the world that can do this.
> (MacMurray 1933, p.134).

This capacity to apprehend certain objects as persons depends upon the similarities between individuals, both in terms of their sensory perception and their capacity for feeling. It is interesting to note that MacMurray stresses the *personal* character of social relations, as in friendship (of course people may *co-operate* without this personal relationship being involved; see Glachan and Light, this volume).

These criteria for distinguishing the physical from the social have certain implications for the possible mechanisms of social cognition since, on this view, the capacity to know people as social objects depends upon the recognition of similarity: 'I am I because I know you and you are you because you know me. I have my being in that mutual self knowledge'. (MacMurray 1933, p.137).

In summary, MacMurray's solution to the problem of the special status of people as social objects has the advantage that it draws into the definition all those properties of humans, including the capacity for emotional expression, that differentiate them from other objects whether animate or inanimate. Objective knowledge depends upon the capacity to stand in conscious relation to that which is recognised as *not* ourselves. Clearly, this entails no necessary dichotomy in cognitive processes between the physical and the social but it does require a distinction between 'self' and 'not self'. Objects are social to the degree that they share properties of self and even within such a definition social objects are only truly social when they are personal, when they recognise one's personhood.

The dichotomy between the individual and the social

Just as explanations of social cognition have generated a false polarity between physical and social objects, so have they emphasised a dichotomy between individual and social approaches to knowing. This split may best be characterised by a comparison between Vygotsky's and Piaget's theories of cognitive development. Vygotsky is widely believed to have argued that cognitive growth is socially determined. His famous aphorism, that any cognitive function appears first *between* two or more people only later to become internalised, suggests that cognitive growth must proceed from the social to the individual level. By contrast, Piaget's concern was to derive the structures of the intellect from their biological roots and this has led some to argue that he stresses the individual in the development of intelligence and knowledge. Piaget's approach has been characterised as if development proceeds from the level of the individual to the level of the society.

However, on examining their positions more closely it turns out that the theories are basically similar. Firstly, both are dialectical, they emphasise the interaction between the individual and the social. Piaget said 'society is like all organisations, a system of interactions in which each individual contributes a small sector which is both biological and social. Development takes place through continual interactions, a dialectical relationship' (Piaget 1966 in Perret-Clermont 1980 p.25).

Secondly, both theories emphasise subject-object relations and both are constructivist, that is they stress the action of the subject in giving rise to knowledge. Where the theories differ is in that aspect of the interaction regarded as primary for purposes of theory building. Piaget accords primacy to the subject; he is interested in continuities between biological and psychological adaptations and in deriving the structures of scientific thought from their origins in individual actions. In the Soviet theory on the other hand, primacy is accorded to the material and social environment. In particular, language is considered an important mediator of reality and an essential instrument for the self regulation of behaviour (see Wozniak 1975, Butterworth 1980). Neither approach rules the other one out, rather each tends to assume the other.

Piaget's (1962) reply to Vygotsky's (1934/1962) criticisms of his theory of egocentric speech makes clear that the apparent confict between the two can be reconciled. Vygotsky, proceeding from the social plane to the individual drew attention to an important developmental continuity between 'egocentric' speech and verbal thought in planning and regulating action. He considered egocentric speech to serve a communication function which first occurs on the intermental plane and only later is interiorised as verbal thought on the intramental plane. Vygotsky's point was that egocentric speech *does* serve a communication function. As Piaget makes clear however, he never intended the concept of egocentric speech to be interpreted as if the child was speaking only to itself. Egocentric speech is meant for others but doesn't necessarily result in any effective communication. Piaget maintains that the pre-school child lacks the intellectual operations of reciprocity and reversibility necessary for the co-ordination of viewpoints and rational communication. So Piaget's position is essentially that the individual requires certain cognitive operations in order to use language effectively and these are acquired during the concrete operational period. Vygotsky's position is that language is necessarily shared, since it can only be acquired in a social context. So, how can Piaget's position which seems to stress the role of the individual in effective communication be reconciled with Vygotsky's which seems to stress the role of social factors?

Vygotsky (1966) was specifically concerned with the development of *higher mental functions,* defined as those mental processes that depend upon speech and language. Leaving aside the issue of whether any such processes actually exist and accepting the possibility that they might, it is clear that since the child uses words before their meanings are fully elaborated, language must proceed from a level where meanings are at their most basic and shared, and may indeed be specified only relative to a particular context and social relation. Thus it is not unreasonable to argue that the growth of cognitive processes dependent on language must proceed from an intermental to an intramental level. Indeed in its most basic form, the meaning of an utterance may not be available to the child at an intramental level at all but may reside only in the social relation and the particular context. (See chapters by Sinha and by Churcher and Scaife). It is only with cognitive growth that the meaning becomes interiorised as an aspect of the cognitive structure. Therefore to the extent that action systems are regulated by language and shared meanings, it is only logical that development must proceed from the shared to the individual level. However, this is a far cry from a social determinist account of cognitive development and it doesn't preclude the necessity for cognitive development in the individual to elaborate the relations implicit in the social realm. The differences between Piaget and Vygotsky appear more as differences of emphasis, particularly with respect to the importance of language as a cognitive instrument, than as differences of substance. Both accounts are poles of a dialectical theory of the relationship between the individual and society.

However, to say that Piaget and Vygotsky may deal with opposite sides of the same coin of cognitive development is not to assert that the contribution of individual and social structures are equivalent. Baldwin (1913) argued that it is necessary to distinguish those social influences in cognition that have their origin in the individual from those that have roots in the social organisation. For Baldwin, the individual is the *particularising* force in the acquisition of knowledge; he (or she) produces new ideas, sometimes on the basis of *generalisations* already available in society. The point of origin of the thought is a single human head but once thought takes on a social form, once it is subject to the generalising force of society, it can live forever. As Baldwin points out, it is difficult to trace our physical heredity back to Aristotle, whereas our social heredity is easily observed.

Society on the other hand is not an original thinker, feeler or doer. Things taken up by society and incorporated in permanent form, as part of the social structure, often are the products of the ablest thinkers. These are transmitted from generation to generation by sometimes laborious processes of construction that may have to wait upon a certain level of intellectual development of the child before they can be truly effective. The transmission of knowledge held by the society nevertheless depends upon cognitive growth in the individual.

Social determinism in intellectual development

There is another research tradition in the study of social cognition which is less concerned with the content of children's minds than with the possibility that cognitive growth may come about through social interaction. This is not so much a theory of social knowledge as a social theory of knowledge and in this tradition a kind of social determinist explanation of cognitive development is being put to the test. Perhaps the clearest examples are the studies by Doise and his colleagues at Geneva, reviewed by Glachan and Light (this volume), and the work of Donaldson at Edinburgh, reviewed by Neilson & Dockrell (this volume). These studies do not readily fit our original definition of social cognition, how children come to know others as social objects. Their concern has been with the mechanisms of 'cold-blooded' cognitive development in relation to social interaction. The hypothesis they wish to test is that the foundations of psychological development are rooted in the social conditions of life.

The essential aspect of Doise's argument is that cognitive conflict created by social interaction between individuals, whether at different levels of cognitive development or simply with different viewpoints, can give rise to cognitive growth. Conflict through social interaction is thought to reorganise the cognitive structures of both participants in the interaction. Glachan and Light's review (this volume) suggests that the experience of cognitive conflict does result in a change in cognitive structures. However, it remains far from proved that such changes are socially determined in any strict sense.

All the studies in this area demonstrate that a minimum level of cognitive competence with respect to the particular problem involved is necessary for the individuals who participate in the interaction, before cognitive restructuring will occur. That is, there is no simple transmission of information from one participant in the interaction to another regardless of the cognitive competence of the individual. Second, even if the experiments reported by Doise demonstrate that cognitive conflict *between* individuals will generate cognitive growth, they do not demonstrate that it is a *necessary* condition. It is quite possible that an individual subjected to conflicting viewpoints in the course of some isolated appraisal of a problem may also experience a cognitive restructuring as a consequence of the *intramental* conflict. However, Doise and Mugny (1977) have shown that collective conflict seems to be more effective in inducing cognitive change than individual conflict in spatial perspective taking tasks, so this could be a matter of degree.

A third issue that arises in the study of effects of social interaction on cognitive change concerns the mechanism of cognitive development. In the studies by Doise *et al*, all the emphasis is placed on the conflict mechanism and indeed they go to a great deal of trouble to rule out imitation as a mechanism of cognitive development. For example, in many of their studies they demonstrate that both the more advanced participant and the less advanced progress in their cognitive development consequent upon cognitive conflict. Since the more advanced participant lacks a model to imitate it is argued that the observed changes cannot have been a function of imitation. Their position holds little or no place for imitation as a mechanism of cognitive development.

This is perhaps surprising because as long ago as 1894 Baldwin, commenting on the social nature of cognitive processes, gave pre-eminence to imitation as the vehicle for social dissemination of knowledge. It seems quite possible that conflict constitutes the motive for cognitive change *within* the individual, an intramental process that requires the individual to recognise the *possibility* of conflict, while imitation may be responsible for the dissemination of knowledge between individuals.

However, where Doise is correct is to argue that the individual and the social constitute different levels of explanation. In his book *Groups and Individuals* (1978) he points out that psychologists are concerned with processes at the individual level while sociologists are concerned with the functioning of society. Society is not simply an additive conglomeration of individuals and each perspective on behaviour constitutes a separate level of explanation although they should be complementary. The cognitive processes of particular individuals are not central to the sociological explanation of group behaviour and the reciprocal argument also holds true. The problem is to find an explanation that can pass from level to level through some intermediary processes and indeed this is the aim of a psychology of social cognition. In the final section we will consider one approach to this problem.

Conclusion

As we have seen there has been a tendency in the study of social cognition for explanatory principles to be polarised with a consequent weakening of the theoretical basis to the subject. How can this tendency be avoided? One approach may come from systems theory. Glassman (1973) has argued that the core of the problem of relating differing levels of organisation is to understand how stability is achieved in living systems at different levels of complexity, for example at the level of the cell, the organ, the organism, the group and society.

He maintains that the degree of coupling or interaction between two systems depends on the activity of the variables which they share. To the extent that there are few common variables, or common variables are weakly coupled to other variables that influence the system, then they are independent of each other. This he calls *loose coupling*. In a fully joined system on the other hand, a perturbation of any one part requires readjustment of all the other variables. For example, social groups may preserve a looseness of coupling between the behaviour of individuals so that even if extreme perturbations in one individual occur, this will not affect the stability of the group as a whole. Living systems can be dependent upon each other but also maintain their independence. This approach does not deny that there are individual contributions to the social structure and that the social structure itself will have properties not observable at the level of the behaviour of the individual organism. This type of explanation has the advantage that it can be applied to a variety of phenomena; for example it offers an explanation as to why monotropism is not necessary for attachments (see the chapter by Smith) in the formation of affectional bonds. It seems that the adult-child system is not so tightly coupled that only one person can act as caretaker nor is the system so loosely coupled that any number of caretakers is possible. Rather, there is an optimum level in which a perturbation of the system, for example through loss of a parent, can be compensated by an adjustment of the system as a whole.

From this perspective it seems unlikely that the direction of effect in cognitive development will either be from the individual to the social level or vice versa, but what will be important will be the nature of the relationship or coupling between the components of the system. The developmental problem is to maintain stability through change. Interactions with the physical *or* social environment can contribute to cognitive growth. For example, certain systems are tightly coupled to the physical environment as in the development of postural control during the sensorimotor period. Butterworth and Cicchetti (1978) showed that both sitting and standing are brought under voluntary control by calibrating the postural system against information for a stable visual surround. This relation to the *physical* environment may have implications for intellectual development since it differs systematically between normal and Down's syndrome (mongol) babies, a population likely to become mentally retarded. In the example of postural control, the coupling can be considered as relatively automatic because the environment invariably contains the stable factors on which the system depends. The child doesn't need to seek out the information since it is always there. Other systems however, may require active coupling because of changes, or fluctuations in the physical or social environment, as in the case of attachment.

So from the perspective of systems theory if we ask, 'Is cognition socially determined?' then the answer may depend on whether we are considering mechanisms or content. From the perspective of mechanism, cognitive development may depend on feedback relations with the physical and social environment to which the individual is coupled. Selecting for pre-eminence only one relation would be to ignore all the other influences in development that contribute to the rise of cognitive processes. If, on the other hand, we were to rephrase the question, 'Is *social* cognition, socially determined?' that is, as a question of content rather than a question of mechanism, then if knowledge of others arises through recognition of the similarity between others and ourselves, social cognition can only arise in a social context.

In conclusion, the numerous conflicts inherent in the study of social cognition emphasise the need for a clearer conceptual analysis of the individual and social aspects of knowing. Hamlyn, in the following chapter, tackles this problem in its philosophical aspects. It is clear that this type of painstaking analysis, together with empirical tests of our hypotheses such as are reported elsewhere in this volume, will be necessary to distinguish the contributions of the individual and the social to the process of cognitive growth.

References

Baldwin, J. M., *Mental Development in the Child and the Race,* New York, Macmillan, 1894.

Baldwin, J. M., *Social and Ethical Interpretations in Mental Development,* New York, Macmillan, 1913 (5th Ed.).

Barker, W. D. L., and Newson, L. J., 'The Development of Social Cognition Definition and Location', in Modgil and Modgil, *Toward a Theory of Psychological Development within the Piagetian Framework,* NFER Publications, 1979, 233-66.

Bower, T. G. R., Broughton, J. M., and Moore, J. K., 'Demonstration of Intention in the Reaching Behaviour of Neonate Humans', *Nature,* 1970, *288,* 679-80.

Broughton, J. M., 'Development of Concepts of Self, Mind, Reality and Knowledge', *New Directions for Child Development,* 1978, *1,* 75-100.

Bruner, J. S., and Lyons, K., 'The growth of human manual intelligence. Part I: Taking possession of objects', *unpublished study, Centre for Cognitive Studies, Harvard University, 1968.*

Butterworth, G. E., 'A Discussion of Some Issues Raised by Piaget's Concept of Childhood Egocentrism', in Cox, M. V. (ed.) *Are Young Children Egocentric?* Batsford Academic, 1980, 17-40.

Butterworth, G. E., and Cicchetti, D., 'Visual Calibration in Posture in Normal and Motor Retarded Down's Syndrome Infants', *Perception,* 1978, 7, 513-25.

Chandler, M. J., 'Social Cognition: A Selected Review of Current Research', in W. Overton and J. McGarthy Gallagher (eds.) *Knowledge and Development Vol. 1. Advances in Research and Theory,* Plenum, New York and London, 1977.

Damon, W., 'Why Study Social Cognitive Development?' *Human Development,* 1979, *22,* 206-11.

Doise, W., *Groups and Individuals: Explanations in Social Psychology,* Cambridge University Press, 1978.

Doise, W., and Mugny, G., 'Individual and Collective Conflicts of Centrations in Cognitive Development', *European Journal of Social Psychology,* 1979, *9,* 105-9.

Frye, D., 'Developmental Changes in Stategies of Social Interaction', in Lamb, M. E., and Sherrod, L. R., (eds.) *Infant Social Cognition: Empirical and Theoretical Considerations.* Hillsdale, New Jersey, Lawrence Erlbaum, 1980.

Glassman, R. B., 'Persistence and Loose Coupling in Living Systems', *Behavioural Science,* 1973, *18,* 83-98.

James, W., *Essays in Radical Empiricism, A Pluralistic Universe,* Longmans, Green and Co, New York, 1947 (first published 1912).

Kuhn, D., 'Mechanisms of Cognitive and Social Development: One Psychology or Two?' *Human Development,* 1978, *21,* 92-118.

MacMurray, S., *Interpreting the Universe,* London, Faber and Faber, 1933.

Perret-Clermont, A-N., *Social Interaction and Cognitive Development in Children,* London, Academic Press, 1980.

Piaget, J., *The Origin of Intelligence in the Child,* New York, Routledge, 1953.

Piaget, J., *The Construction of Reality in the Child,* New York, Basic Books, 1954.

Piaget, J., *Comments on Vygotsky's Critical Remarks Concerning the Language and Thought of the Child and Judgement and Reasoning in the Child,* Boston, MIT Press, 1962.

Piaget, J., 'La Psychologie, les relations interdisciplinaire et le systeme des sciences', *Bulletin de Psychologie,* 1966, *254,* 242-54.

Shantz, C. U., 'The Development of Social Cognition', in E. M. Hetherington (ed.) *Review of Child Development Research 5,* University of Chicago Press, 1975.

Vygotsky, L. S., *Thought and Language,* Cambridge, Massachusetts, MIT Press, 1962 (first published 1934).

Vygotsky, L. S., 'Development of the Higher Mental Functions', in A. Leontyev, A. Luria and A. Smirnov (eds.) *Psychological Research in the U.S.S.R.,* Vol I, Progress Publishers, Moscow, 1966, 11-44.

Wozniak, R. H., 'Dialecticism and Structuralism: The Philosophical Foundation of Soviet Psychology and Piagetian Cognitive Developmental Theory', in Riegel, K. F., and Rosenwald, G. C., (eds.) *Structure and Transformation: Developmental and Historical Aspects,* Vol. 3, New York, John Wiley and Sons.

2 What exactly is social about the origins of understanding?

David Hamlyn

The social nature of knowledge

As I see it, the question in my title is a philosophical one. An answer to it would involve getting clear about how the origins of understanding are to be construed – how, that is, they are to be conceived even as possible. and what makes them possible. I emphasise that point because it seemed to me that one of my main concerns – perhaps *the* main concern – ought to be to explain why a philosopher may justifiably stray into this territory, despite all the appearances, perhaps, of trespassing I have no claim to any expertise about how in fact understanding comes about in individuals, but will argue that this essentially psychological question presupposes an answer, whether explicit or implicit, to the question of how this is even to be construed as possible. My concern is therefore with the concepts involved in the formulations of the problem, the concepts of knowledge and understanding, and with the problems that they entail for a construal of the origins of these things. I am not primarily concerned with the nature of human beings as such.

That leads me to two caveats that I should like to make at the outset. First, if, as I believe, there must be something social about the origins of understanding in the individual, it will clearly be impossible to construe that 'something social' in the sort of terms that may be quite appropriate once the individual participants in the social context have understanding both of each other and of the rest of the world in which they exist. The 'something social' must not be construed in terms of an interactionism which presupposes the very forms of understanding that we are trying to explain through a reference to the 'something social'.

That is not to say interaction of some other kind may not be an appropriate thing to invoke.

Second, it is, I think, possible to construe the opposition between Piaget and Vygotsky, where it exists, as reflecting a difference between two ideologies — individualism versus collectivism. Whether or not that is an exaggerated way of putting it, Piaget's way of considering the origins and growth of understanding in the individual is very much in terms of the relationship that exists between that individual and the environment in which he or she finds him — or herself. That, as I understand the matter, is not the case with Vygotsky. When, however, I refer to the social aspects of the origins of understanding, I do not have it in mind to press the cause of Vygotsky against that of Piaget in that respect. We are, after all, concerned with the origins of knowledge and understanding, in the *individual,* and whether or not human beings are fundamentally social creatures, perhaps even in some respects social products, our problem is still one of how it is possible for knowledge and understanding to come about in *individuals.* For it is to individuals that knowledge and understanding primarily belong, however much it may then exist independently of them. And since understanding involves knowledge, let me say again, as I have done elsewhere (Hamlyn 1978, p.12), that nothing in this depends on whether one speaks of understanding or of knowledge.

Nevertheless, as I said earlier, the philosophical problems about the origins of understanding stem from, and lie in, not what sort of creatures human-beings are, but the very concepts of knowledge and understanding. One can bring out the issues by means of an argument-schema expressed in terms of a number of logical connections or chains of presupposition involving knowledge. If the connections hold they do so irrespective of the nature of the thing to which the concept of knowledge may be applied. Moreover, the presuppositions or implications in question are all meant to be logical or conceptual in nature and do not entail a similar temporal ordering.

The argument-schema is as follows:

(1) To understand anything one has, as I have already said, to have knowledge about it in some respect. I do not believe that that is controversial (at least I hope not).

(2) To know something in this way is to know it as true (or as right or correct). Nothing very much turns on the use of the word 'true' as opposed to 'right' or 'correct'. Since truth is normally attributed to propositions, I do not mean to be taken as implying that knowledge is for that reason restricted to language-users.[1] It is sufficient that what one

knows something *as* should possess the same formal properties as truth has. That is why I am just as happy to speak of knowing something as right, correct, etc. as I am to speak of knowing it as true, as long as the same conformity to a standard of correctness is conveyed.

(3) To know something as true presupposes knowing what it is for something to be true (correct, right, etc.) in some sense of those words and to some degree or other. To say that is simply to point to the fact that someone could not be said to know something as X if he had no idea at all of what X consisted in. Moreover, knowing something as true is not knowing it as any old X; it is knowing it as something essential for it to constitute knowledge at all. One might put the point to be made under this heading by saying that knowing something as true presupposes possession of the concept of truth of something like it to some degree or other. (That can be as indefinite as one likes, provided that it holds good in *some* way.)

(4) The possession of the concept of truth even in this indefinite sense involves in effect the appreciation of the force of a norm or the idea that there or can be standards of correctness. We cannot conceive of that being the case except in creatures which have been brought to see certain ways of doing (or thinking) things as right and others as wrong. It is at this point that the part played by the social becomes evident. I cannot see any way in which the concept of a norm (note that I do not say the norm itself) could be other than social in its origins. To appreciate the force of a norm (and the idea of force in this sense is something involved in the very concept of a norm) is to appreciate whatever it is as, so to speak, imposed, however unwillingly that imposition is accepted. One who had no form of contact with others could have no concept of a norm, and *a fortiori* no conception of truth or correctness.

(5) To be brought to see certain ways of doing (or thinking) things as right (correct or true) or wrong (incorrect or false) thus implies something like correction by others, and more specifically and more importantly, the individual in question seeing that *as* correction.

(6) To see something as correction implies seeing the source of whatever is done as a corrector. Whatever else that involves it certainly involves seeing that something as a being with certain intentions, and thus normally with desires, interests, etc.—in other words as a person or as something person-like. That in turn implies a context of personal relations. It would be unintelligible that someone should come to see another as a corrector except in a context of that sort, however minimal. What is required is an appreciation of the significance of the

act of correction, and that implies seeing the place that the correction has in the relationship with the corrector. It has sometimes been suggested that a machine could perform the correcting role. But any machine complex enough to do the job would in effect be a proxy or substitute person. The correction would still have to be seen as motivated in person-like ways. Personal relations themselves depend on the participants in the relationship seeing each other in certain ways. Hence to appeal to personal relations in attempting to explain some-one's coming to see another as a corrector is not to appeal to something independent of ways of seeing things. One would nevertheless expect all this to emerge out of natural ways of responding to persons when treated by them in a personal way. Indeed, only such a context could provide the conditions necessary for coming to see persons as persons, and thereby make possible the other things connected with that which I have set out. It is, however, important to note that such conditions are not in themselves sufficient for this purpose. Social relations are not sufficient for knowledge even if they are necessary.

What all this implies is, among other things, that knowing any one thing involves knowing a great deal more. For the kinds of 'seeing-as' which I have invoked at the various stages of the argument all imply knowledge. To see X as Y, whatever X and Y are, is not in itself neces-sarily to know something about X, but it does presuppose a knowledge of some kind and to some degree of what it is for something to be Y. I have not attempted at any stage of my argument, therefore, to derive knowledge logically from something that does not involve knowledge. I have not tried in any way to show that knowing something, or any-thing presupposing knowledge, could be reduced to something not involving knowledge, which could thereby constitute an independent but logically sufficient condition for the individual concerned having knowledge. On the other hand, at more than one stage of the argument I made reference to what I may as well now call 'non-epistemic factors' as necessary conditions for the existence of the kind of knowledge in question. Thus I said that knowing what it is for something to be true presupposes a social context, and I tried to spell that out in more detail in relation to the other items of knowledge that that in turn implies. I said, for example, that seeing something as correction presup-poses seeing another as a corrector, and that has as a necessary con-dition standing to the other either in a personal relationship or in a relationship that could become that.

There are, therefore, in the argument-schema that I set out two kinds of dependence of one thing on another. There is a form of logical or conceptual dependence that one kind of knowledge may have on another—something that I believe to be true of all knowledge, although not always in quite the same way as seems relevant in the present context. There is also the dependence of a kind of knowledge on certain kinds of necessary condition without which it would be unintelligible that such knowledge should exist. In the present context, the first kind of dependence is exemplified by the dependence of the knowledge that something is the case on the knowledge of what it is for something to be the case or true. That is a logical or conceptual dependence, since if someone did not know what it was for something to be the case or true he could not, logically could not, be said in any proper sense to know anything. The second kind of dependence is exemplified by the dependence of the knowledge of what it is for something to have the force of a norm on the person who so knows standing in relations to others. This kind of dependence is not simply a contingent of matter-of-fact dependence. It is not simply as a matter of fact that appreciation of the force of a norm is usually dependent on the existence of a social context. I have claimed that it would be unintelligible for it to be thought to exist if that social context did not exist as well. There is nevertheless a difference between the non-contingency attached to this kind of dependence and that attached to the first.

One might express the difference by saying the first turns on certain necessary features of the *content* of knowledge. If it is a necessary feature of what is known (in the sense of the content of knowledge) that it is true (and given what knowledge is, it *is* such a necessary feature if the knowledge is 'knowledge that') then knowledge of anything necessarily presupposes knowledge of what it is for something to be true; and the reason could be simply expressed by saying, knowing that 'p' implies knowing 'p' as true, and one cannot know something as true without knowing what it is for something to be true. This exemplifies, although in a very special way, a principle I have already hinted at—one cannot know one thing without knowing other things.

By contrast, it is not the relation between knowledge and features of its content that produces the non-contingency of the second kind of dependence, or at any rate not just that. It is true that the argument for a connection between knowledge and social context works through the link between knowledge that 'p' and knowledge of what it is for 'p' to be true. The crucial step, however, is made in the claim, that the latter presupposes in any intelligible application, that the knower should have been subject to correction and therefore should have shared in a social context. That claim turns on the sort of thing that truth is and what knowledge of what it is for something to be true must therefore entail.

I would emphasise again, however, that such participation in a social context is merely a necessary condition of being a knower in any intelligible sense; it is not in any way a sufficient condition. Hence, while participation in such a social context—standing in relation to others—will itself inevitably presuppose for its possibility non-epistemic factors such as natural reactions and natural responses through feeling, it is the knowledge that these mediate which is important for other knowledge. For this reason, it is seeing correction *as* correction that is important for the acquisition of the concept of truth, not merely response to whatever it is that is done under the name of correction— although the former (seeing correction *as* correction) will not be possible unless there is the latter (action performed by others as correction and response to it).

What all this comes to in relation to my initial question is that there cannot be knowledge (nor *a fortiori* understanding) in an individual unless and until that individual is in an important sense social, and unless and until that knowledge includes knowledge of what is in an important sense social. It might be thought in saying this I am generating a regress in which the possession of one item of knowledge is dependent on the possession of an item of knowledge of a different kind, and so on. It is perfectly true that it is part of the scheme which I have presented that someone cannot be properly said to have one item of knowledge unless and until he has a great deal more. However, I should like to emphasise a point I have made a great deal of in other things I have written in this area (e.g. Hamlyn 1978). The kind of conceptual dependences with which I have been concerned have no implications for any temporal ordering of items of knowledge, and for the same reason they generate no temporal regress. There was not meant to be any suggestion in what I said that one first comes to see others as people, then as correctors, and thereby one comes to see what it is for something to be true, and so on. The negative way in which I have put the point that someone cannot properly be said to have one item of knowledge unless and until he knows a great deal more, should be taken seriously. What it means is that if we can properly describe someone as knowing that 'p' it must also be appropriate to describe him as knowing other things—and that is all.

The point is, however, quite general. While my argument-schema may suggest that the chain of dependence is one way in ordering, that is not strictly the case as far as knowledge is concerned, although it may be so in relation to non-epistemic factors. It would make no sense to suppose that someone might know what it is for something to correct without knowing anything of how that is exemplified. Hence, if it is right to say someone cannot know that 'p' unless he knows, among other things, what it is for something to constitute correction, the relation can just as easily hold the other way round too. If this is the case, a person cannot know what it is for something to constitute correction unless he knows that 'p', *for some value of 'p';* unless he knows *some* other fact. There can be logical objection to this; the relation of logical presupposition can well be reciprocal. Involved in the claim I am making are (a) the thesis of the non-atomicity of knowledge —knowledge does not come in independent but addable items or lumps which could exist by themselves, and (b) the thesis that something about the social must be included among those things which an individual must be said to know if he is to be said to know *anything.*

Of these theses, the first, as I have already said, seems very plausible in itself, and it may be made even more plausible *via* the consideration that its opposite—the thesis that atomic items of knowledge are indeed possible—faces extreme difficulties over the question of how those atomic items of knowledge are to be individuated. After all, when we say of someone that he knows that 'p', it is in terms of *our* understanding of 'p' that we so describe him. Such a description is compatible with a whole range of different possibilities as far as the individual in question is concerned. It is a great mistake to suppose when we have decided someone knows something or other, that we have determined, anything very precise as far as the person is concerned. There is *no* precise answer to the question of what someone knows when he knows, say, that nothing travels faster than the speed of light, that the earth is round, that Henry VIII had several wives, that men are different from women, that yellow is a bright colour—just to give a few, disparate examples.

If, therefore, it cannot be said exactly what someone knows when he knows that 'p' (except of course that he knows that 'p'), the claim that it is a condition of his knowing one thing that he knows other things is unobjectionable. For the description of 'knowing one thing' has no definite sense such that that condition might by ruled out by it. For that same reason, there is no logical problem about the claim that when someone knows that 'p' he also knows what correction is. For him, knowing that 'p' may indeed involve all sorts of things, but it may indeed involve all sorts of things, but it may nevertheless remain true that he cannot know anything, let alone 'p', unless he knows, among other things, what correction is. For that reason there is nothing wrong in *our* saying just that—that his knowing that 'p' must presuppose his knowing what correction is (if, that is, my argument is valid).

Knowledge is always a matter of degree, in the sense that, while two people may both be said to know that 'p', one of them may know more than the other of what is relevant to 'p' or may know it better. The thesis of the non-atomicity of knowledge has, as a corollary, that there is a certain but indefinite minimum to what a person must know if he is to know *anything*. The second thesis, that there must be something social in what he knows if he is to know anything, points to certain directions in which what he knows must be taken to go. Just what form seeing others as correctors takes in an individual is impossible to say for the reasons which I have been spelling out over knowledge that 'p'.

If my argument is valid, what we are entitled to say is that whatever an individual has it is not knowledge, unless other epistemic factors apply to him in some way, for example unless in some way he sees others as persons. The words 'in some way' in that formulation have to carry a great deal of weight. It remains true that, if someone knows that 'p' at all, it must also be true of him that he knows something of what persons are—and vice versa—for some value of 'p' (that is, if he knows something of what persons are he must know some other fact—and the same applies to animals to the extent that anything approaching the concept of a person gets application).

If someone were still to object to what I have said, complaining that it seems very odd at least to claim that a condition of knowing one thing is that the person concerned must know a great deal more, it could be replied, first, that the only oddity is in accepting the description of the situation at its face value; for it presupposes that 'knowing one thing' is a clear and definite description, which it is not. Second, none of this undermines the thesis that whenever knowledge is ascribable to an individual in one set of terms it must always be possible to ascribe knowledge in some other set of terms. If that general possibility is accepted, nothing remains but to take my initial argument on its merits.

Implications for genetic epistemology

I can imagine a further objection which may seem more pertinent to psychology than the rather abstract considerations I have been concerned with so far. I have insisted that what I have had to say has no positive implications for any temporal ordering of events, and thus *a fortiori* no genetic implications either. There is nothing which a philosopher, *qua* philosopher, can say about what must happen first, and so on. More than that, there is *nothing to be said* on this matter in terms of anything to do with knowledge. The idea of a first item of knowledge has, if what I have said is right, no content. However, it might seem fairly obvious that getting to the point at which ascription of knowledge, even in a minimal sense, is possible in relation to a child, must nevertheless take some time. What are we to say of the child and its 'cognitive state' during that interval of time, however long or short it may be? On that question seems to turn the possibility of a genetic epistemology, at any rate with regard to the beginnings of understanding (for we ought not to assume that what holds good with respect to the beginnings of knowledge and understanding necessaily applies to the later stages too—I shall return to this).

I implied in what I said earlier that, as long as the possibility of knowledge is not ruled out altogether, there must be some sense in which understanding of truth and its conditions is ascribable to the person concerned. We may well want to say that at this stage there is not much on these matters that the child knows, that its knowledge is inchoate to say the least, but that speaking of his or her knowledge of these things has nevertheless a certain sense, however indefinite. Is there not, however, a stage at which not even that can be said, and what marks the transition? One thing is quite certain. It is of no use to say that if we cannot ascribe knowledge we may be able to ascribe belief. That view is implicit in some of the interactional views I mentioned at the beginning, and indeed it is one crucial thing that is wrong with them. They presuppose something like the idea that the child approaches the world and everything in it, including other persons, with beliefs which serve as hypotheses for corroboration or refutation, and that other persons may play an important role in the process. There is much that is wrong in such a view which I have discussed elsewhere (Hamlyn 1978), and I shall not repeat my criticisms here. It is, in any case, clear that only a knower can have beliefs; to believe something one must know at least what is involved in the belief, whether or not the belief can be said to amount to knowledge.

A view at the other extreme is that we do not even know what we are asking in putting these questions.[2] What we are seeking thereby is to describe a state in which the conditions under which alone our adult use of language has sense and application are *ex hypothesi* missing. To ask for a description of a state of mind (if that is the right phrase) before knowledge has come about is to ask for the impossible when the whole of our language presupposes for its application the existence of that very thing—knowledge—which is being supposed as absent.

The question is, however, whether there really is an incoherence in even asking for a description of the state of mind of a preknowledge child, or whether we are not simply being asked to apply language beyond the area of its usual application—a situation in which we have to have recourse, as we commonly do, to metaphor and analogy. I am inclined to think it is the latter which really holds good, but that there is a sense in which it does not matter which it is for present purposes. For we may know that the states of mind of a very young child may admit in principle of description involving serial ordering in time, culminating in something meriting the title 'knowledge', without necessarily being able to provide adequate descriptions of the earlier stages. Moreover, we may know something of the conditions that have to be satisfied before the title of 'knowledge' can properly be bestowed. At the same time, it has to be recognised, since knowledge is for any individual a matter of degree, and since the items of knowledge in the complex that has to exist if knowledge is to exist at all can vary in degree relative to each other, it is not an all or none matter whether and when the title of 'knowledge' can in fact be properly bestowed. Hence it will be impossible to say at what moment knowledge first exists, and equally impossible to say anything definite about the ordering of that knowledge or what immediately precedes it.[3]

Does this mean whatever is or is not possible with respect to later stages in the growth of knowledge and understanding, that there is no place for genetic epistemology at this stage—at the beginnings? No, for it is not the task of genetic epistemology to set out the ordering of knowledge and its preconditions in time—at least not as I understand what genetic epistemology should be on the analogy of ordinary epistemology. For just as ordinary epistemology has as its concern the *possibility* of knowledge and understanding in general, or of the knowledge and understanding of this and that, so genetic epistemology should have as its concern the *possibility* of the growth and origins of knowledge and understanding. Into both these concerns will enter an interest in the question as to what knowledge and understanding actually are, since in order to show the possibility of X it is necessary to be at least relatively clear about what X actually is. This interest in what is sometimes, although in my opinion mistakenly, called the 'analysis of knowledge' cannot however exhaust all that epistemology should have as its concern.

Furthermore, there is a difference between the questions of what makes knowledge in general possible or what makes knowledge of this or that possible, and what makes knowledge, of whatever kind, possible in the individual. The latter kind of question will inevitably demand in the end some account of the conditions which have to be satisfied as regards the individual if he is to have knowledge. Some of those conditions will have to do with the various individual capacities that make knowledge possible—perception, memory, conceptual understanding, and so on. Such an account will clearly have implications for genetic epistemology also, since, if such and such conditions have to be satisfied for the possession of knowledge to be possible, their coming to be satisfied is necessary for the acquisition of knowledge, let alone its subsequent growth.

It will be seen from all the foregoing that I interpret genetic epistemology as a kind of extension of ordinary epistemology, the problem being what makes it possible for knowledge to come about in the individual and for subsequent learning to take place on its basis. Obviously the preconditions for the possiblility of having knowledge apply equally to the possibility of acquiring knowledge, but not vice versa. I am not sure that there is very much to be said about the conditions for the possibility of later learning, although I have tried to make clear certain things about it elsewhere (Hamlyn 1978, ch. 9). The restricted nature of that discussion may (and has) come under criticism for ignoring much empirical material about the conditions under which such learning may best go on. It seems to me, however, that such considerations are in a genuine sense psychological and are not part of genetic epistemology as I have defined the term. Thus, although there are some things to be said within genetic epistemology about the later stages of cognitive growth, the crucial issues are those which arise over the early stages, particularly those over the very beginning. That is why it is so important to try to sort out the issues with which I have been concerned.

It may be suggested, however, that I have offered a prescriptive definition of 'genetic epistemology'. Piaget does not after all define it in that way; nor does Baldwin from whom the term was derived. I am not competent to speak of Baldwin.[4] What Piaget means by 'genetic epistemology' is a very obscure matter. It is not, in his view, to be identified with developmental psychology; for him it is a philosophical discipline, at any rate in some sense of those words. Some of the things

he says suggests his views of the relationship between genetic epistemology and developmental psychology is rather like that between
theoretical physics and experimental physics, that is, as the relationship
between the body of theory in terms of which the facts are to be
viewed and those facts themselves. At other times he seems to see the
difference between the two disciplines as one in the scope of the
inquiries involved. There may also be differences in the traditions to
which the two disciplines belong. That is why, in the context of genetic
epistemology as he sees it, Piaget can, and perhaps rightly, oppose his
position to empiricism and what he calls 'apriorism' (although the latter
involves a confusion as to what *'a priori'* means—it does not mean
'innate'). All this may suggest that in his view genetic epistemology is
just something fitting in with a wide-ranging and abstract way of
thinking about the growth of knowledge.

There is also the fact that the concept of knowledge is in a certain
sense a normative concept—at any rate in the sense that, as I have tried
to point out, it presupposes an appreciation of the force of a norm.
Piaget says that knowledge involves norms of validity, which are the
business of the logician to adjudicate. Since, however, this validity has
to be purely formal it is to be the province of the logician. There are
also required those who are able to adjudicate, as he puts it in an essay
entitled 'Developmental Epistemology' (Piaget 1972), the appropriate
relations between subject and object—and this turns out to mean the
specialist in the field of the science in question. Looked at in this light,
genetic epistemology would appear to be a co-operative inquiry involving psychologists, logicians and specialist scientists, plus anyone else
who might be useful. How they are to proceed remains less than clear.

I suggest that the only helpful way of seeing whether there is a
distinct discipline here, and if so how it is to be identified, is to sort out
the questions there are at stake. Curiously enough, in the essay which I
have mentioned (it is not clear when it was written), Piaget is on the
fringe of doing just that. For he begins by giving as the question with
which classical theories of knowledge have been concerned: 'How is
knowledge possible?'; and he elaborates one or two other questions
along the same lines.

What he finds wrong with classical epistemology is not that
philosophers have asked these questions, but that they have assumed
knowledge to be a state, whereas it is really, he says, a process. On this
last point he is just wrong; the *acquisition* of knowledge may be a
process, but not the knowledge itself. That, however, is of no great
importance for present purposes. He might just as well have said that

epistemologists ought to address themselves to the acquisition of knowledge as well as to its possession. The question with which they would then be concerned would be: 'How is the acquisition of knowledge possible?', as long as that question is construed as being concerned with what gives the concept of the acquisition of knowledge a coherent sense (perhaps against sceptical suggestions that it does not have such a sense). It must not be construed as asking how it actually happens in practice.

It seems to me that the crucial problem in understanding the possibility of acquiring knowledge in this sense is the problem of how it gets off the ground, so to speak. To understand that we need to take into account what sort of thing in general human-beings are, what sort of thing a human consciousness is, and in what sort of capacities that consciousness is manifested; we need, that is, to take into account what a human form of life is.

The necessity of a social existence

The difficulties on which I have concentrated do not, however, lie there, but in the very implications of the concept of knowledge itself (something to which Piaget pays insufficient attention). Hence, if, for example, and to return to my original question, the possibility of knowledge in an individual demands some kind of social existence as far as that individual is concerned, the acquisition of knowledge also demands the acquisition of a social existence of that kind. The knowledge cannot exist before the social existence if the latter is its pre-condition; but that is the only temporal fact—a negative one—entailed by what I have said. It is nevertheless an important fact in itself that any story about the origins of knowledge and understanding in the individual must have as a theme something about the individual's acquisition of a social existence (for there is no adequate sense, I take it, in which children could be said to be born as social beings). Finally, it is important to see in just what respect that theme is a necessary part of the story—and this has been my concern. I shall end with a little more on the subject.

I have emphasised in other things I have written in this area (especially perhaps in Hamlyn 1978) the extent to which a child's growth of knowledge must be seen in terms of an initiation into a public and accepted body of understanding, and the extent to which that depends upon the child's attention being drawn to things and his being put in the way of things by adults. For that to happen it is no doubt important for the child to be treated as a potential member of a community of knowers and thus to an increasingly great extent as a person. That, I know, fits in with some things which some psychologists have said, sometimes for other reasons. It is not quite what I have said here. It is certainly not a necessary condition of the possibility of knowing that 'p' that a child should have been put *by others* in the position of seeing that 'p'. He might, given the satisfaction of other conditions, come to see this for himself (though not, I suggest, if he knew nothing else at all). It is inconceivable, however, that a child should be led to see the force of truth and falsity, without at the same time and along with that coming to see something as true or false. That is to say that the appreciation of the force of a norm is bound to come along with an appreciation of some content of that norm. It is inconceivable that it should be otherwise, given the nature of human consciousness (or indeed of any other consciousness that we could understand).

Hence, while it is certainly not the case that the truth is simply what others tell us or impress upon us, even when we are babies, the paramount importance of what others believe and what for the beginnings of a child's understanding must be obvious. It is only against this background that there can be any subsequent independence on the part of the individual in the acquisition of knowledge and understanding.

I would like to emphasise again, however, that in any adequate account of the origins of understanding in the individual it is not enough simply to make reference to what the role of others is. An account must be offered of the child's response to that of sufficient adequacy to explain how the child comes to see the force of a norm. It must therefore see what it is for others to have wants and concerns, and that is possibly only in a context where those concerns colour, so to speak, the behaviour of those involved. To say this is to say the relations between those concerned, such as mother and child, must be in a genuine sense such as turn on affect or emotion—love being of course the most obvious example. It is quite hopeless to attempt to construe the relations in question in terms of stimulus and response in the ordinarily accepted sense of those terms. Relations so construed provide no foundation for seeing the force of anything, whereas there is an obvious connection between a relation involving love and concern (or indeed the antitheses of these, if it comes to that) and an appreciation of the force of something that may have importance, as a norm usually has and is seen as having.

It is only in a social context of this kind that there can be any intelligibility in the idea of the emergence of the appreciation of the force of a norm. Only with that can one properly speak of knowledge and understanding. Only on such a basis can one conceive of the possibility of subsequent learning. This is the conceptual ordering of these matters. Let me repeat, however, except for the fact that learning implies prior knowledge, there are no positive temporal implications in what I have said. It remains true that even if it is quite impossible to say when knowledge first comes into existence, and even if it will be a matter of degree when it does, it will not be knowledge (nor *a fortiori* understanding) unless the person concerned has the kind of social existence that a relationship with other human-beings involves. That, I suggest is what provides the answer to my initial question 'What exactly is social about the origins of understanding?'

Notes

1. On this see further Hamlyn 1980.
2. Something like that was said by J. Nammour 1973.
3. It equally follows, although it is not my immediate concern here, that there is nothing to be said about how knowledge comes about and that certain conditions have to be satisfied if it is to do so, as my subsequent remarks on genetic epistemology indicate.
4. On whom see Russell 1978.

References

Hamlyn, D. W., *Experience and the Growth of Understanding,* London, Routledge & Kegan Paul, 1978.

Hamlyn, D. W., 'Experience and the Growth of Understanding: A Reply to Mr Cooper', *British Journal for the Philosophy of Education,* 1980, forthcoming.

Nammour, J., 'Resemblances and Universals', *Mind,* Vol. LXXXII, No. 329, October 1973, pp. 516-24.

Piaget, J., *Psychology and Epistemology,* (ed. B. M. Foss), London, Allen Lane, The Penguin Press, 1972.

Russell, J., *The Acquisition of Knowledge,* London, Macmillan, 1978.

3 An ecological approach to cognitive development: implicate orders, joint action and intentionality

John Shotter and John Newson

From the very first days of the child's development, his activities acquire a meaning of their own in a system of social behaviour and, being directed towards a definite purpose, are frequently refracted through the prism of the child's environment. The path from object to child and from child to object passes through another person. This complex human structure is the product of a developmental process deeply rooted in the links between individual and social history.

Vygotsky, 1978, p. 30

Being ecological

In the development of the child, the individual and the social are, we believe, necessarily and inextricably interlinked. In discussing their mutual relations, we shall follow Gibson (1979) and adopt essentially an *ecological* approach. Gibson was, of course, mainly concerned with the study of visual perception. But in attempting to understand the relations between social and cognitive development in early childhood, it may be fruitful to extend his mode of analysis and to generalise his descriptive vocabulary to apply to other modes of perception.

The strength of a thoroughgoing ecological approach is, we feel, that it emphasises the interfittedness of things and directs attention away from the child as a wholly isolated entity (and away from the hidden 'internal processes' presumed to be going on inside her somewhere). It directs us instead towards what is out there *in her world*, at each moment in her development, for her to grasp or 'pick up' (as Gibson puts it), towards the totality in which she is embedded. While such an externalised concern need not in itself be an ecological one, it becomes so if we insist that the child and her world exist only in reciprocal relation to one another, that they are mutually constitutive and mutually defining. Then, what we might call the child's *environment-for-action*, her *effective environment*, or her *Umwelt* (Uexküll, 1957), becomes a very special environment existing just for her. It becomes her world, a world into which she is dovetailed, feels at home, and knows how to operate because it is a world *made* (with the help of others) *by her*. The child then acts as she does in such a world, we might say, in accord with the ecological imperatives it provides; she acts in response to what her world, her *Umwelt* as she apprehends it, offers, demands, or affords.

As 'the first principle of *Umwelt* theory', Uexküll (1957, p.10) states that:

> all animals, from the simplest to the most complex, are fitted into their unique worlds with equal completeness. A simple world corresponds to a simple animal, a well-articulated world to a complex one.

We shall rely upon this principle of reciprocal completeness a great deal in what follows, for we shall take it to mean that the child and his environment, what is inside him and what is outside, interlock in such a way that the structure of one reflects the structure of the other, However, in the case of human *Umwelten*, we must modify Uexküll's principle by extending it in at least two ways:

(1) Human *Umwelten* contain other human beings and thus of necessity, we shall argue, special systems of social affordances which inform the human action within them, systems which include moral orders of often great complexity. They also contain many other humanly constructed artifacts of both an objective and intersubjective kind which 'live on', not just from one moment to the next but from one generation to the next. These accumulate over time in such a way as to give everything in human *Umwelten* an implicit historical aspect— a network of implicit connections and ramifications in time, relating what has been with what might be. For human beings in a society with others, an environment-for-action is not a timeless world, but a space-time (or better, a time-space) structure.

(2) Besides acting in their *Umwelten*, human beings can also act upon

them and make a difference to them, thus creating new conditions for their own existence—not, of course, by creating new worlds afresh, but by remaking or remoulding those they already have to hand. The new effective environment so created is only maintained in existence though if people 'agree', in a special social process, to establish and institute it. Otherwise it fades from existence as soon as the action appropriate to it is complete.

To repeat: it is important to be clear that by the term *Umwelt* we mean the unique environment reciprocally defined by the person actively immersed in it, who as a part of it only exists as such in inter-action with it; an environment which can be 'developed' as the person develops. From within her *Umwelt,* a person's world appears to be full of demands and requirements, opportunities and limitations, rejections and invitations, enablements and constraints—in short, affordances' (as Gibson terms them). And her knowledge of what her environment affords will inform her action in it. So ecologically, what we are suggesting is that the child, as a fragment of biological nature, relates herself creatively to her environment. And that the relation is actively made by the functioning of the natural formative processes constitutive of all human activity (Shotter, 1980); by the operation, in fact, of a form-creating activity continuous with that at work in biological growth and evolution at large. So, although perceptually distinguishable from her environment as an individual, she is not as such physically isolable from it; she exists (as an open system) only in mutual relation to it. Thus, in developing from a simple, undifferentiated being into a more complex, well-articulated individual, a child may also be thought of, ecologically, as at each moment, remaking her world, her own effective environment. This means that her world is not for her as adults experience it. It is her own world and she acts accordingly in *its* terms—not just as she would like or wish, but sooner or later in ways appropriate to what it affords. In fact, as we shall later argue, she experiences such affordances as being 'out there' as external to herself and as a part of the world in which she finds herself placed, and in terms of which she feels she must act—the 'must' being if not a moral must, at least a normative one, there being a usual, normal, or 'natural' way in which to act in one's own world.

Cognitively, in such a view, it is not by observing single people, specific features, or isolated objects that the infant gets to know her *Umwelt,* Building up her knowledge of it additively, piece-by-piece. On the contrary, she only gets to know about the people and things in it as they appear to her in terms of her current effective environment. But she can (under the appropriate conditions) remake that world in the course of her active involvement with the people and things she meets within it, continuing until she arrives at a world in which (for all practical purposes) she can co-ordinate her actions in with those of all other people in her society. Such an achievement is possible for, as Gibson (1979, p. 43) notes in relation to spatial perspectives, although no two individuals can be in the same place at the same time, any individual can be in the same place, position or situation at different times. Thus the 'information' (in Gibson's sense) implicit in the structure of people's surroundings is available for all to pick up and, in principle at least, all may live in similar *Umwelten*.

Though similar, each individual's *Umwelt* will remain nonetheless her own unique environment-for-action, with its own special combination of openings, barriers, offerings, and obstructions. In action, the individual is completely enveloped in it. As such, it is at any moment known to her as a whole, with every part of it related in some way to every other part; she experiences no gaps in it—while sensing at the same time that it contains regions, people, or things with awesome powers to call whatever she knows into question. Indeed, she only possesses her knowledge in virtue of it not being questioned or challenged by powerful others, or by the natural outcome of events as they unfold. Interpersonal assertions of power and the need to negotiate with significant others (to transform the character of what they afford) are inescapably involved in the experience of developing human beings; the legitimacy of one's knowledge always remains open to criticism, correction and amendment.

Hamlyn (this volume) seems to us to be raising similar issues in discussing the thesis of 'the non-atomicity of knowledge': the claim that 'knowing any one thing involves knowing a great deal more' (p. 18). He goes on to list what he calls the non-epistemic factors constituting the necessary conditions for a certain kind of basic knowledge to exist at all *(Umwelt* knowledge in our terms): besides its wholistic quality, it presupposes, he claims, not only a social context in which people are in a personal relation to one another, but also that norms are a part of that context and people can and do act as critics and correctors of one another in relation to those norms; they are concerned with what 'fits' or is appropriate to their shared world in some way— considerations which may, appropriately, also be called ecological ones. Implicit then, in the social processes or practices by which such knowledge is acquired is the possibility of its further change and development; its use is never without risk, its existence remains precarious.

Ecologically, we are proposing that cognitive development can be best understood, not as in the conventional psychological approach—in terms of processes developing independently within the child—but in terms of an evolving context for further action, a change in the effective environment, an expanding *Umwelt.* Thus we take it for granted (as indeed do all caretakers) that, although psychology may not yet possess an adequate account of principles of learning, the potential for the child to develop greater degrees of understanding is nonetheless there, and will function naturally, given that the individual is healthy and intact and appropriately embedded in some coherent cultural context. Ecologically, our task is to specify the nature of that embedding.

The relation between traditional cognitive psychology and the ecological standpoint can be depicted diagramatically as in Figure 1.

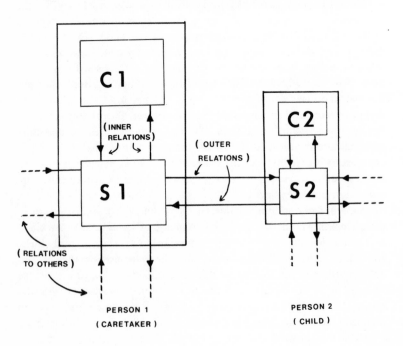

Figure 1.

Traditional cognitive psychology has now set its sights upon discovering the nature of the 'inner computer' (C1 and C2) people use in achieving their actions, and speculation now centres upon the precise kind of data processing operations involved. This is an approach which, incidentally, when set in a social context, tends to pose a number of thorny problems about the relation between the operations and the executive agent on self (S1 and S2) which must somehow direct their overall functioning, and make use of the results they provide. For who or what exactly is it responsible for what is done? Is it the person, or is is her data processing operations which, presumably, to the extent they operate automatically according to program or plan are not under her own self-control? Without at least potential control over every aspect of her own activity it is difficult to see how a child may develop and modify her activity in response to what her circumstances may or may not allow her to do.

By contrast, attention is concentrated ecologically not upon the reciprocal relations between selves and their computers, but upon those between people. And developmental psychology focusses upon the special case in which caregiver (parent) and child constitute *Umwelten* for one another, appropriate to each other's development—caregiver into caretaker, and child into adult, an autonomous new member of the caretaker's society. Central in each person's *Umwelt* is a special kind of personal affordance constituted by another person, establishing the appropriate environmental conditions for the natural functioning of inner developmental processes, howsoever we may choose to characterise them in traditional cognitive terms. And it is our task to attempt to establish for developmental psychology what, in any given society, these environmental conditions are. This task is made easier than the cognitive psychologist's by the fact that the activities constituting them go on out in the open, between people, rather than inside their heads, hidden from direct observation.

Implicate orders and Gibson's 'ambient optic array'

Our interest is, then, in the nature of *Umwelten,* in both their formal structure and in the principle of their making and remaking—in, to use Goodman's (1978) happy phrase, 'ways of worldmaking'. Below, in an attempt to set out an appropriate way of describing the structure of *Umwelten,* we shall explore and generalise (from the physical to the social) Gibson's notion of 'the ambient optic array'.

Though not described as such by Gibson (1979), we shall note (a) that it has a holographic structure such that everything in it is represented everywhere (at all times), and that (b) such an order is best described in Bohm's (1973, 1980) terms as an *implicate* order. People's social surroundings, although not explicitly structured are not, we suggest, utterly without order, and from 'information' (Gibson) implicit in the social activities in which they are involved, that people pick up what specifies their social *Umwelt*. Just as the child comes to appreciate the 'suckability' of a proffered teat or the 'graspability' of a cup handle, so she also apprehends in an equally direct manner, we suggest, the moral force underlying a serious maternal prohibition, and begins to distinguish between a deliberately harmful insult to her person and one which is merely a humourous form of play. She perceives these social barrier reefs and high seas, the harbours, havens, and horizons directly in people's stony silences and fixed expressions, in their nods, winks, grimaces, gestures, stances, and smiles.

Here then, in this section, we shall explore forms of order, implicate orders, appropriate to describing the formal structure of *Umwelten*, and in the next section we shall turn to the intentional processes involved in their construction. All human action is intentional in the sense that it is 'directed'; it 'points to' or 'contains something' other than itself; in short it means, or is a means to something.

Rather than in terms of 'pointing' or 'containing', this property of action is more fruitfully expressed, we believe, in 'specifactory' language (Gauld and Shotter, 1977): to act is to make something other than what it would have been if we had not acted; we give it a structure it did not already possess. So in acting we can be said to be determining or specifying something in terms of the differences we can make to it or in it. Thus any action in progress can, while serving to produce a degree of specification into its content, leave that content open to yet further specification—but only of an already specified kind, what is past determining the style of what is yet to come (Rommetveit, 1976; Shotter, 1980). It is thus that an action in its very occurrence, posits or implicitly specifies a world, a realm of other possible actions serving to specify, articulate, or transform that realm yet further. We shall explore this difference-making, or specifactory property of human action further, in the next section. Let us now turn to the more static aspects of mental phenomena.

Following Piaget (1950), Smedslund (1969) discusses the wholistic, intentional qualities of mental phenomena, and claims that their contents are intrinsically related to one another, by implication, rather than extrinsically related. Having a belief or wish in itself implies, contradicts, or changes the likelihood of many other beliefs and wishes, he points out. A mental phenomenon *A* logically implies another *B* in its very nature, without there being any need of a theory to link them. Only if *A* and *B* are in, say, a cause-effect relationship, and thus by definition logically independent of one another, is a theory necessary to specify the nature of their relation.

Smedslund's claim here is reminiscent of Hamlyn's thesis of the non-atomicity of knowledge: it means for instance, that if a child cries and manifests discomfort, it implies something like 'Give me something different'; it definitely does not imply 'Give me more of the same' (see Lock, 1980, who has explored the implicational structure of many such situations). Implicit in the child reaching for something is the possibility that she wants it, is trying to get it, and will thus try even harder if barriers are put in her way. Acting on those implications, her mother responds to her accordingly. A child, in claiming to know a cat is an animal must, by implication, be assumed to know what in general animals are, what are not animals, and thus, whether the new entity confronting her is an animal or not (ignoring controversy about the law of the excluded middle here); thus her claim may be checked out in her subsequent behaviour. At every moment in their interactions with their children, mothers can be observed as acting upon the logical implications in their child's actions, treating even not well-articulated expressions as if their meanings were clear (Shotter, 1974, 1978).

Children too, clearly act upon what are for them the logical implications in their circumstances: it not being illogical in itself to treat the exit of an object from one's immediate perception as meaning that it has ceased to exist—consider a flame, a puff of smoke, a sound, a touch, and so forth. Clearly the logic of what implies what takes a while and a deal of experience to sort out. In 'failing' to reason as adults reason, the child is not necessarily acting illogically, it is just that they are acting in an effective environment quite dissimilar to that of the adults who test them (Donaldson, 1978). Indeed, the very fact that the child is a human being implies that she is a being capable of behaving logically—a presupposition inherent, as Smedslund (1970, 1977) shows, in all our dealings with our children, whether as researchers or parents. Going even further, knowing how to recognise people as people implies that we already know (but only implicitly) the whole nature of the circumstances in which human beings are constituted as persons—a claim for which Smedslund (1978) also provides evidence. Clearly, to repeat Hamlyn's dictum, knowing one thing *is* to know a great deal more.

Relating these implicational phenomena to the *Umwelt* theory, we can point out that in fact they follow directly from what we have called Uexküll's reciprocal completeness principle. For, to the extent that ecologically an organism's behaviour is fitted completely into its environment, the whole of its *Umwelt* can be said in some sense to be 'known' to it. Although obviously not all explicitly known, anything new is already implicitly known in kind, as the organism can only operate within the capacities it has available for information pick-up, and cannot operate outside of them. Thus for the developing child as for the mature adult, each difference made, each distinction drawn, serves to structure *the whole* of a person's knowledge of his *Umwelt:* if something is not this then, by implication, it must be either that, or that, or . . . The very nature of a person's reciprocal relations to his *Umwelt* are such that whatever he does has implications, connections, and ramifications (implicitly) with everything else within the wholeness of his *Umwelt*. It serves to specify (a) what he might do further; (b) what else he might have done but did not do; (c) what his current place or position in his *Umwelt* is—his situation; (d) how, as a result of his action, his situation is changed and his *Umwelt* differentiated or transformed; and so on.

Gibson (1979), in his notion of 'ambient' as opposed to 'radiant light', captures very clearly the idea of an all-enveloping visual environment, in which at every point (place or standpoint) the whole of one's actual surroundings are implicitly represented. This is caused by light, in being scattered in every direction from the things and objects in that environment, reaching and making a contribution to the light at every point in one's surroundings. Thus, for Gibson, ambient light is *structured* in the sense that, at any given point of observation, there are *differences* between the light coming into that point from different directions (principally differences of intensity), invariant differences. One's environment can thus be specified visually, he claims, by 'picking up' the invariant differences availiable in 'the ambient optic array', differences which will change in an invariant manner as one moves from standpoint to standpoint. To the extent that they are 'there' whether anyone is present or not, as offerings of nature of *affordances,* they are there as possibilities or opportunities for anybody to pick up. Thus on Gibson's theory, the visual world at least is or can be the same for everyone.

Social affordances are a different matter; they can only offer invariant differences for pick-up, clearly, if people act to make invariant differences in their own behaviour, that is, if people act in relation to one another in conventional ways—but more of this later.

A final point of importance to mention here which Gibson makes, is one which we will state but not expand upon: he points out that the invariances specifying, say, an object need not in themselves be obviously patterned, they can be 'formless invariants'. For instance, a single, global change in an optic array may specify *both* an unchanging object *and* the changing of some of its properties (as well as, perhaps, one's own movement in relation to it at the same time). The changed differences in the array overall, intermingled together, need have no discernable form as a whole; different specific forms are, nonetheless, implicated in the structure of that whole, and clearly may be extracted with the appropriate modes of pick-up. We shall return to this most important point almost immediately below.

Strangely absent from Gibson's account of the ambient optic array is any mention of holograms. Holograms are made by using coherent light usually supplied by lasers. No lens is used. A scene is encoded on a photographic plate by recording the interference patterns (differences) made by a (reference or comparison) beam falling on the plate interfering with light from that same beam after it has been reflected from the scene—its original pattern of wave-fronts now being disturbed in a way corresponding to the structure of the scene. If, after having been exposed and fixed, the plate is illuminated with the same laser light again, it serves to reconstruct just the same complex pattern of wave-fronts, carrying in their differences just the same information as the light reflected from the original scene. A virtual three-dimensional display thus appears (Leith and Upatnieks, 1965).

The essential feature of a hologram, which makes it quite different from an ordinary photograph, is that instead of the point-to-point relationship between scene and photograph, there is a whole-to-whole relationship. In the exposure of the holographic plate, each point in the scene reflects light on to the whole plate, while each point on the plate receives light from the whole scene. In other words, on the holographic plate, everything is represented everywhere. As such, the hologram is an example of the same form of order as Gibson ascribes to the ambient optic array, and we may take the hologram as a model for it.

In so doing, a number of interesting features become evident immediately:

(a) Viewing a hologram is like looking at a visual scene through a window; as one moves about, new aspects of the scene come into view while others disappear. Furthermore, just as one may see as much of a scene through a smaller window (even a pinhole, if one moves close enough to it), so a hologram will show the whole scene when cut into halves, quarters, etc. The whole scene remains represented implicitly in the differences still present in every one of its parts.

(b) Another feature apparent in holograms is that the structure visible on the surface of the holographic plate itself bears no formal resemblance to the original scene. Indeed, for scenes of any complexity, the pattern in the emulsion of the plate appears quite random, formless in fact (see Leith and Upatnieks, 1965). The forms it encodes are only revealed when it is 'interrogated' by an appropriate beam of coherent light. The hologram may even encode several different images superimposed upon the same plate, each being recovered by using appropriately different 'interrogation' procedures. Just as, in Gibsonian language, different pick-up procedures may reveal different invariances encoded in the same optic array.

(c) A final point here concerns the nature of the pick-up process, unelaborated by Gibson (1979) himself. In a hologram, the scene is encoded (as an interference pattern) in the differences between the outgoing, incident light of the reference beam, and the incoming, reflected light from the scene. This may give us a clue as to a fuller account of 'information pick-up' than the one offered by Gibson, simply in terms of 'extracting invariants', 'resonating', or 'being attuned'. Instead, we suggest, the pick-up of, say, visual information involves *acts of looking,* such that the relevant invariants are extracted from the relations (or differences) between the activity which we ourselves direct outwards upon the world, and that which results in us from its incoming consequences (Bohm, 1965; Shotter, 1974). Thus the pick-up of information can become, not only a matter of skill, but also a matter of choice and selection as to which of all of the information available we actually attempt to pick up. While looking may be up to us, what we see when we do so is not; the information we pick up is clearly 'there', in the structure of our visual environment—Gibson is surely right in insisting on this.

Bohm (1973, 1980) parallels the contrast between the ordinary photograph and the hologram, with the contrast between the accepted mechanistic order of physics and what he calls the new *implicate order.* In a mechanistic form of order, the world is regarded as constituted of entities which are *outside of each other,* in the sense that they exist independently and are locatable in different regions of space (and time), and interact in ways which do not bring about any changes in their essential natures. This, as Bohm terms it, is an explicate order, in which separately existing, localisable parts, by interacting, form a whole. It was the optical lens, he feels, which served in science to suggest—by its point-to-point imaging, by its use in recording things too big, too small, too fast, or too slow to be seen by the naked eye—that everything can be observed in such a way.

The hologram suggests differently. Holographically, in an implicate order, everything is in some sense enfolded or implicated in everything else; inseparable inter-connectedness is the fundamental reality, and relatively independent, localised parts are merely particular and contingent forms within the whole. Essentially, forms and their influences are not locatable, but are spread out and present everywhere. To the extent that any 'elements' *are* apparent within the whole, their basic qualities and relations with one another will depend upon the whole in which they are embedded; if that changes they will change. In an implicate order, its 'parts' (mostly) exist inside one another, and at any one moment they owe not just their character but their very existence as 'parts', both to one another and to their relation to what were the 'parts' of the whole at some earlier point in time (Shotter, 1975, p. 52).

The study of implicate orders is as yet in its infancy (Bohm, 1980). Yet we hope we have said sufficient here to make clear some of the amazing properties of any environment ordered in such a way, containing (implicitly) properties not locatable but spread out everywhere within it. It remains now to explore not the nature of people's *Umwelten* as passively constituted for them by their physical surroundings, but as constituted for them actively, by the presence of other people within them.

Joint action and intentionality: moral Umwelten

While there are many activities in which we as individuals know what we are doing and why, there are also many others in which we remain deeply ignorant as to what exactly it is that we are doing. Such is the case in *joint action,* in which people must interlace what they do with the actions of others. We remain ignorant of quite what it is we do, not because the 'plans', 'rules', or 'scripts', etc., supposedly in us somewhere informing our conduct are too deeply buried to bring out easily into the light of day, but because its formative influences are not wholly there within us to be brought out. The actions of others determine our conduct just as much as anything within ourselves. In such circumstances, the overall outcome of the exchange is simply not up to us; in fact, it cannot be traced back to the intentions of any individuals. Thus rather than being experienced as a product of those actually producing it, it is experienced as an event which just happens— for example the child is treated just as happening to acquire language —and its occurrence is thus attributed to the operation of an external device (LAD), force, cause, or agency, rather than to the efforts of the people actually involved in it, producing it.

Although unintended and experienced as produced externally, other than by the joint action of its participants, the products of joint action still retain an intentional quality: they serve to specify (see previous section) the style of what further there might be to come. In other words, in joint action each person's act serves to progressively specify or articulate an *Umwelt* within which it takes place. Thus there can be, in Bergson's (1920, p. 188) words,

> a gradual passage from the less realised to the more realised, from the intensive to the extensive, from the reciprocal implication of parts to their juxtaposition.

Such, we suggest, is the process by which an *Umwelt*—experienced as an external world containing a realm of as yet unexperienced possibilities within it—is 'developed'. The process is not one of realising or actualising in it a potential already in existence elsewhere—in some mysterious Platonic realm, for instance—but is one of gradually rendering explicit (collecting and localising) what is already present implicitly (spread out everywhere) within it.

Let us turn now to apply our analyses to some concrete examples. Consider an episode involving Alan (roughly two years old) and his mother:

Alan, playing with a toy train, looks up and sees his mother standing, looking at him. He continues playing for a short time, but now in an exaggerated, 'silly' way. He stops and walks over to her, then stretches his arms up to her in a characteristic gesture. She picks him up, holds him tight, and tickles him. He wriggles and laughs. She does it again. He wriggles again, but this time grimacing and grizzling. She puts him down and attempts to interest him in his train again by 'working' it in such a way as to attract his attention to it. He ignores it. She redoubles her efforts, and this time he begins to show some interest in it. 'Train,' she says. He stops and looks at her. 'Train,' she says again. ''Rain,' he says, beginning again to play with it. 'That's right,' she says, 'train.'

Illustrated in this episode are a number of points. First there is the natural embedding of cognitive factors in the child's social experience. Then there is the way in which real feelings and emotions are inevitably aroused, affording further openings, barriers, and so on, to the continuation of the interaction. Furthermore, in their more deliberate actions the participants offer one another opportunities for different forms of further action, often in the form of invitations to action which may, of course, be deliberately refused. Above all we want to draw attention to the interrelatedness of all these aspects within the unifying flow of a 'spontaneous dialogue' between mother and child, a dialogue of a quite unplanned kind.

We do so to argue against explaining the above episode solely in terms of a 'rule-following' model of human action. Both children and adults are not just rule followers but rule makers. Yet even before they have managed to establish anything like rules, their behaviour is still orderly, each act flows meaningfully into the next. Alan's mother, in acting in response to what he does—in putting him down when he grimaces, in redoubling her efforts when he fails to attend—responds particularly and precisely to him, directly in terms of her immediate perception of him in that situation. If she were working in terms of general rules she would still have to decide (on the basis of information picked up in the situation) *which* of all the rules available to her was the one to apply here, as well as precisely *how* it should be applied. And what applies to his mother also applies to Alan; his actions are also, we suggest, informed by his immediate perceptions: on perceiving himself observed by a powerful other, he acts in a 'silly' way in an attempt to have his behaviour discounted, his behaviour directly informed by his perception of his mother's power to call it into question. Rules are at issue only in a later stage of development, when matters of accountability and responsibility for deliberate action become more prominent (Shotter, 1974, 1978).

Let us consider some further examples:

Child: (sitting in her high chair, grizzling and whimpering, reaches in a grabbing fashion for her bottle, rocking back and forth).

Mother: (gives it into her hand) 'Is this what you want? Suck your nice "bockle" then.'

Child: (throws the bottle down and cries).

Mother: (picks her up, but she 'won't' be comforted—she

possibly 'wanted' to be picked up and nursed, but her
initial behaviour was insufficient to specify that, and
now her mother has made a 'mistake' by acting too late).
Here the (unintended) 'state' that the child is now 'in' has been progressively formed both by child and mother. Clearly, both would like it not
to be as it is; at least we can take it that, implied in what it is to be a
child is the desire to be happy rather than miserable if circumstances
will afford it. And thus the mother continues to experiment, both upon
the basis of 'the state' the child appears to be in *and* the implication
that somewhere is to be discovered the circumstances that will afford
her child an escape from it.

To take another example:

Mother: (offers bottle).
Child: (takes bottle but throws it down).
Mother: (smacks the child and offers the bottle again).
Child: (looks at mother and throws the bottle down again).
Mother: (a contained) 'Grrr . . .'

The 'mistake' initally made by the mother (if indeed it was a mistake)
has been converted into a 'wrong' that the child is now 'in'. And both
mother and child are going to have to take notice of the precise
character of that 'wrong' if they are to deal with it appropriately.
Already specified to a degree, the situation only affords further action
within it of an already specified kind. Of course, with a child, the
mother may 'break' the pattern of action in which they have entrapped
themselves, distracting her child by an utterly 'silly' act:

Mother: (clowning about by popping her tongue in and out, and
             rolling her eyes) 'Look . . . look. The big blue meany is
             coming to get you. Ohoo . . . o.'
Child: (laughs).

Nonetheless, she still appreciates her act as a silly one, that is, as an act
not normally appropriate in the circumstances.

Above we have illustrated activity in which people act spontaneously, without being conscious while acting of having any
particular reasons for their conduct. If asked to account for their
actions they would probably experience difficulty. This is not because
they are unconscious of their reasons and lack the vocabulary and skill
to articulate them, but because they do not possess *the* reason for
their conduct within themselves. The influences determining it are
spread out between them (non-locatable in any real spatial sense),
implicit in the individual *Umwelten* they constitute for one another.
Rather than by reference to their ideas or their knowledge, to anything

in their heads, their actions are explained by reference to the contents
of their *Umwelten,* in terms of the qualities and interrelations of the
entities they contain. And these are the terms in which the people
themselves will account for their actions if pressed to justify them:

Researcher: (to mother) 'Why did you smack her?'

Mother: 'Because she was in the wrong to throw her bottle
down like that . . . wasn't she?'

It is possible, however, to give a much fuller account of why she laid
her hand violently upon the flesh of her child—*the* reason for *her*
reason, in fact.

She did it, we might say, because:

(a) she believed, given her child's initial 'state' that if she offered her
the bottle, she would take it (that she is a human child of a certain age
implies amenability to such offers);

(b) she believes it to be a part of civilised conduct (upon which the
continued existence of the social order depends) that helpful offers
should not be rudely spurned, and if declined, declined politely, that is,
in a way which calls nobody's personhood into question;

(c) she believes the spurned offer did offend her personhood, by
suggesting her incapable of properly appreciating another person's state
(an ability implied in what it is to be a person);

(d) she believes herself to be a victim of an injustice, the social order
has been transgressed, and, she believes, punishment of the transgressor
will restore it;

(e) she believes a smack to be just such a punishment, one which
humiliates her child sufficiently to indicate that she will not tolerate
such treatment; and so on.

Clearly, the implicational structure of the mother's whole
Lebenswelt—not just the *Umwelt* in which she acted, but her social
world as it also appears to her in thought and reflection—is such that
everything in it is connected to everything else. Others are immersed
with her in that same implicate order. Thus it is enough for her to
justify her smack by referring to the child's 'wrong', for it serves to
indicate to others in her *Lebenswelt* what the effective environment for
her action was: her action was indeed informed by her perception. And
we accept, within limits, that persons have a right to act as they see fit.
These 'workings' of daily life are what the child must learn as he
develops into the *Umwelten* constituted jointly by himself and his
caretakers. And they are what he will learn, naturally, as long as the
appropriate conditions for their acquisition are established.

A notable feature of social *Umwelten* is that not only do they provide norms—in the sense of only affording at any moment further action of an already specified kind—but also an (implicit) moral framework, such that certain 'regions' of it offer risks to self or personhood; that is, there are 'places' or 'positions' in which people may 'lose', if not themselves, then at least certain aspects of their personal status, certain crucial rights, duties, privileges, and obligations.

The moral character of human *Umwelten* arises out of the paradoxical fact that, although human beings do not seem to possess any innately determined species-specific way of life, they nonetheless live, when in groups, as *persons* within the confines of a rational social order (Macmurray, 1961). If such an order is to endure, as it is not maintained instinctually, it is necessary for the entities constituting it to recognise transgressions of it, to identify the transgressions, and to have them make restitution and help to reinstitute and maintain the order. Without persons, without entities able to account for their actions, able to relate what they do to the established order, a human social order would fall apart. Hence other social unities—for example mother-child, husband-wife, boss-worker, teacher-pupil—which in theory might constitute the basic 'elements' of a social order, will not do. Such unities would, in their *joint action,* act unaccountably. Not knowing quite who is responsible for what, in any outcome they produced, they would not quite know how to correct it if in some way it was wrong—the position we are now in over juvenile delinquency and vandalism, where we are unclear as to whether society at large, the children, or the parents are 'responsible'.

Persons are the only entities able to account for their actions, to justify, acquit, and redeem themselves, to be able to be responsible and 'to answer for' what they do. Hence the very special status of *persons* within a social order, and the necessity to 'manufacture' persons out of its newborns if the social order is to be maintained. Personhood is a cultural universal (Geertz, 1975; Heelas and Lock, 1981).

Although space precludes any further analysis of it here, we suggest that its development can be understood in terms of the moral affordances—in terms of the rights and duties, etc.—mothers afford or attribute to their children in the course of their interactions with them. As long as the appropriate conditions are established, children will, we have assumed, grasp (or pick up) naturally that which is afforded them by their caretakers, and come to act in ways informed by what they pick up; by the rights accorded them and by the duties demanded of them. At least, this is how, we suggest, those actually entrusted with bringing up children proceed practically; and, initially at least, it is the appropriate conditions for such natural developmental processes which we as researchers wish to understand.

Other ways of learning, other sequences of development may in general be possible; some are demonstrated by laboratory experimentation. In our ecological approach, however, we wish to understand what in particular and how in particular, children in a particular society learn to be members of it, the conditions under which they grasp what is there in their surroundings to be grasped, as well as the conditions under which they may fail. Or alternatively: whether their surroundings are deficient, and what they need is simply not there to be grasped.

Conclusions: hermeneutical explanation as a first step

As psychologists observing mothers and children, we know that in some of the episodes we observe that developmental exchanges are taking place. In a global, not well-articulated way we appreciate the processes at work: we 'see' the child learning an interactional or communicative competence, grasping meanings, expressing intentions, accounting for him or herself, and so on. We want to know the details of the process, the significance of each interactional episode, what it means, what it permits or affords or indicates for the future. The task of transforming a superficial, global, and perhaps misunderstood grasp of things into an accurate, well-articulated account of its actual meaning is essentially a *hermeneutical* one (Taylor, 1971; Gauld and Shotter, 1977; Shotter, 1978).

The search for entirely general laws or rules, for 'objective' presuppositionless knowledge is irrelevant to such a task. Primarily, understandings from within a frame of reference, a tradition, or a culture are what is required. Once discovered, of course, and the frame of reference articulated, then the nature of the frame itself, its necessary and contingent features, the formal and substantive universals it embodies, may be investigated. And finally, the question may be raised as to what must be the fundamental nature of physical reality for such phenomena to be possible. Hermeneutical explanation—the interpretation of what is actually happening or being done may not be the final step in scientific explanation in psychology, but it is we believe a necessary first step. Returning to one of our examples, the 'wrong' in which that mother saw her child, constitutes, we maintain, an initial, irreplaceable, and irreducible datum which any further investigation cannot ignore.

From a practical point of view, (whether proceeding to a deeper scientific analysis or not), the products of a hermeneutical study can be very useful. Having their source in the practices of daily social life, in the spontaneous activities going on between mothers and children in which children develop naturally, they may be turned around to reflect back into those activities. They can be applied both to extend them, and to make their operation amenable to rational deliberation (Shotter, 1978, p. 49). Thus, unlike the 'block diagrams' and 'rule-schema' resulting in the traditional cognitive approach, our more ecological results may be 'put into practice' immediately, as that is the source from which they are derived. Furthermore, our own methodology, to the extent that it also involves the progressive rationalisation of a social practice (child development), achieved in the course of an active involvement with those under study, may be self-developing in the same way, reflecting back both into daily developmental practices as well as the practices involved in their study.

All societies must incorporate in their operational procedures of daily life, devices, 'mechanisms', social practices to do with 'manufacturing' from their newborns the basic elements capable of maintaining their social order, i.e., persons. To the extent that a society remains in existence, these procedures must exist somewhere (nonlocatable) in its ecology, spread out in its constituent interrelations. Thus to us, irrespective of what goes on in people's heads, it seems both an important and feasible endeavour to discover what those procedures are. Thus: ask not what goes on inside people, but what people go on inside of—though if everything is everywhere in an implicate order, it hardly matters, for everything inside is parallelled by what is outside anyway.

References

Bergson, H., *Mind-Energy*, London, Macmillan, 1920.

Bohm, D., *The Special Theory of Relativity*, New York, Benjamin, 1965.

Bohm, D., 'Quantum theory as an indication of a new order in physics. Part B. Implicate and explicate order in physical law', *Foundations of Physics*, 1973, *3*, 139-68.

Bohm, D., *Wholeness and the Implicate Order*, London, Routledge & Kegan Paul, 1980.

Donaldson, M., *Children's Minds*, London, Fontana, 1977.

Gauld, A., and Shotter, J., *Human Action and its Psychological Investigation*, London, Routledge & Kegan Paul, 1977.

Geertz, C., *The Interpretation of Cultures*, New York, Basic Books, 1973.

Gibson, J. J., *The Ecological Approach to Visual Perception*, London, Houghton Mifflin, 1979.

Goodman, N., *Ways of Worldmaking*, Sussex, Harvester Press, 1978.

Heelas, P., and Lock, A., *Indigenous Psychologies: the Anthropology of the Self*, London, Academic Press, 1981.

Leith, E. N., and Upatnieks, J., 'Photography by Laser', *Scientific American*, 1965, *212*, 24-35.

Lock, A., *The Guided Reinvention of Language*, London, Academic Press, 1980.

Macmurray, J., *Persons in Relation*, London, Faber and Faber, 1961.

Piaget, J., *Introduction a l'epistemologie genetique*, Vol III, Paris, Presses Univ. France, 1950.

Rommetveit, R., 'The architecture of intersubjectivity', in L. Strickland, F. Aboud, and K. J. Gergen (eds.) *Social Psychology in Transition*, New York, Plenum Press, 1976.

Shotter, J., 'The development of personal powers', in M. P. M. Richards (ed) *The Integration of the Child into a Social World*, Cambridge, Cambridge University Press, 1974.

Shotter, J., *Images of Man in Psychological Research*, London, Methuen, 1975.

Shotter, J., 'The cultural context of communication studies: methodological and theoretical issues', in A. Lock (ed.), *Action, Gesture and Symbol*, London, Academic Press, 1978.

Shotter, J., 'Action, joint action, and intentionality', in M. Brenner (ed.) *The Structure of Action*, Oxford, Blackwell, 1980.

Smedslund, J., 'Meanings, implications and universals: towards a psychology of man', *Scandanavian Journal of Psychology*, 1969, *10*, 1-15.

Smedslund, J., 'Circular relations between understanding and logic', *Scandanavian Journal of Psychology*, 1970, *11*, 217-19.

Smedslund, J., 'Piaget's psychology in practice', *British Journal of Educational Psychology*, 1977, *47*, 1-6.

Smedslund, J., 'Bandura's theory of self-efficacy: a set of commonsense theorems', *Scandanavian Journal of Psychology*, 1978, *19*, 1-14.

Taylor, C., 'Interpretation and the sciences of man', *Review of Metaphysics*, 1971, *25*, 3-51.

Uexküll, J., 'A stroll through the world of animals and men', in C. H. Schiller (ed.) *Instinctive Behaviour,* London, Methuen, 1957.
Vygotsky, L. S., *Mind in Society: The Development of Higher Psychological Processes,* Boston, Harvard University Press, 1978.

4 Towards a social-cognitive explanation of imitation development

Donald Clementson-Mohr

Introduction

Genuinely momentous research studies, ones that can 'change your mind' about a theoretically relevant problem, are rare in science, particularly so in psychology, So a number of developmentalists, the present author included, were astounded by Meltzoff and Moore's (1977) demonstration that human neonates can imitate.

In that research, Meltzoff conducted several methodologically sophisticated experiments; but the study's basic procedure was fairly simple. The experimenter presents an expressionless face for a short period of time. This is followed by the random-order modelling of lip protrusion, mouth opening, tongue protrusion, and sequential finger movements. The expressionless face is presented again. Independent coders rated videotapes of the infant's behaviour for the appearance of the modelled events. More often than expected by chance, the infants reproduced the gestures when presented.

This finding is at odds with most theoretical perspectives on the acquisition of imitation. Not only was the precocity of their subjects' ability unexpected, but also their imitation of facial gestures violates Piaget's (1962) widely accepted observation that very young infants are able to imitate only the actions of others that they have been able to see themselves perform.

However, it is possible that the implications for Piaget's theory have been overemphasised; that they do at least as much violence to the operant perspective. If the Meltzoff observations are accepted at face value, *and* if science progressed the way that Popper (1962) prescribes, then the study should have signed a death warrant for conditioning explanations of 'generalised imitation' (Gewirtz, 1971). This has not happened of course, and is not likely to; psychology is still in a pre-paradigmatic (Kuhn, 1970) state as a science. Recent failure to replicate (Hayes and Watson, 1979) have been, thus far, less convincing than the original study, particularly since Meltzoff's research was notable for care in execution and painstaking attention to alternative explanations.

There is an urgent need for a comprehensive theory of imitation. The questions about the phenomenon that are at once raised and left unanswered by the Meltzoff study are as broad as the fields of psychology and child development themselves. There is widespread agreement among developmentalists as to an important socialisation role for imitation, but nowhere is there a convincing account of the means by which the mechanism functions. This is the case precisely because the phenomenon has remained refractory to any but surface-level behaviouristic definitions or unmanageably abstract structuralist ones.

This is not to say that these definitional problems are restricted to the practitioners of psychological science. Biologists (Bonner, 1980) are ready to proclaim the crucial import of imitative learning for the adaptation of 'cultural' species (those which transmit information by behavioural rather than genetic means). An emphasis on learning as *the* issue of imitation is probably salutary, but biologists have generally not concerned themselves with specification of how this learning takes place. Since the definition of learning is a task traditionally left to psychologists, that point is better seen as a caution than a criticism. If there is any message made clear by the last twenty years of progress in psychological research, it is that functional definitions are only the beginning, not the end point of behavioural explanation. Given the present rapprochement of biology and psychology, the pressing need for a basis of communication about such cross-disciplinary constructs as imitation is obvious.

Issues and Problems in Definition

The closer one looks at imitation, the murkier it becomes. Aronfreed (1969) considered imitation to present a definitional 'problem'. This remains true because the usual common denominator for biological/psychological discussions is 'behaviour'. Even if that were a useful level of analysis for human action, there is no clear basis for describing imitation as a behaviour without a cumbersome array of operational qualifiers (Foss, 1965). But even with such qualification, there are logical problems with such a description of the imitative act. As Reese (1977) has argued, an act of imitation cannot be legitimately characterised as an isolatable response (in the operant sense) at all. An imitative act is an *abstraction* in that its occurrence definitionally necessitates the presence of an antecedent modelled 'behaviour' as well as the imitative 'behaviour', Hence the behaviourist must either assume that the imitative act is solely in his mind or expand his definition somewhat. The thrust of Neo-Behaviourism has been to follow the latter course.

Thus, most contemporary conceptions of imitation include, as least implicitly, some notion of cognitive processing. Bandura's (1969) definition for social learning theory is illustrative: 'an occurrence of similarity between the behaviour of the model and another person under conditions where the model's behaviour has served as the determinative one for the matching response' (p. 217). Note that while morphological 'similarity' carries the weight of operational definition, cognitive processing is tacitly built in with the concept of 'matching response'. According to Bandura (1977) the similarity is achieved by a series of cognitive processes which transform the perception of the modelled behaviour into a symbolic representation that can be stored and later be used to guide behaviour. This model allows Bandura to make a theoretically critical distinction between *acquisition,* which can be accounted for by attentional and memory process, and *performance,* which is based on motivational processes and motor abilities. The resulting conception of imitation is quite static, based on the additive contributions of relatively discrete mechanisms which are, phenomenally, probably highly interrelated (Brewer, 1974). Moreover, each 'process' is better seen within the model as a performance criterion; the individual is capable of imitation only to the extent that he has been attentive to the model, can retrieve the representation, has the component responses in his repertoire, and is motivated to imitate.

It is not surprising that this model has had great appeal for developmentalists; it parses imitation into factors that have a history of success in producing empirical age differences. Also, the model is sufficiently imprecise to accommodate almost anybody's theory of cognitive processing. That imprecision is of couse a weakness as well. This is no model of mind and behaviour as a coherent unity, but as discrete points in a linear sequence whose only relationship is a simple mechanical one. Bandura's conception is essentially an associationist approach with a great deal of cognitive window dressing in which symbols only aid in the learning and deployment of responses. As Parton (1976) has recently confessed, the theory has no real model of the 'how' of imitation that can account for infant acquisition of the competence. Even so, the problems with social learning theory's conception of imitation are prototypical of many approaches that pointedly disavow behaviourism *per se*. Most offer only scant explanatory improvement. As Weimer (1977) has observed, modern cognitive psychology has repudiated some of the more untenable aspects of behaviourism while retaining its underlying conceptual framework.

Most conceptions of imitation as cognitive porcesses are based on an allegiance to a 'representational' assumption for mind, what Weimer describes as 'sensory metatheory'. This entails a one-way, determinative sequence of perception—cognition—behaviour. Such a perspective on imitation can be much more sophisticated than that of Bandura; Meltzoff and Moore's (1977) explanation of their findings is squarely in the Zeitgeist of contemporary thinking in cognitive psychology. They posit that neonates innately possess abstract representations, cross-modal invariants of perceptual and motor activity. The infant imitator is described as comparing: ' . . . the sensory information from his own unseen motor behaviour to a supramodal representation of the visually guided gesture and construct the match required' (p. 78). The pertinent question here is not whether this is a good explanation of the representational process in imitation, but whether an explanation of imitation should employ the concept of representation at all.

The most obvious defect of the typical representation/matching-process view of imitation is with the standard operational definition drawn in terms of similarity. As Goodman has argued, this is an *inherently* ambiguous criterion. Since everything is, in some respect, similar to everything else, the difficulty lies in specifying what should count as 'similar'. As such, the concept is a rather precarious explanatory perch. For example, Meltzoff and Moore described their neonate subjects as imitating a model, using absolute morphological equivalence as the criterion. Condon and Sander (1974) on the other hand, found a fairly precise synchrony of neonates' motor movements to their mother's verbalisations. This is in one sense not very 'similar' and perhaps that is why the finding has not been described as imitative, though certainly the phenomenon fits the Meltzoff and Moore model very well. In any case, at the point that one can describe the dimensions of psychological equivalence, the concept of material similarity becomes superfluous, a hold-over from a perspective that would define imitation as a response.

By dispensing of similarity as *the* criterion for imitation, the necessity of a representational explanation is eliminated, though it is still possible. If imitation is minimally specified as the intentional use of the action of another to serve as a guide for one's own goal-directed action, it is feasible to assume the existence of a representation of the modelled behaviour which is embedded in the imitator's ongoing activity. The representation would still be externally-derived and determinative of the form of the imitative act. Development of imitation could then be couched in terms of change in the qualities of the represenational mode, change in the skill of application of the representation to problem-solving situations, and so on. As noted earlier, the idea is intuitively compelling, given a long-standing epistemology for psychology which assumes representation of the environment as a basis for all cognitive activity.

It is the writer's inclination to discount such a sensory metatheory in favour of a 'motor' metatheory (Weimer, 1977) based on an active rather than a passive metaphor for mind (Overton, 1976). In part, this decision reflects a judgement that representational explanation is too cumbersome to be valid. But there are better reasons for taking this position than just intellectual taste. For one, it would seem that much of the ambiguity in a cognitive description of imitation or any other activity is to be found in the linking of representation to behaviour, especially in the learning process. Mind and action, like mind and body, are not easily stapled back together, once separated. Even more importantly, the notion of behaviour as necessarily directed by externally-derived representations seems contrary to a conception of mind as a biologically evolved mechanism of adaptation to an environment and of action as adaptational process, and is thus intrinsically unsatisfactory.

Therefore, the idea of imitation as based on imaginal representations of modelled acts can be discarded in favour of an accommodative mechanism, one that allows a process of attunement to the structure of the perceived action. Development would then be most likely to occur in the qualities of the cognitive organisation that is implicit to the accommodative activity.

Piaget's Theory

All of this leads quite naturally to Piaget's theory. The Piagetian concept of imitation (Piaget, 1962) can be seen as describing the route by which an action-based 'representation' (in the sense of a *fit* to external reality rather than a mirror of it) is achieved, releasing the child's intellect from being at the mercy of every inconsistency encountered in his activities. This is a specialised case of the more general cognitive function of achieving equilibrium with the environment. Thus, definitionally, there is little that can be said about the Piagetian concept of imitation that is not dependent on developmental status except that, in general, imitation is an act of motor correspondence to the configurational properties of an external model's activity. The more commonly known Piagetian definition of imitation, based on the relative weighting of the adaptive functions, is avoided here because in the first eight months of life they are not differentiated in the activity of the infant. Thus, to assert that imitation involves nearly pure accommodation can be misleading and it does have the unintended effect of downgrading the importance of assimilatory structures for imitation. It should be remarked, however, that this idea is quite widespread precisely because it is the one Piaget himself emphasised.

But in his description of imitation in the early months of life, more important for Piaget than the question of the relative balance of assimilation and accommodation is the problem of the roots of imitation. Piaget posits that the beginning of imitation is quite simply when accommodation to a model goes on past perception, and therefore imitation cannot be accounted for by an appeal to perceptual mechanisms. Although, like perception, imitation is concerned with figurative knowledge, the mode of imitative knowledge is grounded in action. Thus, by the eighth month of life, a great deal of sophistication in imitation can be observed, based on general intellectual development. But imitation is still quite conservative; only actions that the infant has previously performed serve as a basis for imitation.

As always for Piaget, the route to overcoming such limitations is in the infant's own activity. The infant maps his acts on to his environment and there is a resulting differentiation of intellectual function. This leads the infant to become interested in practising his own schemas which produces further differentiation. Imitation gradually becomes a function in its own right and a general 'method' of accommodating to new models. The imitative competence becomes quite exact as the infant's internal mapping is completed. As the infant nears the middle of the second year of life his map of self is so well co-ordinated with his schemas that he can imitate the gestures of body parts he cannot see *if* he has made the movements previously.

This ushers in the close of sensorimotor development in which the mechanics of imitation become complete. While imitation is influenced by later cognitive development, it always remains a sensorimotor knowing process. The hallmark of imitation at this age is that it can be deferred, one of several new representational capacities that appear around or after the middle of the second year. These include the imitation of new models even though the movements have not been made before and involve body parts that cannot be concurrently visualised; the immediate imitation of complex models; and the systematic imitation of object-models. It should be emphasised again that the developmental basis of the child's capacity to represent non-present events is to be found in previous imitative activity and not in perception. Conceptually, the description of the development of infant imitation is all quite tidy and self-contained.

Concerning the years following the child's acquisition of representation, the tight interlockedness of Piaget's explanation for imitation development appears to slip a bit. The relationship between the development of imitation and other aspects of the child's cognitive functioning is not clearly drawn. Where the connections are made, the reasoning seems forced and after the fact, as if Piaget never actively came to intellectual grips with the phenomenon. Piaget actually had very little to say about imitation after the age of two or so and this should come as no great surprise. As noted previously, sensorimotor intelligence, the basis of imitation across the life-span, has reached its zenith at the point that internal representation is accomplished. Changes in imitation after that level will eventuate because of changes in the cognitive system which are not directly related to the sensorimotor imitative mechanism. Its over-riding developmental significance as an activity is gradually overshadowed by the burgeoning importance of the more 'conceptual' aspects of mind. In imitation, as in all intelligent acts, Piaget is quite firm about the 'subordination' of sensorimotor intelligence to the operative.

What, then, is the nature of developmental changes in imitation after the age of two? One specific change is in the relation of the imitative act to the internal image of the model. In stages one to five of the sensorimotor period, there is, of course, no image involved at all. In stage six, the image is intrinsic to the imitative act. As the child moves into pre-operative thought, imitation *always* follows the image, or rather is a continuation of it. The imitative act draws upon the image (based on previous imitations) of the model, not the model itself. A consequence of egocentric thought at this age is the non-consciousness idea that there might be some theoretically important differences of imitation. For example, even though imitation has become the 'vehicle' of the child's inter-personal relations with resulting differential imitation along status relation lines, the child seems unaware of the distinction he is making and there is little imitation of detail. At the age of seven or so, imitation is described as becoming reintegrated into intelligence as a whole. Imitative acts become more strategic and discriminative, based on needs arising from the child's ongoing activity. Why and how the advent of operative intelligence should make this difference is never made clear. The weakness of Piaget's discussion of the pre-operational child's imitative predilections may arise because his arguments here are not buttressed by his exquisite natural observations.

Criticisms of the Piagetian Model

In the terms used earlier, Piaget's investigation of the development of imitative behaviour can be seen as an attempt to reduce the ambiguity of a strictly behavioural explanation. It would be difficult to gainsay his success in that task. Piaget's account of infant imitation is still *the* definitive study, the yardstick by which present studies are measured and interpreted. Even so, this discussion of Piaget's theory might seem too detailed were it not the case that his conception of imitation is still routinely misunderstood (Brainerd, 1978), which can mask its tremendous heuristic potential. Much can be learned from thoughtful criticisms of Piaget's conception of the imitative act. The greatest value of a rich theory like Piaget's may lie where it seems most unsatisfactory.

One important difficulty with the Genevan case has, quite simply, to do with descriptive limitations of the phenomena that Piaget chose to include as instances of imitative behaviour. Imitation defined solely as accommodation served his theoretical goals very well; there is no doubting the coherence of his arguments. But in terms of the child's ongoing adaptive activity and its explanation, it is not a very interesting definition; it deliberately excludes phenomena that might intuitively seem imitative to non-orthodox admirers of the structuralist point of view. For example, if the child elaborates the model in any way, then the activity is assimilative and out of the imitation bailiwick. But this effectively excludes most learning; and as suggested earlier, learning would properly be at the heart of an explanation of imitation. Further, is there something special about imitation as a learning process? Since

Piaget has only rarely concerned himself with problems of learning, the idea that there might be some theoretically important differences between instrumental and observational learning seems never to have captured his interest. To do so would have been to inquire into the nature of assimilation and Piaget has evidently found it preferable to treat the concept as a given.

On the grounds of theoretical parsimony, one can understand why Piaget chose the conceptual route for imitation that he did. However, if there is anything that is abundantly clear from the best of the edifice of research on observational learning (Zimmerman, 1977), it is that children of a wide range of ages can learn surprisingly complex behaviour patterns in modelling situations. It is difficult to imagine how Piagetians can ever take a clearly defined stance on the limits to observational learning without coming to grips with its mechanism. Given Piaget's clear disposition to view imitation as intentional investigation, there doesn't seem to be a strong case that the tenets of his theory demand the strict accommodative view. The decision to cloister infant imitation at the figurative knowledge end of his theory appears to be tidy but somewhat arbitrary, and has had the effect of sealing off the construct from potentially interesting avenues of research.

This difficulty with the Piagetian conception may be viewed in methodological terms rather than solely on theoretical grounds. If we assume that imitation logically includes those instances when the child not only accommodates to the behaviour of another but uses it, like a *tool*, then the problem may be the criterion Piaget used for selecting imitative events. With only a few exceptions, he focussed on relatively contextless gestures and instrumental acts. By doing so, he assured that the simple cognitive accommodation explanation would be the most parsimonious and could thus retain the concept of imitation at the most abstract levels of his theory, freeing him to weave these acts into his more general model of cognitive change.

Piaget's case would have been far more compelling if it had included an explicit role for the social context of mental development in general and the imitative act in particular. The simple brute fact is that the greatest number of Piaget's observations concerned acts of imitation within a social context; that he was *interacting* with his children did not attract theoretical concern. This is probably another case of a definitional rigidity resulting from avoiding an alternative that was seen as conceptually more pernicious. Piaget was very explicit, repetitiously so, in his rejection of social explanations of the acquisition of imitation. The vigour of his attack on this point of view leads this author to suspect that Piaget was attempting to avoid any possibility that he might be seen as approving of a role for an extra-system mechanism for imitation development. It is clear in his writing on imitation that he resolutely rebuffed any notion of a socially determined explanation for mind and that resolve has not diminished (1971).

However, there is a genuine theoretical difficulty with this position since Piaget does not lean toward the notion of imitation as being the 'vehicle' of social relations in the post-infancy years. This is hardly in line with theoretical demands for continuity in development. Moreover, there is no theoretically specified mechanism that 'attaches' the imitative act to interpersonal relations in those later stages of development. This makes the non-social nature of imitation in infancy even more of a glaring problem. Casting the imitative act in terms of a social event seems called for if the Genevan case is to achieve coherence.

Explicitly to include social factors in Piaget's conception of imitation would certainly involve an elaboration of the theory, but it would not necessarily do harm to its constructionalist essence. It is certainly not suggested here that the Piagetian mode of thinking should be distorted to accommodate such paradigmatically alien factors as personality attributes of the model and the reinforcement histories of the relation between model and observer, although these are 'social' factors that have indeed made a difference for children's imitative performance. Such concepts can be seen as rather static metaphors for the qualities of an ongoing interaction system (Bell and Harper, 1977), the construction and maintenance of which is an active function of the child's input even in the first few weeks of life (Trevarthen, 1977). If so, then why not consider imitation from a perspective that emphasises the active context of structuring social as well as physical reality?

The essential tension for a definitional description of imitation development is thus in the determination of the nature of the interlocking relationship between its cognitive and social components. There is no theory in psychology which comprehensively deals with the cognitive/social nexus in any context, except as discrete factors. This has been a long-standing conundrum for psychology and is particularly evident in the study of language. It may well be that the 'mystery' of language acquisition will remain such until this issue is resolved. It is an outsider's perception of the language acquisition literature that the recent concern with language as communication has precipitated the most meaningful breakthroughs in this area of inquiry by emphasising both the social and cognitive aspects of the process (Bruner, 1978).

Comparable advances in the study of imitation may await the adoption of a similar perspective.

Bruner's Theory

Bruner (1972) is the only theorist who has ever assayed a social-cognitive argument concerning imitation. He did so from an explicitly comparative perspective on ontogeny. As Bruner reminds developmentalists, evolution does not operate solely on finished behaviour systems; the evolutionary history of a species is profoundly implied in how its immature state is 'managed'. It is not unreasonable to expect that a conceptual purchase on imitation development might emerge from informed speculation on its adaptive function. The phenomenon is pervasive throughout the higher primate species and, as an intentional mechanism of learning, probably does not appear in non-primates at all (Wilson, 1975). The argument is not that an evolutionary/comparative approach to imitation is a royal road to the understanding of its underlying processes. Rather, the perspective does provide a frame of reference, a place from which to commence the discourse.

For example, this line of thinking opens the door to such questions as: why does man imitate? And by specifying the evolution-related 'whys' of imitation, reasonable speculations can further be made about the 'who' of the imitative cogniser. As Shaw and McIntyre (1974) have pointed out, cognitive psychologists have generally limited themselves to the 'what' and 'how' questions (the algorithms) concerning the organisational processes underlying behaviour. They argue that, without specifying the 'who' (the algorist), any model of cognitive activity is hopelessly incomplete. Extending their argument, it is an assumption taken here that the qualities of the human algorist involve limitations on cognition that are best explicated by attention to the likely demands of evolutionary adaptation, not strictly logical/computational ones. To some minimal extent at least, the imitative algorist must be found in the phylogenetic history of our species, part of the primate 'plan'. Precisely this argument has been explored by Bruner (1972).

In an elegant and brilliantly reasoned essay, Bruner places the imitation mechanism squarely in the cultural evolution of man, which was characterised by a shift from fixed linear relationships to social systems based on reciprocal exchange. It is Bruner's thesis that these changes were accompanied by parallel changes in patterns of 'managing immaturity'. Specifically, this entailed '. . . the appearance of a pattern involving an enormous amount of observation of adult behaviour by the young, with incorporation of what has been learned into a pattern of play' (1972, p. 4). Imitative behaviour is thus classified as 'serious' play, incorporating what is observed into the solution of a task. It is only in a playful context, in which means are not firmly tied to ends, that the observed activity can be successfully used in problem-solving. Bruner has tested this latter notion (Sylva, Bruner, and Genova, 1976) and found some support for it.

According to Bruner, manifestation of this intriguing interrelationship of imitation, play, and problem-solving requires particular sorts of social context. In part, there must be an emancipation from the attentional demands of rigid social bonding. Bruner observes that a number of primatologists are convinced that the observational mastery of complex tool skills depends on the focussed arena of mother-child interaction but the evidence for this hypothesis is limited (Wilson, 1978).

Bruner marshalls an impressive array of comparative evidence and evolutionary reasoning to support a general argument that man's capacity for imitation evolved in tandem with his communicative skills and cerebral cortex. All three can be seen as part of general reciprocal adaptation to an existence increasingly dominated by the cultural mode. Bruner especially emphasised the link of imitation to tool-using/problem-solving, the former being a necessary route to a repertoire of skills in the latter activities. Bruner also asserts that it is the nature of the primate bond that produces special social regulative demands on the developing organism which are met, in the absence of ritualised instruction (even among human groups, a comparative rarity, given the history of our species), by imitation. Thus imitation cannot be fully understood by recourse only to the intellectual qualities of mind; explanation requires attention to intimate social relationships as well.

These are bold and stimulating ideas. Perhaps too vague for some tastes, they contain a broad range of general research directions to be pursued, if not specific hypotheses to be tested. It would be gratifying to be able to report that the ideas have indeed been heuristic. They have not. Why? A number of reasons are probably involved, but the most complete explanation would have to include the fact that Bruner's insights on this topic tend to violate a pervasive set of assumptions about the nature of human cognition. These can be described fairly simply. For one, mind is generally viewed as a unitary matter of 'practical intelligence', which makes possible learning, problem-solving, tool-use and making, and so on. This same basic intellectual capacity, whatever theoretical form it takes, is assumed to be involved in the learning of social regulatory mechanisms. Mind can be quite variously differentiated, but it is of a single kind.

Thus, social interaction itself enters into the development of mind solely in a supporting role. For example, social factors can provide the motivation to solve problems, serve as an elaborative context for the problem and its solution (such that each is recognised as such), and provide experienced guidance for the solution of problems. But social interaction is seen as extrinsic to the meaning of the problem-solving mechanism.

Bates' Theory

Imitation is generally viewed as a highly efficient route by which social interaction can have the above-mentioned cognitive facilitation effects; in fact, it ususally is seen as a *critical* mechanism in this respect. But it is also ubiquitously described as a relatively 'primitive' mechanism of learning, with no intrinsic complexity as psychological process. This is true even when morphological similarity is *not* crucial to the definition of imitation.

An illustration of the latter point can be found in Bates' (1977) thinking on imitative learning. Bates' treatment of imitation elaborates that of Bruner and also differs from it in interesting ways. Bates is far more concerned with the cognitive mechanisms of the imitative act. The processes of imitation are seen as largely determined by man's capacity for drawing *arbitrary* relationships between events. Imitation entails the acquisition of end-means relationships without a prior analysis of the means. More specifically, imitation involves the creation of an iconic motor analogue (through some unknown matching process) between a perceived sequence of behaviours which comprise a means-ends relationship and an internal behaviour scheme. Furthermore, in order to be considered as a true instance of imitative process, the observer must use a representation (in the Piagetian sense of the term) of a model's behavioural sequence that is not yet fully assimilated. In this case one can often detect such an imitative process through behavioural adjustments on the part of the observer, bringing his behaviour increasingly in line with that of the model.

Although there is a distinct flavour of associationism to Bates' concept of imitation, it clearly also depends on constructive cognitive processes on the part of the observer. The centre of emphasis is on the representational activity itself, unlike mediational approaches. Recall that Bandura was forced to divide imitation into learning and performance in order to account for deferred imitation. Because cognitive processing is definitional to Bates' conception, this distinction is not necessary. However, it is the case that an important aspect of Bates' thinking is her emphasis on the idea that imitative behaviour need not be performed in order to be counted as an instance of imitation (as in Bandura's model). It is with this notion that Bates explains individual differences in imitative language performance (Bloom, *et al.*, 1974). The differences may only be in the timing of the overt imitative act. What is commonly distinguished as imitation may refer only to those instances in which means-ends relations are re-presented in behaviour before sufficient analysis has taken place.

Like Bruner, Bates strongly stresses the role of tool-using/problem-solving activity in her conception of imitation. There seems to be good *a priori* cause for taking this position. The general hypothesis, that an explanation for much of the ontogenetic character of mind can be found in an innate readiness for the cultural mode, seems unassailable. From this point of view, imitation comfortably enters the picture as a mechanism for the transmission of cultural skills from one generation to the next. Certainly if imitation did not exist, then something functionally similar would have to be available to replace it. Virtually no modern developmental psychologist questions that direct experience is an insufficient explanation for the child's acquisition of all the skills he uses. But how much of a role should be given over to the problem-solving situation for a sufficient explanation of imitation?

Bates and Bruner differ in that regard. Bates would reduce the nature of the imitative mechanism to a schematic of the functional properties of a problem-solving act, the connection of ends to means. Thus, she places her conception square in the 'practical intelligence' tradition. Bruner would seem to prefer to introduce unique qualities of social interaction into his conception of imitation, but he never delved into the nature of such a mechanism. So, by default, he conforms to the same tradition of assumptions concerning mind. This is even more clear in the research of Kaye (Kaye and Marcus, 1978) who, working in Bruner's (1973) tradition of skill acquisition, studied imitation in a fashion that leaves it indistinguishable from instrumental learning. The imitative mechanism is, in effect, virtually reduced to the skills that are learned with it. One is left with a sense that a postition like that of

Bates is inevitable if the definitional emphasis for imitation is restricted to the intellectual context of the problem-solving situation.

The Phylogeny and Ontogeny of Social Intelligence

Now it would be simply wrong to deny that the evolution of human culture has taken much of its form because of man's technological propensities. It is hard even to conceive of culture as a concept outside of man's exogenetic adaptation to his environment. Yet, culture is not co-extensive with technology; a better, more inclusive definition of culture would deal with the system of shared meaning that links technology to the fabric of social existence (Geertz, 1973). The 'who' of the imitative algorist is a communicator as well as a problem-solver. It is interesting to speculate then, that the power of the human problem-solving capacity derives from the general planfulness of human social activity, not from the demands of problem-solving situations. That is to say, the use and learning of cultural skills may be only meaningfully conceived of within the webs of significance that comprise the totality of any individual's cultural milieu. If so, the fullest conception of the development of mind and imitation would account for the social interchange qualities of cultural transmission as well as its immediate functional properties.

That last line of reasoning can be employed while still retaining an evolutionary perspective. Humphrey (1976) has argued that the evolution of man's unique cognitive capacity was probably not in the sphere of 'practical invention' because the evolving hunter-gatherer simply did not need such a powerful mechanism in order to enhance physical survival. Rather, the adaptive basis for creative intellect can be found precisely in the cognitive skills which maintain the transactional quality of social interaction. In a fashion that is analogous to the notion of pre-adaptation in evolutionary biology (Gould, 1977), Humphrey advances the hypothesis that social intelligence is applied to problem-solving activity and that this accounts for the complexity of human cultural skills and their ontogenetic acquisition. In a sense then, the fullest flower of mind as a problem-solving mechanism is an evolutionary accident, a social by-product which would have never eventuated through a direct selection process.

There are implications of these ideas for a theory of imitation. Unlike the conception of Bruner, in which the suggestion is that phylogenetic changes in human social structure *facilitated* the use of imitation for means/end skill-learning in human ontogeny, Humphrey raises the possiblity that the ability to interact within human social structure is *intrinsic* to mind and hence, the imitative act. But in what terms should this notion be advanced?

Towards that descriptive end, one can extrapolate from Humphrey's ideas three relatively simple and inclusive statements about mind, social interaction, and imitation. First of all, social intelligence is probably both innate (in the sense of a cognitive readiness for social exchange) and, theoretically at least, differentiable from practical intelligence. Furthermore, the development of mind is best understood as an integration of practical and social intelligence. And finally, if both of the previous statements are provisionally acceptable, then it is likely that the development of such a phenomenon as imitation should not be studied as a matter of practical intelligence alone. Nor would it seem wise to empirically pursue the construct as if it were a discrete and primitive mechanism with a single thread of development.

That the human infant is innately prepared for, and disposed to, social commerce is an idea that seems to have found its time, given the increasing evidence of social precocity in human infants. In the study noted earlier, Condon and Sander (1974) found that adults synchronise their body movements both with their own speech and with the speech of others. In a stunning demonstration of interpersonal co-ordination, the investigators found that newborns display the same sort of fine-tuned synchrony of their bodily movements with the speech of their mothers. Even more overt social co-ordination has been observed at this age. Trevarthen (1977) found evidence of 'conversations' in the inter-actions of mother-neonate dyads in which the infants took an active, albeit limited role in the exchange. One interesting aspect of this pervasive social readiness on the part of the human neonate includes motor control of communicative acts among which are the same behaviours that Meltzoff and Moore (1977) employed as modelling stimuli. Trevarthen reports the incidence of such 'gesturing' behaviours as occurring when the child is *socially* excited. Thus, not only is the social engagement that would seem to be required for an act of imitation available at birth, but the motor programmes are as well.

Although Bruner (1973) has found evidence for an innate inten-tionality in skilled (non-social) action, it is not necessarily the case that the neonate's social intentions are based on the same mechanism. For example, Trevarthen (1978) argues that there are at birth, two primary modes of mental functioning which are relatively differentiated for several months. One is 'subjective' which involves, in part, a motoric map of self. The other is 'intersubjective' which entails innate intentions to communicate, but the resulting interaction is phatic, for its own sake only. The subjective mode appears to be dominant in the first few months of life.

The proposition advanced earlier, that practical and social intelligence are integrated in ontogeny, is supported by Trevarthen's observations. He argues that at the age of six months or so the infant undergoes a rather thorough-going reorganisation of mind, based on a melding of the subjective and intersubjective in the child's activity. This results among other things in the child's active engagement of the mother in communication patterns focussed on what the infant is doing. This is secondary intersubjectivity, which is characterised by 'triadic and co-operative play with and about things and experiences shared' (p. 127). It is this mode of functioning that Trevarthen posits as the primary basis for the dynamics of development. The child at this age is no longer interested in 'chatty' communication with the mother though he will do so with a stranger. Clearly the primary relationship is providing a frame for the infant to structure his activities, just as Bruner (1972) has suggested. The secondary intersubjectivity transformation appears to extend to imitative learning as well; at the same age that phatic communication is falling out, the infant is showing a distinct preference for imitating modelled actions with objects over those without (Abravanel, *et al.,* 1976).

The advent of secondary intersubjectivity may perhaps be best described as a matter of arriving at a shared metric to serve as an interpersonal framework, one that is parhaps more flexible than the tight-knit inter-co-ordination reported by Condon and Sander. In the months preceding the integration of the subjective and intersubjective modes of functioning, Trevarthen reports that the infant's social interaction with the mother is becoming rhythmical, with breaks in which the infant appears to be attempting to bring context into the 'conversation'. Moreover, the infant begins to exhibit pre-speech in these interactions, making speech-like movements of lips and tongue in response to vocalisation. These observations help to make sense of the finding of an upsurge of imitation of auditory (especially vocal) stimuli at this age (Maratos, 1973); true communicative intent appears to be awakening.

The idea of a broad-based integration of social and practical intelligence appears quite plausible in the light of these data. But for integration to be theoretically meaningful as a developmental mechanism, differentiation must be implied as well (Werner, 1940), and this ensures that a particular integration is almost never a one-time affair in ontogeny. Hence, there is no good *a priori* reason to expect that such an inter-co-ordination would be anything but a cyclic phenomenon, punctuated by major shifts in the complex of: (1) the child's cognitive organisation and the problems he seeks out, (2) the nature of the social interactions in which he engages and, (3) the qualities of the particular social/cognitive fulcrum of their harmonisation. Of course, not everything psychological must be related to everything else, but it is not unreasonable to expect certain genetic regularities along these lines.

What sort of developmental sequence is likely to best describe this ongoing integration of social and practical intelligence in ontogeny? The evidence is patchy but what there is suggests that the most fruitful conception is one that emphasises the acquisition of 'control processes' (Brown and DeLoache, 1979) which have to do with the conscious deployment of social skills. These self-regulation mechanisms are probably best viewed as an emergent feature of the dialectics of mutual interaction (Bruner, 1978; Marvin, 1977; Wertsch, 1978). It is the mechanism of such 'meta-skills' and how they are employed to facilitate learning within social and non-social settings which should properly be the focus of research on the development of imitation, not attempts to directly elicit out-of-context imitative acts.

Conclusion

Thus, what probably best separates the relatively mature human problem-solver from other primates is the presence of control processes which guide the child's learning activity, including imitation. Although chimps have been observed to imitate with some measure of planfulness (Wilson, 1978), what an older pre-school child might (rarely) do that a chimpanzee would never do is to strategically *seek out* someone to watch in order to learn from, or in a certain sense be instructed by that model. In this way, Bonner's conception of instructional transmission of knowledge serving as the basis for the interface of human intellect and culture can be preserved; recall that formal instruction is a comparative rarity for our species. Bonner did assume that man's great propensity for imitation is linked to instruction but the relationship is probably closer than that. Tutoring itself can be seen as only a little more than imitation skills turned around, both based on abilities that are achieved rather early in development and are probably related to role-taking skills (Shatz and Gelman, 1973). Intuitively, the only important difference between the imitative and tutoring events would seem to be that the latter necessarily involves an intention on the part of the model/tutor to facilitate learning. For learning to take place, both events require an intention to learn on the part of the imitator/ learner.

A broad outline of possibilities for empirical research of such an approach to imitation readily suggests itself. Imitation is a social event and will undergo a successful developmental investigation only within the context of naturalistic and semi-naturalistic observation of meaning-ful social interactions. The emphasis must be firmly on the mutual regulation of observational learning and only minimally on what the imitative behaviours 'look like'. While imitation can presumably occur in any non-stressful social context, it would seem most likely to be profitable to break down the communicative and learning parameters of the tutoring situation (Wood, Bruner and Ross, 1976) as the proto-typical setting for imitative learning to most effectively take place.

The motivation for conducting research of this kind would properly be quite high. When imitation, its development, and precise relationship to the tutoring process are well understood, psychology will have taken a giant step towards a comprehensive explanation of mind and its relation to culture.

References

Abravanel, E., Levan-Goldschmidt, E., and Stevenson, M. B. 'Action Imitation: The Early Phase of Infancy', *Child Development*, 1978, *49*, 1032-44.

Aronfreed, J. 'The Problem of Imitation' in *Advances in Child Development and Behaviour*, Academic Press, 1969, Vol. 14.

Bandura, A. 'Social Learning Theory of Identificatory Processes' in ed. D. A. Goslin, *Handbook of Socialisation Theory and Research*, Rand McNally, 1969.

Bandura, A. *Social Learning Theory*, Prentice Hall, 1977.

Bates, E. 'The Emergence of Symbols', Paper delivered to Minnesota Symposia of Child Psychology, Minneapolis, 1977.

Bell, R. Q., and Harper, L. V. *Child Effects on Adults*, Wiley, 1977.

Bloom, L., Hood, L., and Lightbown, P. 'Imitation in Language Development', *Cognitive Psychology*, 1974, *6*, 380-420.

Bonner, J. T. *The Evolution of Culture in Animals,* Princeton University Press, 1980.

Brainerd, C. J. *Piaget's Theory of Intelligence,* Prentice Hall, 1978.

Brewer, W. F. 'The Problem of Meaning and the Inter-relations of the Higher Mental Processes' in eds. W. B. Weimer and D. S. Palmero, *Cognition and the Symbolic Processes,* Erlbaum, 1974.

Brown, A. L., and DeLoache, J. S. 'Skills, Plans, and Self-Regulation' in ed. R. Siegler, *Children's Thinking: What Develops?,* Erlbaum, 1979.

Bruner, J. S. 'Nature and Uses of Immaturity', *American Psychologist,* 1972, *27,* 687-708.

Bruner, J. S. 'Organisation of Early Skilled Action', *Child Development,* 1973, *44,* 1-11.

Bruner, J. S. 'Learning How To Do Things with Words' in eds. J. S. Bruner and A. Garton, *Human Growth and Development,* Oxford University Press, 1978.

Condon, W. S., and Sander, L. W. 'Synchrony Demonstrated between Movements of the Neonate and Adult Speech', *Child Development,* 1974, *45,* 456-62.

Foss, B. M. 'Imitation' in ed. B. M. Foss, *Determinants of Infant Behaviour,* Wiley, 1965, Vol. 3.

Geertz, C. *The Interpretation of Cultures,* Basic Books, 1973.

Gewirtz, J. L. 'Conditional Responding as a Paradigm for Observational, Imitative Learning, and Vicarious Reinforcement' in *Advances in Child Development and Behaviour,* Academic Press, 1971, Vol. 16.

Gould, S. J. *Ever Since Darwin,* Norton, 1977.

Hayes, L. A., and Watson, J. S. 'Neonatal Imitation: Fact or Artifact?', Paper delivered to Society for Research in Child Development, San Francisco, 1979.

Humphrey, N. K. 'The Social Function of Intellect' in eds. P. P. G. Bateson and R. A. Hinde, *Growing Points in Ethology,* Cambridge University Press, 1976.

Kaye, K., and Marcus, J. 'Imitation Over a Series of Trials without Feedback', *Infant Behaviour and Development,* 1978, *1,* 141-55.

Kuhn, T. *The Structure of Scientific Revolutions,* University of Chicago Press, 1970.

Maratos, O. 'The Origin and Development of Imitation in the First Six Months of Life', Unpublished paper, University of Geneva, 1973.

Marvin, R. S. 'An Ethological-Cognitive Model for the Attenuation of Mother-Child Attachment Behaviour' in eds. T. Alloway, P. Pliner, and L. Krames, *Attachment Behaviour,* Plenum, 1977.

Medawar, P. 'Does Ethology Throw any Light on Human Behaviour?' in eds. P. P. G. Bateson and R. A. Hinde, *Growing Points in Ethology,* Cambridge University Press, 1976.

Meltzoff, A. N., and Moore, M. K. 'Imitation of Facial and Manual Gestures by Human Neonates', *Science,* 1977, *198,* 75-8.

Overton, W. F. 'The Active Organism in Structuralism', *Human Development,* 1976, *19,* 71-86.

Parton, D. A. 'Learning to Imitate in Infancy', *Child Development,* 1976, *47,* 14-31.

Piaget, J. *Play, Dreams, and Imitation in Childhood,* Norton, 1962.

Piaget, J. *Biology and Knowledge,* University of Chicago Press, 1971.

Popper, K. A. *Conjectures and Refutations: The Growth of Scientific Knowledge,* Harper, 1963.

Reese, H. W. 'A Learning-Theory Critique of the Operant Approach', Paper delivered to American Psychological Association, San Francisco, 1977.

Shatz, M., and Gelman, R. 'The Development of Communication Skills', *Monographs of the Society for Research in Child Development,* 1973, *152.*

Shaw, R., and McIntyre, M. 'Algoristic Foundations to Cognitive Psychology' in eds. W. B. Weimer and D. S. Palermo, *Cognition and the Symbolic Processes,* Erlbaum, 1974.

Sylva, K., Bruner, J. S., and Genova, P. 'The Role of Play in the Problem-Solving of Children 3-5 Years Old' in eds. J. S. Bruner, A. Jolly, and K. Sylva, *Play: Its Role in Development and Evolution,* Basic Books, 1976.

Trevarthen, C. 'Descriptive Analyses of Infant Communicative Behaviour' in ed. H. R. Schaffer, *Studies in Mother-Infant Interaction,* Academic Press, 1977.

Trevarthen, C. 'Modes of Perceiving and Modes of Acting' in eds. H. L. Pick and E. Saltzman, *Modes of Perceiving and Processing Information,* Erlbaum, 1978.

Weimer, W. B. 'A Conceptual Framework for Cognitive Psychology: Motor Theories of the Mind' in eds. R. Shaw and J. D. Bransford, *Perceiving, Acting, and Knowing,* Erlbaum, 1977.

Werner, H. *Comparative Psychology of Mental Development,* Harper, 1940.

Wertsch, J. V. 'Adult-Child Interaction and the Roots of Meta-Cognition', *The Quarterly Newsletter of the Institute for Comparative Human Development,* 1978, *2,* 15-8.

Wilson, E. O. *Sociobiology: The New Synthesis,* Belknap, 1975.

Wilson, E. O. *On Human Nature,* Harvard University Press, 1978.

Wood, D., Bruner, J. S., and Ross, G. 'The Role of Tutoring in Problem Solving', *Journal of Child Psychology and Psychiatry,* 1976, *17,* 89-100.

Zimmerman, B. J. 'Modelling' in eds. H. L. Horn and P. H. Robinson, *Psychological Processes in Early Education,* Academic Press, 1977.

PART II

ORIGINS OF SOCIAL COGNITION IN INFANCY

5 The primary motives for cooperative understanding

Colwyn Trevarthen

This paper proposes a new theoretical basis for a mental biology of infants. It rests on the belief that the human brain has systems which integrate interpersonal and practical aims together from the first few months after birth. Evidence for this belief comes principally from close observation of how young infants behave in interaction with other persons and with objects (Trevarthen, 1977; 1979; Hubley and Trevarthen, 1979; Trevarthen and Hubley, 1978), but it also has support from studies of human brain growth (Trevarthen, 1980a).

Infants actively use human companions to gain knowledge from the time their minds recognise objects of knowledge, even from before they can effectively manipulate things. Through mental partnership with caretakers they may have the effects of acting when direct action is impossible for them. But specification of how they do these things is extremely difficult.

The main difficulty with infants is the baffling mixture they exhibit of psychological immaturity and readiness for a mental life in company of other persons. Scientific research trying to explain infant behaviour is caught between two needs. It feels it has to prove by objective measurement of responses in well-defined conditions of stimulation that infants have psychological powers. But there is an equally compelling need for a subjective evaluation of what it is that makes infants exert such remarkable degree of control over the physical and social environments in which their perceptions and skilful behaviours develop. Psychological studies of infants have been conservative, and deliberately neglectful of the second of these needs. Strenuous efforts have been made, and are still being made, to reduce explanations for

such easily observed phenomena as the smile of greeting to physiological or physical (for example, 'information processing') levels, even
though this kind of behaviour can only have subjective value. The
objective features of a smile, whether physical or psychological, are
entirely secondary to its psychological function in communication of
affect. Only the mind of another person can be affected by a smile. To
smile effectively, an infant must understand other persons.

In the last fifteen years there have been many signs that developmental psychology is undergoing a revolutionary change of concepts.
It would appear that the way is open now for deliberate research on
the subjective function of infant actions. I believe that to understand
what infants do we must give up a motiveless psychology. The mind-
clearing reductionism of the behaviourist school has done its work.
Now we need to recover a more balanced holistic perspective on the
mental life of infants. We must analyse for objective details, not to
eliminate subjectively observed mental processes, but to find out how
the processes of this level may be regulated from inside the subject.

I shall ascribe motives for action which are expressed by infants of
different ages, attempting to find the functions of such motives in the
development of infant consciousness and of actions with purpose.
Special attention will be given to the adaptations of babies to human
co-operative social life, because this is the area of mental life in which
they have greatest mastery.

The Meaning of the Word 'Motive'

In the dictionary, definitions of 'motive' centre on an internal cause
of a subject's action:

> 'that which moves or tends to move a person to a course of
> action';
> 'having the quality of initiating movement or action';
> 'a desire, fear, reason, etc., which influences a person's volition';
> 'the whole of that which moves, excites or invites the mind to
> volition'. (Shorter Oxford English Dictionary)

In notebooks he wrote not long after returning from the voyage of
the *Beagle,* Darwin wrote on the importance of inherent motives, and
on their capacity to change. In the notebook labelled 'Old and useless
notes about the moral sense and some metaphysical points written

about the years 1837 and earlier', he states:*

'Every action is the effect of a motive . . .'

'Motives are units in the universe.'

He defined character and aptitude for a given behaviour, the internal cause of it, as:

'the condition of mind which leads to motion being inclined that way'

and observed that:

'From contingencies a man's character may change—because motive power changes with organisation'

Here Darwin is concisely expressing a concept of motivational 'schemata' transformed by learning.

Darwin did not believe that the inherent motives of mankind are simple. It is relevant that much of his evidence for motives in human beings came from observing the behaviour of his sister's children when they were babies. Later he and his wife Emma made meticulous observations of their own numerous infants. Some of these observations were reported in a famous paper in the philosophical journal *Mind* (Darwin, 1877). They reappear in the study of emotional expressions which was also published near the end of his life (Darwin, 1872). In many ways, the theory of emotions presented in this book is more conservative and physiological than the speculations of the notebooks written about forty years earlier which have an astonishingly modern psychological ring, as Gruber points out in his essay on the early notebooks (Gruber and Barrett, 1974).

It would seem that dictionary definitions and Darwinian evolutionary theory both perceive motives as interior processes of a subject, features of the subject's organisation, which anticipate and interpret consequences of behavioural action. They do not necessarily take into account, especially in their innate and inexperienced forms, the limitations or advantages of actual external reality, either in detail or immediately. As consequences of action are taken into account, behaviour may become guided by more elaborate purposes which have more complete or more accurate reference to external circumstances, but motives have inherent freedom from the specific or particular conditions for their expression. We frequently want much more than we are capable of achieving. Motives, it should be stressed, are distinct from emotions which transmit the colour of motives to others so they can know what we want. This we consider below.

---

*The following quotations are from Gruber and Barrett, 1974, pp. 388-99.

Relations of Motive to Intention, to Perception and to Experience

Behaviour which regulates itself by anticipating a rich and intricate awareness of a field of possibilities for action is said to be intentional. Human intentions are largely shared and conventionalisation plays an important part in the specification of intentions. Intentions relate on one side to motives, from which they originate, and on the other side to perceptions of relevant distal objects. In the course of intentional activity, motives may be changed by perception of shifting goals. However, as we have seen, motives can arise in absence of perceptions of relevant objects or situations, and even in absence of means to act. They have self-generative and self-regulatory powers on their own. On the other hand, while a motive may be unchanging or stable through a variety of circumstances, the choice of a particular form of intentional action satisfying that motive is largely free. Indeed, volitional freedom depends upon the inherent unspecificity of motives with respect to means.

An important conclusion from this line of thought is that psychological development results from changes in motives themselves, as well as from changes in the power of perceptual or motoric mechanisms which serve motives. The effects of every action are projected back into the motive from which it arose and they transform the motive or cause it to differentiate. For example, the motive for prehension, by causing the arm and hand to act into spatially projected mental images of tangible goals, enriches awareness of graspable objects. This feed-back of effects into motives generates new intentions. However, once again, the perceptual input is not sufficient to determine either the original form of a motive or the direction in which it will develop. We must expect primary motives to originate in morphogenetic processes of the immature brain which are initially free of regulation by perception and unable to produce any act. Many acts of infants should be expected to be expressions of such inexperienced and ineffectual motives.

Motives, being internal to a subject, the core of the subject's intrinsic mental organisation, are correspondingly less dependent on experience than are the specific intentions by which motives gain active expression. Intentions always have specified external goals. These must have been perceived in the past through uptake of information in patterns of stimuli coming from outside the subject. More specific and more intricate motives acquired by learning may combine with others derived from less defined experience to set an ideal and general aim for purpose. One may feel a wish to enjoy Chopin; or to have a successful summer holiday. The satisfaction of any motive or desire through action will depend upon awareness of the circumstantial conditions (knowledge) that effects the movements of an appropriate skilful act (ability). Actually playing an *etude;* swimming without stepping on a sea urchin, or finding the bar in the right company are effective and appropriate behaviours to satisfy the wishes mentioned.

The difficult task for developmental psychology is to determine how effective human consciousness starts. In what way are inherent motives predisposed to form the comprehensive, precise and meaningful concepts of adults, beings who live within an historically created and increasingly sophisticated system of knowledge and beliefs? Ideal and general motives, open to transformation by experience, give rise to concepts, inferences, knowledge. We ask how these arise in the child's mind. Are there autonomous 'instincts' for them or are they learned or imitated from others older and more experienced? Do they depend on growth of a general cognitive capacity or are they special features of an inherent ability to share as well as to communicate?

Motives for Co-operative Intentionality

Human beings neither know nor perceive as isolated individuals. It is a favourite trick of philosophers to postulate an isolated thinker or rationaliser—a being who knows. The philosophical knower tends to be an inactive thinker of thoughts. This trick backfires. In the end the fund of knowledge is something we must both act upon and share. These same constraints appear in the genesis of knowledge. Piaget insisted that infants must *act* to know. Now we must emphasise again, as Vygotsky and Guillaume did, that they must *share* to know.

Some of us in Britain now interested in how infants acquire concepts and intentions have learned much from the analysis of the self as an agent, by the late Edinburgh philosopher, John Macmurray. We have been influenced by the primacy he gives to interpersonal understanding (Macmurray, 1957, 1961).

Macmurray is a Kantian and motivation has a favoured place in his metaphysical system. He observes that empirical concepts are derived from experience—learning to distinguish significant others (things and persons) that will occur again and again, but also states:

'These empirical determinations are possible only because there are pure concepts which are not produced in this way, but are completely general, and presupposed in all experience.' ('Self as Agent', p. 49)

Furthermore, in learning, he states:

'The pattern of motivation must remain unalterable.'

Thus Macmurray believes that our unalterable pattern of motivation generated pure concepts that are presupposed in all experience.

I wish to make one important qualification of these statements of Macmurray. When attempting to assess the motives of newborn infants that are independent of experience, it is necessary to recognise the special, highly specific forms of directive power that inheres. Human motives are *not* 'completely general' at any stage of life, except with respect to those highly particular contingencies of experience which cannot possibly be anticipated in antenatal developments. Red mail boxes are not known *a priori*. Nevertheless, the motives of infants may have highly specific orientation to perception of certain definite categories of event, or equally definite effects of action. Darwin's 'units of the universe', may be highly specific in adaptation. For example, the appearance of a happy and friendly human face would seem to be very clearly defined in an infant's mind. Thus 'general' becomes almost a worthless description for primary motives. We must try to define the *special pre-adaptive forms of motive*, by description of their actual organisation and by tracing the developmental processes to which they contribute. The only way to do this is to accept the principle of natural selection and to suppose that inherent motives have both a fitness to their environment and the capability of causing development of adaptive (beneficial) forms of activity.

Macmurray emphasises the mutual adaptation of world and subject. Action is contrasted to mere movement by being addressed to an object in the world. Thus 'self' and 'other' are mutually adapted. Whitehead (1925) expresses the same idea in his philosophy of 'organisms'.

For a psychologist, Macmurray's most significant contribution is his incorporation of a theory of personal relations within a general philosophy of intention (Macmurray, 1961). He places the 'I-Thou' relation in command of human motivation. He examines that form of intuitive knowledge which establishes a bond between the motivated self and the motivated other. For him 'personality' is not, as in both contemporary psychology and popular usage, just an individual's distinguishing characteristics that have been acquired in the course of development. It is the natural and necessary condition for a human of being a person in relation to other persons.

Whereas in Natural Law intuition must satisfy how things happen in reality, in Moral Law intuition must satisfy others and their view of how things *ought* to be. Macmurray defines three modes of life from which arise three moralities: the *communal*, (which is positive with respect to others), the *contemplative* (which is negative with respect to others and submissive to experience), and the *pragmatic* (which is interpersonally negative and aggressive to experience). Macmurray, who was close to the Object Relations School of psychoanalysts (Kline, Winnicott, Fairbairn) portrayed the infant as adapted to form an inter-personal relationship with the mother while being helpless in action and weak in powers of thought.

To comprehend infant motivations we certainly must follow Macmurray and consider the demands of the communal mode of existence. Developmental psychologists are fond of searching for 'biological' and 'social' causes of development as if these were different. But there are complex biological aspects of social life, and interpersonal life has its own special causes and functions. The demands of communal existence are not adequately described as 'social' because they are fundamentally interpersonal. They may, indeed, set intimate person-to-person relations in conflict with relations to society at large. They may be antisocial. In infancy there is an important sense in which social and interpersonal relations are opposed, with the former having far greater life value.

Motives and Emotions. Communicative Expression of Feeling and of Fact

Macmurray is lead to reject the traditional opposition of 'reason' to 'emotion', claiming that there is emotional as well as pragmatic reasoning. How are we to integrate emotions with our theory of motives for cognitive and interpersonal activity?

The motives for co-operative life require communication of the intensity, urgency or risk of states of mind (feelings, interests, impulses to act, purposes, intentions). Emotions expressed in facial movements, vocalisations, and so on, specify to others the energy, directions and changes of direction of such states of mind, especially in their inter-personal aspects. Evidence that emotional states and forms of movement to express them are innate supports the concept of innate motives.

The fact that emotional expressions may be cultivated in art and language has been taken as evidence that feelings are acquired. An actor has the ability to 'generate' signs of emotion, intentionally, for presentation to an audience, and he can confine his expressions with training. We are all similarly trained as we live in society to express our feelings 'properly' with cultivated facial expressions, gestures, quality and manner of vocalisation and posturings. But, even actors 'inventing' passion draw on a universal code of expression that all humans understand without training. The emotional expressions of an infant, and of any person who does not act a part, are a direct output of that subject's inevitable state of mind in those circumstances. There is an intricate set of guidelines built in for generation of universally comprehended signs of feeling. But what of other aspects of motive—to what extent is their communication innate?

Expressive movements of human eyes, face and hands are also adapted to communicate interest, decision, purpose. Language is a specialised cognitive and performative mode which adds representational power to these expressive behaviours. It is important to note that speech and gesture are to a considerable degree complementary in ordinary discourse. The vocal apparatus and the hands have a high degree of equivalence for learning language expression. The hands may be trained to substitute for speech in writing and in sign language. This would seem to be evidence for an underlying general expressive system, co-ordinating significant body parts.

Music, in contrast to language, cultivates a wide range of expressive behaviours which contrast predictable and emotive images in sound. These images portray body motion, movements of the vocal tract and movements of the hands on musical instruments. Homologous visible images of movements are cultivated in dance and theatre. Music has language-like evolution—it is conventional and historic; but it is tied more closely than language to the basic motives of human expression, and it is weaker than language in semantic reference to topics. It lacks the equivalent of words with sharply defined meaning in relation to experience. Dance and song have to do with the recollection of mood and impulse, whereas language is usually concerned with recollection of events and identities, and with specification of interpersonal or practical actions in a well-defined context for interaction. Poetry, like music, is not primarily concerned with argument or transmission of information. It is emotive like music. These universally important areas of human communication show up the powerful functions served by exchange of feelings in linking minds together.

Observations of natural uses of language in conversation (in contrast to attempts to formulate rules for logical or persuasive discourse with precisely defined reference), brings out evidence of psychological processes that regulate the intentions of speakers as persons co-operating or competing, rather than the truth or falseness of their statements in relation to 'reality'. Obviously people understanding each other in conversation have immediate intuitive grasp of the co-operative motives of language. They detect and use these motives. Intentions to communicate in particular ways are both immediately perceived and involuntarily produced.

The evidence from comprehension and use of language by children is strongly in favour of there being well-organised linguistic motives in a child before the lexico-grammar of adult society has been acquired. Current studies of this pre-verbal language behaviour are concerned with the relation of grammatical and lexical conventions in adult language to motives of infants for co-operation and to the organisation of intentions with respect to others and with respect to circumstances. (Halliday, 1975; Bruner, 1975; Bates, 1976). But the issue is still obscure. No one has explained the relationship between the so-called 'grammar of action' and the power of language to instruct and to inform, let alone its power to amuse, delight or offend. Attempts to unify the social, the personal and the cognitive or the pragmatic in a theory of protolanguage flounder because they have no clear concept of the primary motives for transmission of feelings and purposes between human subjects. Co-operation in intricate, consciously determined behaviours requires communication at all levels of motivation, from the most interior and autogenous to the most fitting to outside reality. Before words are used the basic intersubjective functions of language in dialogue are understood by the child. This fact is gaining increasing recognition by students of the earliest phrases of language acquisition. Unfortunately, there is virtually no research on the musical or theatrical abilities of infants.

Limitations in Scientific Study of Infant Motives

By the nature of their development and at the stage they are in relation to experience, it is certain that infants are less adapted to reality than are older children or adults. They have to learn more specific

adaptations. But that is not the question of greatest concern. To understand how psychological development moves in any direction—towards
attainment of knowledge, of language, or moral sense or any other
human faculty—we have to understand the fundamental state of free
and effective activity that, independent of experience, is pre-established
in the infant brain. The only useful sense of 'innate' in psychology is
this; to describe the psychological processes at or shortly after birth, so
that their active orientation to particular kinds of experience can be
understood. We need to comprehend the infant as a psychological
organism and to do this we must use an appropriate paradigm in our
research.

We cannot hope to see how the motives described above direct
human communication without having some awareness of how we may
become trapped in an inappropriate scientific paradigm. Conventional
scientific methods may actually obscure the very data we seek. It now
appears that exaggerated realism and reductionism, which limit psychological sciences generally, have had a particularly deadening effect in
psychological research on infants.

To set out to measure innate actions of infants, and then select only
effective actions is absurd. An infant may well have, on his own, no
effective actions whatsoever, save those 'physiological' reactions of the
reflex nervous system that keep his body alive. Infants are, in fact,
exceedingly helpless and dependent organisms that need help even with
their organic maintenance. They cannot survive alone.

To look for perception of objects by an infant who can perform no
act is to look for an ideal philosopher who is capable of pure contemplation; of reflection on the meanings of things having had no
experience or very little. Perhaps recent studies of orienting and
exploring reactions have led some psychologists to a too-free attribution of ideas and concepts to infants, even though many experiments,
notably those of Bower (1974) and his colleagues, have proved that
infants perceive much more of their world than had been suspected
for many decades.

The experimental method in psychology is not always well adapted
to analysis of complex mental events. It frequently amounts to an
effort to prove the incapacity of subjects to have motives in unnatural
circumstances. While controlled experiments to find how infants
respond to well-defined stimuli are essential to analyse the structural
and functional limitations of motives in behaviour and the progressively
strengthening articulation of motives with reality through perception
and motor co-ordination, use of procedures to avoid observing the free

cause of motivated behaviour is immediately destructive of understanding, and in the end self-defeating. After many such experiments
have been performed, their collective import leads, little by little, to a
much less restricted form of conclusion. The various findings correct
one another's limitations. But nevertheless, the resultant fund of
understanding is disjointed and somehow colourless. It pleases only the
experts.

In contrast to the above tactics we may ask what the motives are of
juvenile organisms of a species that has evolved for a unique kind of
co-operative life, in which every phase of life will depend on action and
reaction with others of like mind. That is a reasonable quest for a
scientific psychology. What do we find when we simply look for
evidence for such motives?

Paradoxically for any theory that takes physiological homeostasis as
the model for motive, infants have a strong preference for achieving
interactive relation with other persons. Interaction with persons appears
to be simple for them and to give its own reward immediately. It is
constituted to be a primary drive to actions. Empiricist psychology
considers that awareness of persons is so complex it must be derived
from experience. Infants, it is said, discover persons by interacting with
the special stimulus and response properties of humans. It is supposed
that this creates person awareness out of knowledge of much lower
order, and that self-awareness comes by experience of the difference
between consequences of one's own motives and the motives of others.
This is the area where most progress may be expected by adopting a
free and speculative scientific perspective and attempting to understand
the innate foundations of motives that may be specifically adapted to
the growth of interpersonal understanding.

In the last ten years a richer understanding of the infant mind has
been achieved by methods which allow infants to exercise cognitive
regulation, prediction and problem-solving, and also by recording signs
of their emotional response to cognitive changes. Signs that express
emotion and that generate a response to a human perceiver (rather than
in a physical measuring instrument) have been particularly informative.
Although one might easily believe the opposite from the form of most
reports of research in infant psychology, few, if any, of the experiments
on which our present knowledge of the capacities of infants less than
four months of age to discriminate objects and to perceive their
phenomenal status depends, have employed responses that are immediately necessary to the physiological well-being of the infant or that
are capable of changing the physical condition of the world. The most

fruitful paradigms have used perceptual regulating movements (eye fixations, looking away, head rotations), artificial perception-regulating prostheses (sucking on a pressure transducer), autonomic correlates of change of central state of orientation or alertness (heartbeat, respiration), movements of prehension, and expressions of emotion (especially smiling and fretting or crying). When single behaviours are recorded, while some very clear results have been obtained, there are frequently paradoxical trends which can be resolved only by looking at combined behaviours. For example, looking at, then smiling is different from looking at and frowning or grimacing. Smiling without looking at is different from smiling while maintaining regard on another's eyes.

Other difficulties are due to researchers taking insufficient interest in the natural complexity of infant actions, which are often described as 'random'. Much needless controversy has come from assertions in the literature that movements in the same approximate form must always mean the same thing (for example, arm extension means reaching), from the use of crude categories covering a rich range of motivations (for example, presence or absence of 'vocalisation') and from the persistent illogical belief that demonstrating failure of an infant to respond in an experimental situation is proof of incapacity. To perceive evidence from their movements that infants are cognitive beings, it must be accepted that they may be coherent agents, with inherently well-formed co-ordinative structures pre-adapted to acting in response to the world.

How Motives of Infants may be Observed

Put very simply, to find out what somebody wants to do, whom you cannot ask, you have to watch what they choose to take an interest in, how they act to gain a particular objective. A great deal of information can be obtained about a subject's motives by seeing which options are taken up from many available, and especially by observing the effects of removing options or blocking courses of action. You can offer pairs of alternatives as in discriminatory experiments, but this is a laborious way to explore free motives. Piaget's 'clinical' method set up situations in which the manipulative actions of infants and the utterances of older children were systematically chanelled. He did this to answer questions about the logico-mathematical 'concepts' that the young subjects are moving to sustain or test.

Vigorous action to overcome obstacles is a sign of strong motivation.

When a subject adopts different means, different forms of action in one direction of purpose, this helps define the underlying motive. Use of alternative modalities of perception to know a single object and spontaneous substitution of modalities indicates a cognitive representation of the object itself. The motive is to 'observe' or 'have' the object, not to 'see' or 'smell' or 'feel' it.

When all is said and done, the most intimate evidence of motives comes from highly 'subjective' manifestations—the expressions of feeling and emotion. Expressions of pleasure, delight, triumph, exuberance all indicate motivational success or prospect of success. Displeasure, anger, sadness, depression or fear indicate motivational disorganisation, failure, or risk of failure. Self-absorbed behaviour, fatigue, sleep, indicate a motivational retreat, and disorganised violent activity of panic is usually interpreted as both an attempt to beat off threat and an appeal to someone to help.

Luckily for our purpose, babies have abundant and usually very clear expressions of feeling. Their feelings, as expressed in facial movements, vocalisation, body movements, orienting movements, are closely integrated with the expression of what they want to do in exploratory or prehensile behaviour and in communication. Moreover, there is a vast amount of information available on what infants do and on what interests they have at different ages. We need a theory of motives to pull the criss-crossing strands of data on motoric, cognitive and social achievements into a coherent representation of the 'strategy of development'. It is extremely important that close correlations exist between periods of rapid or conspicuous change in motoric, cognitive, or interpersonal and social capabilities and interests. I believe this to be evidence for a co-ordinating system of the brain that regulates development in cerebral psychological components and ensures their integration by means of systematic changes in its own organisation.

To illustrate my claim for infant motives, I shall briefly review evidence that the intrinsic generators of action undergo self-regulated change in infancy, and attempt to identify the principal motives and the functional relationships that form between different types of action generators.

Major Developments in Motivation in Infancy

For convenience of description and to have a framework on which to formulate a theory of infant development, I shall divide the two years

Table 1: Behaviours revealing developments in primary motives of infants

Time	Behaviours	
BIRTH Neonate	(birth arousal—release of prefunctional signs of motives). Withdrawal within maternal care. Motives become 'hidden'. Occasional visual exploration and face regard. Smile rare. Pre-reaching, 'magnetic' imitation of face and head movements.	Negative
Phase I (10 weeks) — 5	*Primary Intersubjectivity, Affectional Play* Responsive smile, pre-speech, gestures, coos. Intent eye-to-eye contact. Protoconversation, play. Increased strength proximal musculature.	Positive
— 10	Withdrawal from eye contact. Watching mouth and hands. Intent regard to objects, visual exploration and tracking. Controlled reaching (from 16 weeks). Markedly improved visual acuity and accommodation.	Negative
Phase II (20 weeks) — 20	*Games, Teasing* Laughs to physical teasing, peekaboo, etc. Responds to ryhmes in action play. Babbling. Manipulation of objects and systematic exploration of effects in Routine acts.	Positive
SIX MONTHS — 30 weeks		

Negative

Intense possession of mother. Dependence on her. Less co-operative.
Anxiety with strangers in some cases.
Fine manipulation. Independent mobility by crawling.

Positive

Secondary Intersubjectivity, Co-operative Play
Acts of meaning (protolanguage) and co-operation in object play
(person-person-object interaction)
Obeys instructions, makes requests, points, asks for help, etc.

Negative

'No!' period. Refusals to comply. Considerable comprehension of
words frequently used by familiar persons in familiar contexts.

Positive

Pretend Play
Symbolic representation of actors and of actions with objects.
Increasing vocabulary of words used with gestures in acts of communication.

Phase III
(30 weeks)

Phase IV
(40 weeks)

30 — 40 — 50 — ONE YEAR — 60 — 70 — 18 MONTHS — 80 — 90 — 100
weeks

of infancy into four periods, each longer than the last by the addition
of ten weeks. This division is not only somewhat artbirary with respect
to the times of division between periods, it is also highly speculative,
especially for the second year. I have insufficient experience of
behaviour in this period to give a more accurate account. I know that a
much more complex set of stages could be described. Nevertheless, I
think that the main structure will stand after further research and that
the principle of spontaneous transformation of motives will be
sustained.

I have taken each period to represent the attainment of a new level
of cognitive and behavioural function and a new complexity of
expression for two fundamental motives; that to master objects in the
environment, and that to obtain a community of motives with others.
It seems most logical and convenient to describe the development
observed as the building up of progressively more effective motives to
act co-operatively in doing anything and everything.

Infancy is a time when capacities to act change radically. At each
change in motoric efficacy, to looking about, reaching, sitting up,
crawling, walking and so on, there is a revolution or transformation of
the field of co-operative action, as well as in cognition of objects.
However, I believe that the great changes in mental processes of infants
are directly concerned with, or regulated by, intrinsic communicative
powers that are independent of particular movements for their
beginnings. They would arise in a limbless infant. The biggest changes
of infant behaviour are anticipatory to entry in the course of childhood into the explicit world of meanings, a world in which co-operative
functions are mediated by language and symbolic actions. Mature
human co-operation always requires this level of mutual awareness.
Adult motives for action are dominated by social or cultural creations
in which many subjects must co-operate, and for the invention and
development of which many more have co-operated in the past. These
motives simply could not exist without creating rituals, artifacts,
symbols and some form of language.

Table 1 summarises the following brief account of developments in
infant behaviour which reveal motives for human co-operative life. An
extensive review of the literature on infant perceptions, motor co-
ordination, learning and motivation, as well as on their interpersonal
and social adaptations, is in press (Trevarthen, Murray and Hubley,
1981). In perusing the following, the reader will note how easy and
natural it is to describe details of infant behaviour as if they often are
motivated interpersonally.

Phase 1: Primary Interpersonal Life (0 to 10 weeks)

The neonatal period (0–5 weeks) is a predominatly negative one for interpersonal and exploratory life. It is a time in which the more complex motive structures for engagement with the world distant from the body are defensive. The neonate is, at the same time, highly efficient in response to direct holding and at obtaining care required for regulation of general states of arousal, for feeding and for protection against threatening conditions. This demanding of attentions reinforces the new mother's condition of increasingly strong 'maternal preoccupation'. Although much of a neonate's time is spent in sleep, there is evidence that highly complex mechanisms for recognition of and response to other persons exist in a shadowy prefunctional form in the first weeks.

First, the evasive looking away, curling up, fussing or sleeping behaviours are frequently specifically directed *away* from face-to-face approaches of persons, including the mother. These movements are selectively negative. Neonates may reject being spoken to, may avoid eye-to-eye contact, may struggle when picked up. They respond positively to holding, cuddling, rocking, and such, which permits them to shut out more complex engagements. On the positive side they may, in brief periods of a 'quiet alert' state, show strongly oriented 'searching' gaze to a person's face, and listening to a voice. It is reported that neonates may become synchronised in their body movements to the rhythm of adult speech (Condon and Sander, 1974), but I doubt that this is the full story. Condon's method applying descriptive and analytical kinesics (a science of motor rhythmic patterns) obscures the motivational significance of expressions and it is biased to a description of the mother. It is not applied by him, or by other followers of the micro-analytic method, with equal interest in patterns of behaviour that are initiated by the baby and shadowed by the mother.

A newborn baby may orient to and track an object with his eyes and turn head and eyes to a gentle sound (for example, a bell). Loud sounds and visual stimuli indicative of suddenly approaching large objects cause startle and distress with defensive actions.

Many movements of young infants take the form of feeble and unpredictable response to imposed stimuli; nevertheless, neonatal movements do regulate experience. The clearest response of a neonate is frequently to *avoid* stimuli. They are described as trying to maintain integration, to reduce the impact of strong stimulation that causes their co-ordination to be disrupted. Newborn babies, however, may move their receptors to choose particular forms of stimuli, that is, to *increase* the effect of some stimuli relative to other stimuli. These orienting and attending responses habituate readily. Eye, ears, hand are moved so that frequently experienced stimuli are less sought after and novel ones are chosen. While this may aid enrichment of experience, it will also limit development of more complete awareness of recurring events. Older infants explore and orient more efficiently and experiment more assiduously, which gives evidence of their greater awareness of events.

When the attention of a neonate is caught by an object, elementary reaching and grasping movements (pre-reaching) may be well-formed and precisely co-oriented with head and eye. The grasping of the hand is integrated with the climax of the arm extension and there are frequently associated mouth movements. However, pre-reaching is stereotyped and ineffectual. It is not modulated, or modulated very weakly and late, to allow tracking or correction of position of the extended arm.

Conditioning experiments prove that even neonates may learn quickly. What they learn depends on what they want to perceive. Intake of experience by learning may be described as the satisfaction of constructive motives. One-month-olds exhibit clear expressions of pleasure at gaining the effect they predict and displeasure at failing (Papousek, 1969). There is no support for the theory, expounded forcefully, indeed rhetorically, by Watson in his book *Behaviourism,* that the primary motives of human mental life and for conditioned responses are simple (Watson, 1930). However, early manifestations of complex inherent interest of infants in the comings and goings of objects with differing properties and usefulness are obscured by the diffuseness of infants' perceptual discrimination and recognition, and the even weaker differentiation of their intentional actions. While the interior causes of both perception and voluntary action are already active in the infant a few weeks old, giving proof of formulated motives that seek occasions for their satisfaction, independent movement and active perception of the uses to which objects may be put are both severely limited.

Neonates may intently watch exaggerated mouth and tongue movements and hand movements, and occasionally they even imitate. This proves that they have at least rudimentary structures for representing these parts of the bodies of others as equivalent to matching parts of themselves. Both eye-to-eye contact and imitative responses are slow and erratic in newborns; they give the impression of being effortful, and they are often followed by distress. The regard of a neonate has been described as 'locked-on'.

Neonates do not usually smile to a person to whom they are oriented. Usually the gaze is expressionless or concentrated with a 'frown' (knit brow) (Oster, 1978). They may make small smiles when they are visually oriented to a face, or hear a voice or both, and when touched around the mouth while not looking at the face, and smiles and hand gestures also appear in light states of sleep.

Notwithstanding the evasions and diffuseness of acting which characterise much behaviour of neonates, the most extraordinary complexity and vitality of behaviour can be observed in the first hours after birth, before the first feed. Immediately after birth babies look about with cyclical bursts of well-co-ordinated conjugate saccades, orient to and make pre-reaching movements to nearby suspended objects or into the air. They react quickly to a human voice by looking to see the speaker (Alegria and Noirot, 1978) and they may make elaborate expressive movements when hearing a voice or watching a speaker's face. These movements include smiles, coos, lip and tongue movements related to articulatory movements of speech (pre-speech), fine gestures of the hands, including index finger pointing, hand-waving, and so on, grimaces and eyebrow-raising or knit brows. Facial expressions of neonates and premature infants include almost the full repertoire of expressive motor units seen in adults (Oster, 1978). All these activities appear to be less easily observed in the next three weeks. They appear to be inhibited or inactivated then.

At about four or five weeks there is a pronounced change in the positive orientations of the infant, and by six weeks highly responsive 'social' smiling is easily elicited. Visual attention is more positive and eye movements are better regulated to obtain a fixation. Experimental studies indicate that infants of this age have considerable powers of discrimination, for tastes, sounds, colours, textures, forms, etc. They certainly recognise differences between familiar and unfamiliar persons. Objects may be intently regarded and tracked, but are frequently ignored in favour of interpersonal contact at this age. Reaching is generally limited to awkward arm extensions, though occasionally, in a quiet baby, a complete pre-reaching pattern may be aimed to a fixated object by a two- to three-month-old.

In face-to-face interactions of six- or eight-week-olds with the mother a complex interchange of expressions may be observed. These have been shown by Lynne Murray (1980) and Ben Sylvester-Bradley (1980) to be regulated not only by the mother's compliant adaptation of forms of utterance to a range of expressions of the infant and by her shadowing or imitation, but by recognition by the infant of the human significance of the mother's expression and by a strong motivation in the baby to obtain a positive interaction between complementary states of communicative initiative. If the mother is emotionally withdrawn or if she is made artificially unresponsive in an experiment, the infant shows avoidance leading to distress (Murray, 1980). This proves that the elaborate 'protoconversational' address and reply of happy exchanges with six- to ten-week-olds is something the infant wants to obtain. When either the baby or the mother are abnormal in motivation, the pattern of behaviour of the baby may be very different, with more negative behaviour (gaze avoidance, grimacing, crying, sleeping, tension).

In this period, imitation of the mother by the baby is not easily elicited, though the baby may show intense interest in mouth and tongue movements and in hand movements. Eye-to-eye contact is easily obtained with most two-month babies and it is followed by smiling, vocalisation, gestural movements and pre-speech. Withdrawal or disinterest on the part of a recognised partner may lead to sadness or a depressed withdrawal.

Clearly the motive to obtain contact with a person and engage in an expressive exchange of interest and pleasure, is strong. It is stronger than all other forms of complex mental activity of which a two-month-old is capable, except perhaps visual inspection of nearby objects, especially those in motion or undergoing change. This is a fruitful period for experimental studies of object perception and recognition, as long as stimuli are undergoing the right kind of transformation. Nevertheless, interest is not sustained for an object that has gone out of sight as it may be, and emotionally, for the mother when she vanishes.

While neonates are sensitive to the quality of holding and dependent on sensitive gentle care for development of well-organised crying-free states, regular sleeping, settled feeding and weight gain, etc., two-month-olds have more complex interpersonal needs. Their motivational development is shown in their reaction to face-to-face orientation with the mother and it is affected by her manner of responding—by the support she offers for the infant's seeking of love and companionship. Depression, bereavement, and such, causing the mother to be withdrawn and sad lead to withdrawal of the infant and floppiness, sleepiness or fretfulness and tension. Anxious hovering and excessive fussy touching may also lead the infant to be avoidant, unsmiling and silent in the mother's company. The same baby may respond positively to other persons. In extreme cases of cruelty or neglect the baby may lose all positive affect, or even die without 'organic' explanation.

Phase II: Object Prehension and Games (11 to 30 weeks)

It might be expected that the complex positive response and interaction with the mother of two-month-olds go on to develop quickly into even more positive enjoyment. But this is not so. About ten or twelve weeks after birth a normal happy infant is looking less at the mother, seeking less strongly to catch her eye for smiling and chat. The amount of time spent in eye-to-eye contact may be greatly reduced, as may by smiling and vocalisation. After a brief fixation of the mother's eyes the baby looks away. The baby's manner is frequently intensely preoccupied. Meanwhile, objects are looked at and tracked with increased intensity and awkward movements towards reaching take place. The hands are frequently held fingering each other, or one or both go to the mouth to be sucked. However, the baby does still show ready smiling to the mother to greet her, and to other persons, including strangers. A sense of humour is indicated by a chuckling laugh, frequently excited by teasing with surprise movements of the baby's body, or of the partner's face or hands. The mother, though frequently puzzled by the difficulty she has in getting sustained attention to herself, is in no doubt about the baby's attachment to her. She has the impression that the baby needs her but that it is more difficult to keep going direct play, face-to-face. She has become, somehow, a less acceptable mirror to her baby's feelings.

Considerable increase in body size in the second and third month is associated with better sitting posture and more mobility of the hand. The arms are twice as robust at eight weeks as at four. However, before sixteen weeks they are incapable of a well-directed extension to an object. Prehensile movements take the form of stiff extension, grabs or swipes. There has thus been a loss in fluency of co-ordination of reach and grasp since the neonate period, in spite of marked developments in visual discrimination and orienting and visual understanding of objects. However, the hands frequently grasp objects (such as clothing) when they come into contact with them. Once grasped, objects are taken to the mouth. Usually the grasped object is not looked at.

When approached and spoken to the infant may 'shut out' by looking down and concentrating gaze on moving feet or hands. There are thus numerous signs of a complex negative motivation towards intimate personal rapport. If the mother sits further away (say at two metres) the baby may look at her much more willingly. Unfamiliar persons may be given an alert stare or even a smile and greeting vocalisations when they come close. At the same time, the baby becomes extremely interested in objects being presented by the mother. This she may exploit, to 'keep in touch' with the baby's interests. Hand-clapping can cause the baby to laugh as can vigorous body play (bouncing, throwing up in the air).

After sixteen to twenty weeks, reaching after objects becomes much better directed. One day, the arms are extended to nearby objects with a jerky movement which is well-aimed, even showing accurate anticipation of the velocity of an object moving into the reaching space (von Hofsten, 1979). Object perception is well developed with consistency of size and form, and directly perceived objects are tracked behind screens and through erratic courses. From this point infants become better able to anticipate or imagine the course of displacement of objects taking indirect or curved trajectories behind screens. Increased efficiency in orienting to objects and in tracking their displacements and an ability to grasp at seen objects and bring them to the mouth greatly enriches the underlying motives to obtain knowledge of the properties of objects.

Infants are usually noted to first laugh heartily about three months of age. By five months they respond hilariously to many sorts of teasing. This playfulness is a puzzling but major element of the co-operative sense of infants from the time they are efficient at reaching and grasping objects. The laughing response and the way the baby waits for repetition of the teasing event causes parents, siblings and all other familiars to play games.

Throughout the next few months elaborate and increasingly ritualised games are played by most mothers with the baby. Penelope Hubley and I (Trevarthen and Hubley, 1978; Hubley and Trevarthen, 1979) have evidence suggesting that under five months or so games tend to arise as a result of systematic variation in the interpersonal contact (person-person games). Then, objects are increasingly introduced to catch a baby's attention and are manipulated as toys by the partner (object-person games). However, even a three-month-old will laugh at the movements of a ball animated by a playmate. The movements others transmit to objects and the aim of other's interest indicated by the direction of gaze or the movements of hands may become the focus of close attention. Games appear to be generated from this interest in what others do. While capable of intense concentration on the 'activities' of objects, alert to many interesting events, and aware of familiarity and novelty, the six-month-old fails to understand instructions and rarely imitates acts performed on objects by companions.

When a mother teases an infant she makes a joke out of the feelings, actions or interests of her baby, gently thwarting or negating what the baby wants or expects. That this is a source of pleasure indicated by laughter is proof that the baby is interested in the clash or mingling of intentions (Trevarthen, Murray and Hubley, 1981). The baby is also interested in playing with the mother's body, enjoying the fact that her eyes, mouth or hands may move in reaction to being touched, bitten or vocalised about. Vocal play becomes increasingly elaborate with extreme variation in intonation, rhythm and voice quality of the mother's utterances and the gloss of ritualised movements by songs, chants or rhymes, usually of traditional form ('peek-a-boo', 'round and round the garden', 'clappa clappa handies', 'pop goes the weasel', etc), is clearly appreciated by the baby. This is a rich and fascinating aspect of the impact of culture in the life of infants that begins near the middle of the first year.

In general, after the somewhat avoiding, preoccupied air of four- and five-month-olds, six-month-olds seem more easy-going and cheerful. They are exceedingly alert and eager to observe changes in objects which others are moving as well as to experiment with effects of their own handling of objects. As in Phase I, a relative negativity of motivation towards others is succeeded by a strongly positive period.

Phase III: Development of Co-operative Understanding and Expression of Meanings (weeks 31 to 60)

Once again, one would expect the eager and confident manner of a six-month-old to lead to increasing ability to relate to others and to co-operate with them. But, once again, there appears to be a rather difficult or anxious period in which games become frustrating for the baby and unfamiliar persons threatening. The much discussed 'fear of strangers' of seven- or eight-month-olds is simplistically presented by many psychologists as a reflection of developments in powers of perception, or as due to over-learning of the relation with the mother. Almost invariably stranger-fear, indeed the emotion of fear itself, is thought by experimental psychologists to be due to a general perceptual or cognitive change. In fact, it appears to have more complex implications and to be related to a major reorganisation in motivating structures that were highly differentiated at much earlier stages, The psychoanalysts of the Object Relations School note that infants become highly susceptible to anxiety at absence or loss of a loved one at this age. We observe that an intrinsic change in motivation profoundly affects the way in which infants communicate, and this transforms the responses to familiar companions as well as to strangers.

After about nine months babies become markedly more interested in the purposes of others as indicated by their actions, their expressive movements and their utterances (Trevarthen and Hubley, 1978; Trevarthen, 1979b). In particular, there begins to dawn in the child's mind a new kind of interest in what others know about or are doing to objects. Truly co-operative activity with a toy or set of toys becomes possible.

In games, partners may play mutually acknowledged roles, but in serious constructive action involving two persons there must be a deliberate identification or comparison of the other's purpose with one's own. Instead of sensing the effect of another's actions through alternations in the consequences of one's own actions, one has to anticipate and make way for them to act alternately or confluently with oneself. There must be a more independent representation of what they want to do or what they want one to do.

Recently this period, the last trimester of the first year, in which infants seem to grasp the meaning of another's actions in a new way, has received intense attention by students of early language. The realisation that language has strong intersubjective foundations has encouraged a search for interpersonal and pragmatic antecedents of language functions before words are used. It has been observed that after nine months or so, appealing, demonstrative or indicative gestures addressed to the attention of another, the uttering of exclamations, requests, commands in subtly modified forms of vocalisations combined with the non-vocal expressions, all become commonplace in the daily life of babies with their familiars and in familiar circumstances (Halliday, 1975; Bruner, 1975; Bates, 1967). The exclamatory or request utterances of infant protolanguage clearly conceive of others having interests, purposes and helpful powers. In the other sense, there comes an eagerness to deliberately receive gifts, help, instruction and information given by these others. There is also a new interest in one-year-olds to make certain imitative responses; vocalising or doing things like others. Although neonates can imitate expressions or gestures they can never imitate what one is doing to an object, and babies usually resist invitations to imitate after they are six weeks old until, as one-year-olds, they begin to try to be other people doing particular things.

Halliday (1975) suggests that vocalisations of protolanguage, acts of meaning without verbal form which become common after about nine or ten months, may have a 'preview' or 'trailer' at five months. This kind of foreshadowing or premature emergence of motives into a sketch of the form they will later assume more strongly is characteristic of development, at least in infancy. It is evidence of elaborate prefunctional morphogenesis of motivational structures (Trevarthen, 1980a).

Phase IV: Development of Symbolic Representation and Verbal Communication (61 to 100 weeks)

In the second year, infants become capable of playing with objects with awareness of what they signify, and of pretending that an object is something else. They can use objects of definite and familiar use or meaning to represent complex actions or experience metaphorically. That is, their impulses to know or do become invested in objects that are uniquely associated with these experiences or actions, as shared with other people. This development is, once again, most strongly apparent within the strongest, most trusting interpersonal relationships that have been established with the mother or other most familiar and attentive persons. In the same family context the understanding of words that are frequently heard in use steadily grows. Once more, the co-operativeness on which this development in motivation is dependent seems to undergo a negative or withdrawn phase before blossoming into a new richness, spontaneously.

The negativity, unco-operativeness, touchiness and unpredictability of fifteen-month-olds is famous. This Spitz describes as the period of the 'No!', that is, of refusal to comply (Spitz, 1957). The now-walking baby likes to be close to mother in unfamiliar territory, but at the same time often tends to walk away, in the 'wrong' direction. Likewise, communication and co-operation in dressing, feeding, and so on, may be difficult.

After eighteen months there is a great increase in vocabulary (in the words a child utters) and a new freedom in representational play. Observations of inventive play by Fiona Grant (Grant and Trevarthen, 1980) indicate that creativity or inventiveness is much higher in the presence of the mother. She is frequently sought to obtain help or complementary action in the execution of a familiar ritual (for example, putting a hat on the head or on a doll's head) or the reciting of a story. Current studies of this period indicate highly systematic changes in motives for co-ordinating awareness, understanding and intentions with others, as well as an enormous increase in awareness of the shared world of symbols. It leads into the toddler period when speaking children move towards co-operative play with peers—but this takes us away from infancy.

The above summary is a hastily prepared sketch. It doubtless requires careful revision to incorporate many fine observations already in the literature. But such correction will not affect my most important claim: that a more coherent and intelligible description of infant mental development can be given in terms of a 'rhythm of approach and with-drawal' (Winnicott, 1974), a fluctuation in innate motives for affec-tionate and co-operative action with others and a progressive building of intentions that give expression to these motives. This claim is in opposition to attempts to explain developments in infancy as due to maturation in perceptual or motor structures, to learning of increasingly elaborate cognitive rules, to logical refinement or enrich-ment of cognitive concepts, or to development of representations of reality by incorporation of evidence from acts performed on objects. The growth of interpersonal functions cannot, I claim, be reduced or transformed into any or all of such objective, impersonal or rational elements.

In middle infancy, before language develops but not independently of the foundation of language, an organisation of motives appears that may explain the genesis of communal knowledge, technological practice and morality. By showing powerful motives for co-operation in purpose or sharing of motives with others, infants about one year of age indicate that we had to acquire the cultural artifacts—languages, systems of belief, metaphorical games, moral codes, technical and scientific traditions, and so forth—without which human life is unthinkable. At the end of infancy, toddlers with a rudimentary grasp of a true language are inveterate imitators of roles and tasks, as well as sayings. Their fantasy world is a collective human creation, richly affected by the culture into which they were born.

Conclusion

It is proposed that the prime regulator of mental development in infancy is the system for interpersonal motivation which comes to vigorous life in the behaviour of two-month-olds, and that soon this becomes elaborated, by differentiation of the awareness of circumstances for action within it, into the mechanism of co-operative understanding which is the essential generator of culture in the human social world. Lacking this mechanism, animals are incapable of sharing understanding of symbolic objects. They cannot grasp the motive of another for attaining an objective. Human social life has features shared by no other form of life on earth because human beings possess this unique mental equipment. Their social behaviours include true language and related ways of communicating with conventional symbols, but they cover a far wider range of co-operative enterprises, all of which depend upon inherent motives which are manifest in infancy. These motives are not rigidly prewired and they are elaborated in response to experience throughout the life of each individual, but they have strong control over the course of mental development.

In the historical development of understanding, the accumulated skills, memories, habits and values passed on from generation to generation become the means for translating permanently established motives for acting in association with others into adaptive forms of intention that benefit the whole of human society.

Scientific study of the primary generative motives of infants, whether experimental or descriptive, will require precise analysis of fine details of behaviours, as well as a conscious effort to study the co-ordinations between different actions of infants on their own and between the actions of infants and others when they are in communication. Considerable progress has been made to satisfy these requirements in recent years and micro-analytical techniques are rapidly improving. Now we need concepts that will give us ways of unambiguously describing the subjective value of the more complex of these co-ordinations.

Appendix: Tentative Lists of Motives Implicit in Actions of Infants

A similar list of adaptive motives of infants has been presented elsewhere (Trevarthen, 1980b). Of course, the real motives of infants may require a different, surely a longer, description and they will be organised in a hierarchy or a network. Many may co-occur and their interactions will propel development in particular directions. The list merely indicates the range of distinct impulses that underlie how infants behave.

I. Motives behind the behaviours of infants prior to the development of effective prehension and of play with intentions. (First four months —Primary Intersubjectivity.)

A. MOTIVES TO KNOW THE EXTERIOR PHYSICAL WORLD AND THE BODY—SUBJECTIVITY

1. To seek unambiguous information, permitting detection of layouts and events in a single egocentric field, in which the sensory modalities becomes increasingly specialised as differentiation proceeds.
2. To gain prehension of small objects perceived as discrete from their background, by virtue of independent motion or by a boundary of high perceptual salience. To develop skill in knowing and using objects.
3. To increase awareness by learning to attend to novel events and places, registering their occasional recurrence and their association with forms of exploratory or performatory action.
4. To maintain a coherent state of well-being while carrying out the above (i.e., to avoid fearful and painful experiences).

These emphasise the subject-centred view of experience. Infants, by acting under the above motives also generate a particular awareness in others, the human environment in relation to which interpersonal motives have evolved.

B. MOTIVES TO COMMUNICATE WITH PERSONS— INTERSUBJECTIVITY

1. To co-ordinate closely with holding, feeding and cleaning movements of the mother and to obtain her presence by expressing alarm, hunger, pain. To learn to sense her presence and her identity.
2. To seek proximity and face-to-face confrontation with persons; to watch, listen to and feel the pattern of expression and become engaged, especially with movements of face and hands. To listen to the voice.
3. To respond with expressions of pleasure, then with manifestations of special human expression such as gestures and utterances, these being co-ordinated from the start with concurrent or intervening interests towards impersonal surroundings and objects that might be commented or or used co-operatively. Some forms of expression are clearly pre-adaptive to acquisition of cultivated forms of communication, including a true language. Most important are pre-speech movements of lips and tongue, cooing vocalisations associated with pre-speech, and gestures

of the hands. These signs of expressive motivation lack support from mental representations of conventional topics.

4. To exhibit emotions in relation to one's cognitive and praxic performances, such as 'deep serious intent' or 'pleasure in mastery', so that others may know one's state and direction of mind.

5. To engage in reciprocal give and take of communicative initiative, seeking to complement the expressed psychological state of the partner. This may involve both synchronisation of motives or states of excitement and alternation in address and reply. Both partners must adjust to the actions of the other.

6. To express clear signs of confusion or distress if the actions of the partner become incomprehensible or threatening.

7. To avoid excessive, insensitive or unwanted attempts by others to communicate, thus to retain a measure of personal control over one's state of expression to others.

II. Motives in the development of behaviour towards co-operative understanding (Secondary Intersubjectivity—months 4 to 15), and the use of symbolic actions and speech (second year).

A. MOTIVES TO BE AWARE AND TO KNOW AND USE THE PHYSICAL WORLD

1. To develop understanding and control of the world and of objects and their uses. To explore the use of objects as instruments or as intermediary in production of a desired result.

2. To withdraw from action and simply perceive or recollect experiences in tranquility (contemplation).

B. MOTIVES FORMING COMPANIONSHIP AND TRUST WITH PERSONS AND FOR CO-OPERATION

1. To form a bond of friendship and mutual trust with those who regulate their sharing of motives with one most surely, and with whom one is most familiar. To show affectionate recognition of them and to appeal for help from them when fearful or hurt.

2. To react with humour or annoyance to the efforts of others to involve themselves with one's purposes by means of various forms of teasing.

3. To join in overlapping or complementary forms of expression,

leading to dance-like or song-like performances involving confluent patterns or rhythmic movements.

4. To show, at times, a limited independence, by avoiding or ignoring attempts by others to obtain face-to-face play.

5. To regulate interpersonal actions with others by laughing, teasing or mocking.

6. To avoid playful interaction with 'strangers' who do not share a common context of experience, and who have not learned particular conventions or rituals.

C. MOTIVES FOR ACTING LIKE OTHERS AND FOR TAKING INITIATIVE IN CO-OPERATION

1. To enlarge one's own motives for dealing with people and events by seeking to observe and to match, or even imitate exactly, the expressive or praxic acts of others—that it, to accept the other as a potential source of motives for oneself.

2. To gain familiarity with habitual acts of caretaker/companions, especially the mother.

3. To learn by example from the acts of others.

4. To govern the degree of mixing of actions with the aid of rule-bound games learned together.

5. To assume, at times, deliberate control over the actions of another and thus to reverse the reciprocal relationship of co-operation to determine what another will do.

6. To contribute imaginative innovation to co-operative activity with others.

D. MOTIVES FOR DEVELOPMENT OF COMMUNICATION WITH SYMBOLS

1. To extend play with another to incorporate an object which may be exchanged, shared or modified by joint action within the convergent attentions of both subjects.

2. To express by vocalisation or by gesture acts of meaning that transmit distinct states of excitement, of purpose and of interpersonal relationship.

3. To use expressive acts or use of objects increasingly as symbols for transmission of information about one's own mental states (of recollection, of feeling, or of purpose) to others. To represent in this way familiar jointly recognised items.

4. To develop a vocal and gestural 'vocabulary' by imitation of symbols used by companions in co-operative activity.
5. To practise the skills of speaking and to gain words.
6. To become increasingly part of a culture in which expressions of consciousness and purposeful action of objects is constrained by habit and tradition.

References

Algeria, J., and Noirot, E. 'Neonate orientation behaviour towards the human voice', *International Journal of Behavioural Development*, 1978, *1*, 291-312.

Bates, E., *Language and Context: The Acquisition of Pragmatics*, New York and London, Academic Press, 1976.

Bower, T. G. R., *Development in Infancy*, San Francisco, W. H. Freeman, 1974.

Bruner, J. S., 'The ontogenesis of speech acts.' *Journal of Child Language*, 1975, *2*, 1-19.

Condon, W. S., and Sander, L. W., 'Neonate movement is synchronised with adult speech: Interactional participation and language acquisition', *Science*, 1974, *183*, 99-101.

Darwin, C., *The Expression of Emotions in Animals and Man*, London, Methuen, 1872.

Darwin, C., 'A biological sketch of an infant', *Mind*, 1877, *2*(7), 285-94.

Gruber, H. E., and Barrett, P. H., *Darwin on Man*, London, Wildwood House, 1974.

Halliday, M., *Learning How to Mean*, London, Edward Arnold, 1975.

Hofsten, C. von, 'Development of visually directed reaching; the approach phase', *Journal of Human Movement Studies*, 1979, *5*, 160-78.

Hubley, P., and Trevarthen, C., 'Sharing a task in infancy', in I. Uzgiris (ed.) *Social Interaction during Infancy—New Directions for Child Development*, 1979, *4*, 57-80.

Macmurray, J., *The Self as Agent*, London, Faber, 1957.

Macmurray, J., *Persons in Relation*, London, Faber, 1961.

Murray, L., *The Sensitivities and Expressive Capacities of Young Infants in Communication with their Mothers*, Ph.D. thesis, Edinburgh University, 1980.

Oster, H., 'Facial expression and affect development', in M. Lewis and R. A. Rosenblum (eds.) *The Origins of Behaviour: Affect Development,* New York, Plenum, 1978.

Papousek, H., 'Individual variability in learned responses in human infants', in R. J. Robinson (ed.) *Brain and Early Behaviour: Development in Fetus and Infant,* New York, Academic Press, 1969.

Spitz, R. A., *No and Yes: On the Genesis of Human Communication,* New York, International Universities Press, 1957.

Sylvester-Bradley, B., *A Study of Young Infants as Social Beings,* Ph.D. thesis, Edinburgh University, 1980.

Sylvester-Bradley, B., and Trevarthen, C., ' "Baby-talk" as an adaptation to the infant's communication', in N. Waterson and K. Snow (eds.) *Development of Communication: Social and Pragmatic Factors in Language Acquisition,* London, Wiley, 1978.

Trevarthen, C., 'Descriptive analyses of infant communication behaviour', in H. R. Schaffer (ed.) *Studies in Mother-Infant Interaction: The Loch Lomond Symposium,* London, Academic Press, 1977, 227-70.

Trevarthen, C., 'Communication and co-operation in early infancy. A description of primary intersubjectivity', in M. Bullowa (ed.) *Before Speech: The Beginnings of Human Communication,* London, Cambridge University Press, 1979(a), 321-46.

Trevarthen, C., 'Instincts for human understanding and for cultural co-operation: Their development in infancy', in M. von Cranach, K. Foppa, W. Lepenies and D. Ploog (eds.) *Human Ethology,* Cambridge, Cambridge University Press, 1979(b), 530-71.

Trevarthen, C., 'Brain development and the growth of psychological functions', in J. Sants (ed.) *Developmental Psychology and Society,* London, Macmillan, 1980(a), 46-95.

Trevarthen, C., 'The foundations of intersubjectivity: Development of interpersonal and co-operative understanding in infants', in D. Olsen (ed.) *The Social Foundations of Language and Thought: Essays in Honor of J. S. Bruner,* New York, W. W. Norton, 1980(b), 316-42.

Trevarthen, C., 'Basic patterns of psychogenetic change in infancy', in T. Bever (ed.) *Dips in Learning,* Hillsdale, N. J., Erlbaum, 1981 (in press).

Trevarthen, C., and Grant. F., 'Infant play and the creation of culture', *New Scientist,* 22 February 1979, 566-9.

Trevarthen, C., and Hubley, P., 'Secondary intersubjectivity: Confidence, confiding and acts of meaning in the first year', in A. Lock (ed.) *Action, Gesture and Symbol: The Emergence of Language,* London, Academic Press, 1978, 183-229.

Trevarthen, C., Murray, L., and Hubley, P., 'Infant psychology', in J. Davis and J. Dobbing (eds.) *Scientific Foundations of Clinical Paediatrics,* London, Heinemanns Medical Publishers, 1981 (in press).
Watson, J. B., *Behaviourism,* Chicago, University of Chicago Press, 1930.
Winnicott, D. W., *Playing and Reality,* Harmondsworth, Penguin, 1974.

6 How infants see the point

John Churcher and Michael Scaife

Quand le doigt montre la lune, l'idiot regarde le doigt

Introduction

The fact that people can point out remote objects for each other by means of gestures (looking, pointing, and so on) poses a developmental problem. Insofar as such gestural communication constitutes a preparation, in normal development, for the use of language, it raises the problems of *referring* and of *signification;* at the same time, analysis of its structure will reveal its dependence on a particular level of *spatial* understanding. Finally, the communicative gestures do not occur in a vacuum, but have social and emotional value.

This chapter begins with a discussion of referring and its possible precursors in development, followed by an account of Piaget's use of de Saussure's concept of the sign in the context of sensorimotor intelligence. The comprehension of pointing and looking gestures as signs, then as a formal spatial problem, is briefly discussed to introduce the evidence from observations of infants. Some methodological problems are mentioned, and then we try to explain the observations. The chapter concludes with a brief discussion of some of the conceptual issues raised by this work.

Referring

The recent renaissance of interest in the pragmatics of communication, particularly in the transition from pre-linguistic to linguistic communication in children, has restored to respectability questions concerning the relationship between the means of communication and its objects (in both senses of 'objects': the aims of communication, as well as what it is all about). Examples are Bruner (1975a,b) and Bates *et al.* (1975). But in developmental psychology, despite acknowledgements to particular 'philosophers of language', this is often confused by a syncretic equation among a number of terms: reference, referring, 'referencing', etc. (For a clear-headed review, see McShane, 1980, chapter 2).

Thus it is still necessary to recall the basic distinction made by Strawson (1950): if reference can be regarded as a relation holding between some linguistic expression (called a referring expression) and some thing, process or state of affairs (called the referent), this is only so in a derivative sense; what is primary is the communicative act of *referring:* this is not a relation between words and the world, but something that people *do* with words. Confusion between these concepts arises partly from the terminology, partly because they are closely connected: in referring one typically constructs or makes use of referring expressions, and according to certain rules.

We can characterise referring more precisely by stating the various conditions an act must satisfy in order to count as referring (what Searle, 1969, calls 'Rules of reference'). For our purposes, these can be reduced to three.

The first condition of referring is its immediate aim or end: when I refer to something I *identify* it for you. But what does 'I identify it for you' mean? It means something like this—I get you to think of it, or selectively attend to it. The second condition is a restriction on the means of achieving this end: not only do I intentionally identify something for you, but I do so partly by means of your recognition of my intention. Thirdly, referring only occurs as part of a larger communicative act, such as making a statement, asking a question, and so on.

What do these conditions imply when we try to identify the earliest occasions of referring involving a child? The first implies recognition of the other as a psychological subject, and awareness of objects as potentially objects of the other's thought or attention. It also implies the performance of some overt action, perceivable by the other, whether it be verbal (such as a speech act) or non-verbal, or both at once.

The second condition can normally be satisfied only by using shared assumptions about the way acts are to be interpreted, that is, by acting according to the 'conventions' or social rules which govern the meanings of acts.[1] Most of the time it is only *because* we use mutually recognised *conventions* that we are able to *use* each other's *recognitions* of our intentions (Searle makes this explicit as a separate condition on referring: his sixth 'rule'). But this ability to use a convention in *producing* a communicative act implies a complementary ability to *comprehend* such an act produced by another; and vice versa. Before a child can do either, she must be able to do both.

Thus there is a large gap between the observation that infants and adults spend some of their time together looking at or interacting with the same things, and the conclusion that they are referring to anything. But this is as far as the 'philosophy of language' will take us, for the question is now the developmental one—how does the ability to take part in such a social practice arise (how is it reproduced in the infant)?

We can imagine that there might develop *precursors* of referring which fail to meet some of the above criteria, but which are developmentally continuous with referring proper. If an infant searches for something, and someone seeing this intervenes to put the thing in her hand, she is thereby confronted with the social meaning of her own action; it has several times been suggested that this kind of feedback from adults progressively forms not only the infant's knowledge of the particular conventions in use in her culture (the language, manners, etc.), but also her reciprocal awareness of communication intentions, indeed her very awareness of herself as a subject (see Lock, 1980, chapter 3). If this is true, it is an important restatement of the problem, but not its solution (we still don't understand what it is about infants, and the social practices into which they are born, that makes this possible); but whatever the mechanism, such gestures by the infant would then be precursors of referring acts. As for comprehension, if it is possible to get an infant to look at some particular thing or place *without* using her recognition of the intention to get her to do it, again it may be that whatever makes this possible for the infant is also a precursor of the comprehension of referring. At its most passive this might involve the infant in merely suffering herself to be carried and placed in front of an object; or having something placed before her, and attending to it. More interesting would be a reaction to someone looking or pointing in which, without recognising any communicative intention, she would nevertheless try to look in the appropriate direction. It is this latter possibility that will be discussed in detail in this chapter.

Sensorimotor signs

As we have seen, referring normally presupposes certain conventions or social rules governing the way acts are to be interpreted. While there have been various attempts to theorise these, I want to discuss only one of them here—the semiological approach of de Saussure (1916: 1974)— mainly because of its relevance to Piaget's ideas on sensorimotor intelligence. De Saussure theorised the conventional rules of language as an abstract system *(la langue)*, separable in the theory from its actual historical use *(la parole)*. The fundamental element in this system is the 'sign', which consists in the combination of a particular 'signifier' and a particular 'signified'. What is signified is not some thing, but a concept, an abstract object; the signifier likewise is an abstraction, but a different one: the abstract representation of a class of linguistically equivalent speech-sounds (a 'sound-image'), or (in semiotics generally) of marks on paper, gestures, etc.[2] Signs can be 'arbitrary' (as in natural language 'tree' or 'arbre' may signify the concept of a tree); or (what for de Saussure is the converse of arbitrary) 'relatively motivated' that is, determined by associative connections.

The concept of motivation in de Saussure is worth clarifying. He introduces it in what at first sight appear to be two quite distinct senses.[3] Firstly, it conveys the idea of a 'natural' associative connection between signifier and signified, for example, between a picture of a tree and the concept of a tree. Secondly, it applies to a sign to the extent that its signifier breaks readily into serial elements, and thereby associates with other signs, for example the word 'farmer', as 'farm + er' associates with 'farm', 'farmyard', and so on, and, through the suffix, with 'gardener', 'labourer', etc. But it is essentially the same concept of 'association' that is being used here, in the first case between signifier and signified, that is, within a sign, and in the second case between one signifier and another, that is, between signs.

The utility of this concept of motivation in a discussion of the development of communication is that it in principle allows signs to be theorised in terms more general than any that linguistics itself can provide. Now the fact that de Saussure may have been thinking of psychology in some narrow sense as the possible source of such a theory, or that many of his followers have tended to play down this aspect, for fear of 'psychologism', is not the main point; the concept of association in this sense, as the limitation of arbitrariness, does not by itself impose any particular solution. What matters is that it creates the possibility of some way of understanding the functional and developmental continuity between the use of signs and the rest of life, while respecting the peculiarly systematic nature of signs.

Piaget (1936: 1953) attempted to make this connection in this account of sensorimotor development. In order to understand his use of de Saussure's ideas, it is first necessary to understand that for Piaget a sensorimotor scheme is an essentially *relational* entity, definable only by its relations with other schemes. This is not stated in his formal definition of assimilation, nor made clear in his discussions of the co-ordination between particular schemes, which are often discussed as if they could be distinguished simply in terms of which muscle-groups are active, or even which sensory modalities are involved. However, when addressing the question of the criteria for the individuation of schemes (how do we know when we are dealing with one scheme or two) Piaget is explicit:

> The criterion of this distinction is the following. When the sensorial movements and elements are associated which do not yet present themselves, by another road, in the isolated state, we shall say that there is a single schema. We shall say, on the contrary, that co-ordination between schemata exists when they are able to function separately in other situations. For example, putting the thumb in the mouth constitutes a single schema and not a co-ordination between the sucking schema and the manual schemata because, at the age at which the child learns to suck his thumb he knows, it is true, how to suck something other than his thumb, but he does not know how to accomplish in other circumstances, by means of his hand, the action which he performs in putting it into his mouth ... On the other hand, the behaviour pattern consisting in grasping objects seen (4 to 5 months) may be cited as an example of co-ordination between heterogeneous schemata, for grasping objects independently of sight constitutes, as early as the fourth month, an autonomous schema and looking at objects independeptly of prehension is prevalent from 1 to 2 months. (Piaget, 1936, 1953, pp. 131-2)

Thus, analogous to a system of signs, there is always a *system* of schemes, each element identifiable only in relation to other elements, even if this systematicity is at first found only at a biological level (in morphology, and the differentiation of reflexes). This enables Piaget to introduce signification in the following way:

To assimilate a sensorial image or an object . . . is to insert in in a system of schemata, in other words, to give it a 'meaning'. *(ibid.,* p. 189)

Piaget argues that each developmental transformation in the system of schemes involves a corresponding transformation in a system of signs. Sensorimotor signifiers are called by Piaget 'indices',[4] and this term is used in two senses:

Concerning the ("index"), this is the concrete signifier connected with direct perception and not with representation. In a general way we shall call (index) every sensory impression or directly perceived quality whose signification (the "signified") is an object or a sensorimotor schema. In the strict and limited sense of the word, an (index) is a perceptible fact which announces the presence of an object or the imminence of an event (the door which opens and announces a person). *(ibid.,* pp. 191-2)

In stage II of the sensorimotor period, these indices are of the type Piaget calls 'signals': during the functioning of any scheme a complex pattern of sensorimotor processes is maintained and reproduced; when the scheme is not functioning, but some *part* of that pattern is recreated by other means (for example, by putting an infant into the characteristic posture for nursing). *the part signifies the whole*—this whole being the scheme itself, whose assimilatory functioning is now set in motion and thereby 'completes' the sign. But such a signal is limited in utility by its motivation: the only associative relations it has are with the other states capable of initiating the same scheme (for example, the nursing posture is in this way associatively related to a touch on the lips, since either will trigger the same primary circular reaction, and be assimilated by it).

In stage III, the indices accompanying the secondary circular reactions again consist in those perceptual fragments capable of reactivating the whole scheme; but now, because the secondary reaction aims to reproduce some 'interesting sight', this 'interesting sight' is included in the signified. And to the extent that the secondary circular reaction involves the beginnings of a differentiation of the end (reproducing an 'interesting sight') from the means (reproducing the action itself), the signal now enables anticipation of a future event, but only as part of an imminent action.

In stage IV the schemes become more 'mobile', that is, capable of forming temporary co-ordinations, and therefore more numerous and varied ones. A greater number of means-end co-ordinations implies a variety of means to each end, hence a growing independence of the end from any particular means, externalisation of the end as object, and a degree of separation between signifier and signified, allowing anticipation of future events as independent of the ongoing action (though still dependent on a future, deferred action to which the ongoing action is a means). Thus the sight of a cushion, or a cup, may signify the act of grasping a watch that was hidden beneath it; the creak of a door may signify watching someone enter the room later on. These are the signs that Piaget calls indices in the strict sense.

What level of sign is necessary in order to understand pointing or looking gestures? Suppose an infant often beholds such gestures at the same time as 'interesting sights' (or sounds, etc.) occur in her peripheral field. It would in principle be possible for her to develop a secondary circular reaction of turning the gaze aside in order to see. Here the sight of the gesture would come to signify both this turning and the 'interesting sight'.

The spatial problem

As far as signification is concerned, then, we might expect an infant in stage III to be able to look somewhere away from the gesture itself—but where? *How* does the gesture specify something spatially? How do we know where to look in order to see what someone else is looking or pointing at? Clearly, as adults we are often assisted by the context of conversation and/or action, sometimes to the extent that the number of possibilities is reduced to one. But this need not be the case, and a simple thought-experiment reveals our ability to use much more abstract spatial information when necessary.

Imagine two people in a bare room (see figure 1). Each can successfully identify for the other, by looking and/or pointing, a very large number of locations (strictly regions) on the walls, ceiling or floor. Given that this holds regardless of the dimensions of the room, or of the position within it adopted by the two people, we have an effectively infinite mapping of gestures into locations (or regions); the only obvious geometrical interpretation of this mapping is the intersection of the room-surface with the euclidian straight line (or bundle) given by the oriented axis of the gesture.

In order to explain this capability psychologically, we must suppose

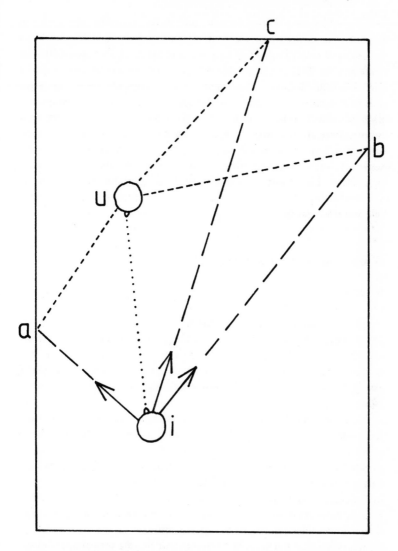

Figure 1. Idealised plan of two people (*i* and *u*) in an otherwise empty room. Using orienting gestures, *i* can identify for *u* any location (region) on the room's surface (except when occluded by the body of *i* or *u*); e.g. the arbitrary locations *a, b* and *c.* For *u* the direction of such a location (region) is specified only by the intersection of the room's surface with the straight line (bundle) given by the oriented axis of the gesture.

(a) the ability to construct such an axis at the site of the gesture itself, (b) the ability to extrapolate it across empty space, and (c) the ability to determine the intersection of this extrapolated line with a visible surface. The first of these involves at least perceiving the axis of a pointing arm or finger; at most it involves somehow determining the axis of symmetry of a sphere with superficial annuli (the eyeball, with its pupil and iris). Determining the sagittal axis of the head seems to be intermediate in difficulty. The question of interest is: which of these abilities, if any, must involve *representation* of a straight line, in Piaget's sense of mentally representing or imagining something absent from perception. I shall return to this question of spatial representation; for the time being, this purely formal analysis is sufficient to introduce the relevant observations.

Observations of infants' reactions

In the last few years there have been a number of attempts to study the genesis of this kind of communication in infants; we shall only discuss studies of comprehension, and start with our own work (Scaife, 1976; Churcher and Scaife, 1979). The starting-points for this work were our thinking about the spatial problem, plus the results of Scaife and Bruner (1975), which showed that the gaze-direction of infants as young as four months can be influenced by the gaze-direction of an adult.

We began our studies of infants' reactions to such gestures working independently and informally, each with different infants. After a year's observations of a few infants from birth, in their own homes, we decided to collaborate in a longitudinal laboratory study, hoping both to reproduce and film what we had already observed in the home and, in the light of the theoretical analysis, to try to test rigorously whether the infants' comprehension was fully generalised, and therefore involved an understanding of the spatial problem.

We persuaded ten women to bring their infants into the laboratory at approximately three-week intervals for a period of four to five months; at the start of the study the infants ranged from fourteen to twenty-two weeks old.

We tested the infants in a room partitioned by a black cloth screen, in the middle of which was a horizontal aperture NF camouflaged by black gauze (see figure 2). The infant sat in a suitable chair or on the mother's lap facing the experimenter, about one metre from the middle

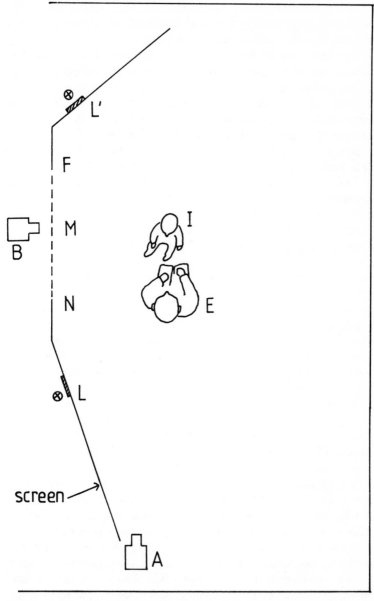

Figure 2. Plan of observational situation. The experimenter (E) and the infant (I) were traced from a video frame provided by the overhead camera; other features are positioned to scale (see text).

of the aperture. Contours were visible on the screen, including the boundary of the aperture, but these were relatively inconspicuous, and the infants rarely looked at them spontaneously.

Spotlights covered by infra-red filters at L and L' illuminated the infant's face with infra-red light, producing bright corneal reflections whose apparent positions relative to the pupils helped us estimate eye-position independently of head movements. We recorded from three video cameras simultaneously. One at A gave a broad view of the proceedings, while an infra-red camera hidden behind the aperture at B gave a close-up view of the infant's face. A third, overhead view of both participants, came from a camera in the ceiling.

Each session started with a calibration routine: we would shake a toy rattle for a few seconds at L, N, M, F, and L' respectively. As the infant looked at the rattle in each position, we were able to obtain positions of the corneal reflections for each of these directions. Once the infant appeared to be settled, and attentive to the experimenter, he was presented with a series of trials. A 'trial' consisted of an attempt to get the infant to look at one of the locations F or N, the experimenter either turning head and eyes to look there, or pointing as well as looking. On some pointing trials we pointed with a short wooden rod held in the hand, on others we used the hand alone. We nearly always said something like 'Look!' while making the gesture, and generally tried as hard as possible to coax the infant into looking at the chosen place. The timing of each trial was determined by our judgement of whether the infant seemed to be ready—a criterion that is hard to describe and which we had to learn. We always began with head and eyes alone, then added pointing, and finally pointing with the rod; and with each type of gesture we indicated the near position (N) before the far one (F). Sessions lasted from twenty to forty minutes, normally allowing each condition to be tried several times.

It is important to note that we were trying to get the infants to look not at clearly identifiable objects, but at 'empty' regions on a blank screen, that is, locations scarcely distinguishable except *as locations.* Also, as the diagram (reconstructed from the overhead video) shows, while N may well be within the infants' effective visual field, F is extremely peripheral when the infant looks at the experimenter's face.

Our observations fall into four kinds. Firstly, by far the most common reaction of all infants at all ages observed, was to look only at the experimenter—at his eyes or pointing hand—punctuated by looking down, or away from the experimenter in a way quite unrelated to the gesture. In a word, the appearance of total incomprehension.

Secondly, by the time the infants were only twenty-two weeks old, all but one had clearly shown a form of reaction on at least some trials which we will call 'Simple Appropriate': the infant looks horizontally away from the experimenter, on the correct side and in the correct plane, but not normally to the correct location. When the gesture had been presented with head and eyes only, the typical form of this reaction was a single, horizontal saccade, either without head movement or with a rapid, simultaneous head-rotation in the same direction, the infant turning her eyes through the same small angle (ten to thirty degrees) regardless of which location had been indicated by the gesture. When the gesture had included pointing, the infant would look at the pointing hand or rod, then make further horizontal saccades angularly beyond the hand, but, again, not to the specific location being indicated. Essentially this confirmed what we had already seen in the home.

Thirdly, on a few occasions some infants at twenty-seven to thirty-one weeks clearly attempted incompatible reactions to the same gesture. For instance, one infant began to reach for the pointing hand, suddenly stopped in mid-reach with a marked change of facial expression, withdrew her hand and looked out towards the screen in the way we have described (see figure 3).

But none of these observations suggests that the infants really know *where* to look. Such evidence is only afforded in our experiment if an infant correctly and differentially looks at N or F according to which we indicate.

This fourth class of observations is of just such differentiation *on successive trials,* in other words, we have excluded sequences of trials showing correct localisation of both N and F but with other trials intervening. This 'Spatially Differentiated' reaction first occurs at very different ages in different infants, but by forty weeks we had seen it in half the infants. The infant seems to know just where to look, and moves with the same characteristic speed and assurance as in the 'Simple Appropriate' reactions. When turning through the larger angle to F a blink often occurs during the synchronised head-and-eye saccade. For each infant, the age at which we first observed the 'Simple Appropriate' and 'Spatially Differentiated' reactions (if at all) is given in Table 1.

In a series of studies, Butterworth and his collaborators have made independent observations which confirm, complement and considerably extend those described above. They have, so far, only studied looking and not pointing gestures. In many respects, the conditions under

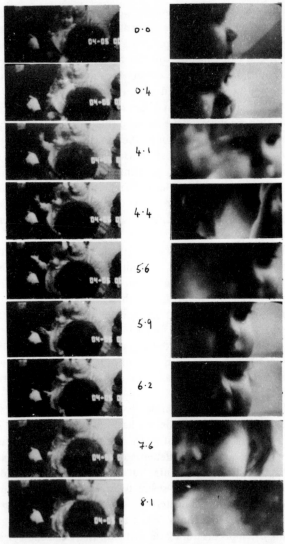

Figure 3. An infant of twenty-nine weeks starting to reach for the pointing hand, suddenly pausing, then turning to look away from the hand on the appropriate side. Note the change in facial expression as the reaching is interrupted. The two sequences of frames are from cameras A and B (see fig. 2). The printed numbers give the elapsed time in seconds. The bright object beyond the pointing hand is not visible to the infant.

Infant Number	Observed		First Occurrence of Simple Appropriate Responding		First Occurrence of Spatially Differentiated Responding	
	From	To	HE	HEP	HE	HEP
1	15	32	15	15	–	–
2	16	33	16	21	–	–
3	16	33	16	16	24	24
4	17	34	27	17	–	–
5	18	33	27	–	–	–
6	14	39	21	17	–	–
7	15	41	15	15	41	29
8	18	39	18	22	39	–
9	21	38	21	23	–	27
10	22	46	22	22	28	46

all data are given in weeks of age

Table 1. Ages at which each infant first showed criterial responses.

which their observations were made are similar to our own; their work has appeared in full elsewhere (Butterworth, 1979; Butterworth and Cochran, 1980; Butterworth and Jarrett, 1980), so only a summary of the main differences is given in Table 2.

The most obvious difference is the presence of target objects. As a result of our pilot studies, we found that when pairs of clearly visible target objects were used, we were unable to interpret the infants' reactions unambiguously: were they looking at the objects because these were salient in their own right, or because we were pointing them out? In particular, it seemed to us that the infants' tendency to look back and forth between the two objects as if comparing them, or establishing some relationship between them, might be obscuring any tendency to look preferentially at one or other of them in consequence of our gestures. In omitting objects, and in using a relatively featureless screen, we were trying to isolate the gestures as the only source of spatial determination. Such a move, whatever its success or failure from our point of view, may of course alter the meaning of the entire situation for the infant.

Study	Churcher and Scaife	Butterworth et al.	Lempers	Murphy and Messer
Design	Longitudinal	Cross-sectional	Cross-sectional (+ short-term longitudinal)	Cross-sectional
Infants' ages	4–10 months (at 3-week intervals)	6, 12, 18 months	9, 12, and 14 months (also 18, 24, 30, and 36 months)	9 and 14 months
Who presented the gestures	Experimenter	Mother	Experimenter	Mother
Target objects	None (Blank screen)	Two in variable positions	Three in fixed positions	Three in fixed positions
Types of gesture	Looking (head and eyes), pointing (head eyes and hand)	Looking (head and eyes)	Looking (eyes; head and eyes), pointing (hand) (Attempted to separate movement and gesture)	Pointing (head, eyes and hand?)
Method of recording	Video	Video	Experimenter judgements	Video, also judges hidden behind each object
Where	Laboratory	Laboratory	Home	Laboratory

Table 2. Comparison of studies on infants' comprehension of looking/pointing gestures

Given the differences, the agreement on essentials in our observations is the more remarkable. Firstly, the description of the dynamics of the infants' reactions closely fits our own:

> Typically, the baby would fixate intently on the mother's face while she was turning to a target, then after the mother's movement stopped, the infant would make a ballistic eye and head movement to foveate a target in the appropriate direction. (Butterworth and Cochran, 1980, p. 262)

Secondly, what we have called 'Simple Appropriate' reaction seems very similar to the shift of 'about forty degrees' described by Butterworth and Cochran when the target object was out of the infant's field of view. Finally, they found that if two objects in the visual field on the same side were separated by sixty degrees, infants would sometimes correctly differentiate them, that is, would show 'Spatially Differentiated' reaction. Butterworth and Jarrett (1980) call this 'geometric compensation'. (If the objects were separated by only forty degrees, this did not occur; which would be consistent with the assumption that the closer together their images on the retinae, the stronger the tendency for reactions to the objects themselves to obscure reactions to the gesture.)

As for the ages at which the reactions appear, in our study the first infant to show a 'Spatially Differentiated' reaction did so at twenty-four weeks, whereas not until forty weeks had half (5/10) of the infants shown it; Butterworth *et al.* report statistically significant differentiation in the twelve-month-old group, but not in the six-month-old group. (However, see the remarks on methodology, below.)

A thorough study of the comprehension of pointing by infants aged nine, twelve and fourteen months was done by Lempers (1976) (see also Lempers *et al.*, 1977), who tried systematically to separate out various component 'cues' in the gesture, particularly those provided by movement as opposed to static posture. His observations are consistent with those described above; however, perhaps because he analysed the spatial problem loosely in terms of 'distance', and appears to have ignored angles, it isn't clear whether or not he observed 'Spatially Differentiated' reactions.

Murphy and Messer (1977), who studied production and comprehension of pointing by infants of nine and fourteen months in interaction with their mothers, did consider angles, but only those subtended at the infants' eyes by the pointing hand and the target object. The larger this angle, the more 'difficult' the task, as measured by the lower probability of looking at the target.

Methodological problems

This kind of research is almost impossible to do. The compromises one is forced to make are many, various and serious, and there isn't space to treat them all adequately here; instead, we will briefly mention some of the more salient ones.

In our own study, we repeatedly compromised between 'clinical' and 'experimental' method. For example, in attempting to devise an accurate objective measure of gaze-direction for the unrestricted infant, we had to accept the presence of visible contours on the screen; however inconspicuous, these affect the rigour of our test of 'generalised comprehension'. In fact, the technical limitations of that measure of gaze-direction forced us back to our own observational judgement of where the infants looked. The numbers shown in the table express our agreement on a series of 'clinical' judgements, after repeatedly viewing and discussing the videotapes together.

But it is not just a question of technical limitations; deciding whether, and where, an infant is looking is not the same as deciding on the instantaneous orientation of his eyes, because 'looking' is a complex involving not just aiming the eye, but characteristic patterns of eye- and body-movement. Looking in this sense could not be measured by any eye-movement recorder, and our observations of it will not necessarily be made more 'objective' by any quantification, or other 'operational' convenience. Our ability to discriminate the different reactions did not ultimately depend on the precision of our measure of gaze direction; we tried to arrange the situation so that the effect would either be clear or non-existent. When 'Spatially Differentiated' reactions occur they are clear; but they only occur rarely. The lesson is: when simple observation was the best means available, we should have stuck to it.

Butterworth and his co-workers (also Murphy and Messer, and to a lesser extent, Lempers) are trying to obtain statistically significant results; in order to reject the null hypothesis they are obliged to treat successive observations on the same subject as samples from a single 'population'; i.e. they assume the same competence (plus 'noise') is being tested on every trial. The fact that nearly everyone does this doesn't make it right. There are two objections to this assumption. Firstly, to the infant, for whom the experiment is part of 'real life', every trial may be a unique historical event, whose meaning depends on its context—including the other trials in a series. If someone asks you your name, or the way to the station you might answer (depending on the circumstances); if they repeated the question many times in close succession, your remaining dumb most of the time would hardly constitute statistical evidence against the hypothesis that you understood the question and are able to answer it. Secondly, to the extent that the gestures are more or less ambiguous to the infant, the probabilistic approach fails to allow for the possibility that one extended 'performance' (sequence of responses) may be manifesting two or more distinct 'competences',

How can these observations be explained?

It seems that Piaget's concept of secondary circular reaction would be sufficient to account for the 'Simple Appropriate' reaction. The infant turns in order to reproduce some effect (which need not be simply the sight of an object, but may include, for example, social reactions from the other). Whether there is a visible object there or not is not critical: the circular reaction, being in this case a ballistic movement and thus having its end-point pre-programmed, does not require an external end-point to 'terminate' it (cf. Butterworth and Jarrett, 1980). And the level of significance peculiar to the secondary circular reactions, that of the 'signal' seems to be adequate: the sight of the gesture signals the imminent functioning of the scheme which will assimilate this sight, plus any 'interesting sight', by the act of turning the gaze aside in a certain way. And although the signal is not yet properly mobile, it can be ambiguous, as figure 3 beautifully illustrates—the sight may simultaneously signify for the infant two incompatible schemes.

It is different when we come to the 'Spatially Differentiated' reaction. Here the infant seems really to be solving a problem, and it is hard to see how this is done without involving the representation of a straight line, as discussed above. According to Piaget and Inhelder (1956), this doesn't otherwise appear until much later.

In stage III of the sensorimotor period, at which the secondary circular reactions appear, the spatial 'groups'[5] are 'subjective', that is, there is no differentiation between displacements occurring in the actions and the displacements of objects. The infant's understanding of the trajectory of a moving object that disappears is limited to a continuation of the bodily movements of accommodation that were made before it disappeared (that is, the tracking movements which kept it in or near central vision). Can the subjective groups explain the 'Spatially Differentiated' reaction? To answer this question, we have to consider pointing and looking separately.

In the case of a pointing gesture using the arm, what are the 'movements of accommodation' the infant can make? As the arm is being extended, she can track the hand (or any other part) until it stops moving; or, if the arm is already extended (see Lempers, 1976), she can shift her gaze along it as far as the hand. In the former case, smooth pursuit eye-movement may be involved; in the latter it will not, as in the absence of moving targets smooth pursuit is known not to occur except under special conditions. (See, for example, Young, 1977; also Trevarthen *et al.*, 1975). So the first restriction on continuation of the movement of accommodation is that any smooth pursuit component will not be continued as such. In the case of saccades, 'continuation' in Piaget's sense can only mean repetition, that is, more saccades in the same direction. But what does the same direction mean here?

In the general case, changing the point of binocular fixation in three dimensions involves (i) a conjugate binocular saccade; (ii) an independent binocular vergence movement, superimposed on (i); (iii) a saccadic movement of the head; (iv) accommodation of the lenses; (v) a vestibular eye-movement added to (i) and (ii) to compensate for (iii); and (vi) a whole series of little-researched postural adjustments.[6] Now there is nothing odd about the idea of a single sensorimotor scheme, in Piaget's sense, doing all of these in stage III—this is what the co-ordination of schemes by reciprocal assimilation in stage II is all about, although Piaget didn't analyse this particular example in detail. And it might even be that any smooth pursuit has already been integrated into this totality, the subjective displacement group thereby allowing saccades and smooth pursuit to the equivalent for the purpose of 'repeating' the whole act.[7]

Now if repetition meant going back to the starting position of the act and repeating the whole complex, there would be no problem. But to carry the gaze *beyond* the hand, *and along the same straight line in space,* would involve the co-ordinated extrapolation of different trigonometrical functions for different components. That is, equal intervals along the straight line correspond to variable saccadic angles, vergent angles, and focal length adjustments. And the rates of verification are different for different components, and while vergence and lens-accommodation may be reflexively yoked there has to be independence between these and saccades, as each straight line implies a unique ratio between these rates of variation, and because the same systems are used to sample points anywhere within a three-dimensional visual space, not just along a particular line.[8] In other words, the component schemes have to be systematised (differentiated and co-ordinated) at a higher level than that of the subjective group, one where there can occur co-ordination of movements without their actually having to be performed.

Can 'objective' groups help? Stage IV is the stage of transition from the subjective groups of stage III to the objective groups of stage V, that is, to groups which though still dependent on perception (cf. the 'representative' groups of stage VI), refer to the displacements of perceived objects as independent of the subject's action; 'changes of place' are henceforth distinguished from 'changes of state'. A relevant example of the 'autonomous trajectory' achieved at this stage is given by Piaget:

> But the pertinent experiment is one that can be made by dis-
> placing objects in a straight line behind the child .... For
> instance, at 0;9(12) Laurent is in the garden, seated in a carriage
> and unable to see behind it because of the half-raised hood;
> nevertheless when someone walks quietly from left to right, or
> vice versa behind his carriage, he follows the movement on his left
> with his eyes to the point where he no longer sees anything, then
> turns abruptly to the right to rediscover the moving object.
> (Piaget, 1937: 1955, pp.167-8.)

Here the trajectory of an object is maintained for perception while the activity of accommodation is interrupted and the infant completes the group of displacements by a different route from that followed by the moving object. This is quite similar to what 'Spatially Differentiated' reactions would be *with visible targets:* the gaze leaving the hand or face to alight on the appropriate object, just as in Piaget's example it leaves the disappearing figure to intercept it where it reappears further along its independent path. In either case the co-ordination of visual schemes must have progressed to the extent that a movement of accommodation can now be continued along a straight line, in the temporary absence of a visible straight edge, which we saw above is not trivial. In the course of what activity could such a co-ordination have developed? We can only speculate: perhaps in watching people approach objects; perhaps in simultaneously watching and listening to conversations.

So for the case of pointing, we may conclude that while the

original movements of accommodation specify a straight line, this accommodation can only be continued as straight by co-ordinating independent visual schemes at the level of objective groups. In the case of looking, all the above difficulties concerning extrapolation apply, only there is an added difficulty—the original movements of accommodation cannot uniquely specify a line in the first place. Instead, the line has somehow to be constructed as an axis of symmetry of the eyeball, or at least of the head.[9]

But whether pointing or looking are used, if there are no targets to look at the task is surely more difficult: the infant has to search such a large surface for its point of intersection with the extrapolated line, and to do this would disrupt the extrapolating activity. In fact, there is little evidence of searching, the movements being quick and precise. Thus the possibility seems to remain that the infant in this situation, deprived of perceptual props, is somehow making the co-ordinations 'in her head', and genuinely imagining a line she cannot see.

Summary and discussion

As early as two to four months, infants will sometimes respond to pointing or looking gestures intended to get them to look in a certain direction by turning the gaze away from the face or pointing hand, and to the appropriate side, but apparently without any further differentiation of direction, as if grasping that the gesture signifies something spatially separate from itself and to be seen somewhere on that side ('Simple Appropriate' reaction). Sometime during the second six months, infants will occasionally demonstrate that they also know roughly where the line of sight goes, since they correctly differentiate gestures to different places on the same side and in the same horizontal plane ('Spatially Differentiated' reaction). In neither case does this imply 'referring', though it may be one of the developmental precursors of referring. The 'Simple Appropriate' reaction is entirely consistent with Piaget's stage III, in respect both of the type of signification (signals), and of spatial cognition (subjective groups). The 'Spatially Differentiated' reaction is consistent with stage IV (indices, and the transition from subjective to objective groups), but only when the gesture is pointing and target objects are present; when looking alone is used, the line of sight must be entirely constructed, and when there are no target objects the line must be co-ordinated with the perceived environment, there has to be the 'mental representation' of a straight line.

The currently fashionable resort is to Gibson's notion of 'direct' perception, where the most intractable of developmental problems can ultimately be solved by denying that it really is a developmental one— the solution, it is declared, has been there all along: a certain pattern of stimulation simply 'specifies' a certain perception, or 'affords' a certain action. (For example, see Butterworth, 1982, or Brown, 1980.) Gibson's theory is important and in some respects unavoidable: we can no longer ignore the generality of the concept of 'invariants', or the insistence on an 'ecological' optics. But we should not allow Gibson's iconoclastic zeal to lead us into yet another biologism, in which everything of importance is preformed and the problems of development are unloaded on to evolutionary biology (where they remain developmental problems, but someone else's). That there is a complex pre-adaptation evident in morphogenesis and in 'behavioural embryology' does not mean that development is reducible to the mere expression of this pre-adaptation over time.

How then, without Gibson, do we cope with the apparently precocious representation of straight lines described above? We have no answer, because we hardly begin to understand its functional importance in the infant's life. Instead, here are three ideas which we believe point in the right direction.

The first concerns the concept of representation itself. It is essential, as Sinha (1981) has recently argued, to see representation as a *material* process, whose material basis is not confined to the physiology of the individual, but includes other individuals, cultural artifacts such as tools, or paper, or even the air we vibrate when we speak. From this standpoint, representations are both supported and constrained by material structures in the brain *and elsewhere*. Of course, not just any material structures will do, and brains in particular play a unique role; but the brain is no more nor less a part of the material support of representations than is any other part; the representational structure of reality is no less material than its atomic, mechanical or physiological structure. This argument is developed more fully by Sinha (1981 and this volume); and its purpose here is to erode the idea that representation only takes place 'in the head'.

The second point concerns the individual and the social in Piaget's theory.[10] From the period of concrete operations onwards, Piaget makes no theoretical distinction between the co-ordination of operations within the individual, and their co-ordination between individuals in social co-operation; at earlier periods, however, the child's social understanding is limited by partial egocentrism, that is, the incomplete awareness of the relativity of her own point of view, and further limited in the sensorimotor period by the lack of properly differentiated signifiers, such as those which can be fully differentiated from their signifieds because they are representations of them, in Piaget's sense.

But why must co-operation be reciprocal in order to count as true co-operation? An adult or older child can so structure the possibilities for the infant, that the infant becomes able to 'do' things she cannot 'do' without that social support (Bruner has aptly called this 'scaffolding'). To insist at every stage that the infant should do everything 'by herself' in order for it to count as competence, is a perversity systematically prevalent in much developmental psychology. We know perfectly well the infant cannot survive outside society, that is, outside the social practices involved in reproducing people. As Wallon said, to remove a child from society would be equivalent to removing its cerebral cortex.

We can separate the utility of the concepts Piaget discovered, from what Piaget himself did with them, and see that the profound egocentrism (i.e. indifferentiation) of sensorimotor intelligence is entirely compatible with a radically social theory of development. The world that schemes assimilate is both physical and social; a pointing finger is both a physical object to be grasped, and a social sign to be interpreted, in other words, a material representation to be 'grasped' in the other (derivative) sense. Neither of these senses of 'grasping' is more fundamental than the other, and each is sensorimotor functioning in Piaget's sense.

The last point concerns the purely cognitive nature of the analysis. The concept of attention serves to obliterate the emotional aspects of communication—why is the child playing this game at all? Objects in the child's visual world aren't just objects in the physical sense, things seen; they are also things shown, presented in some way, whether by setting them in front of the child, or the child in front of them, or indeed by pointing them out. The place I look at is not only the place where you may find some neutral object of my attention, but also the place where you may find the object of my desire (or fear, anger, and so on), the place where you would have to put yourself if you were to become that object, and the place you would be looking at if you could stand here and imitate my posture, that is, if you were to become me. The infants may not just be looking for whatever happens to be over there, but also for what they have just lost as a result of our looking away from them; they may be seeking to re-establish a relation between themselves and us, as well as to establish a relation between themselves and a third 'object'. This is an eternal triangle, which psychoanalysts have attempted to theorise (for example, with the concept of 'identification'), and which we should not ignore. (e.g. Lacan, 1973: 1979.)

Margaret Donaldson, trying to explain a similar discrepancy, between Piaget and Inhelder's mountain task and Martin Hughes' policeman task, argues that pre-school children possess

> an ability to decentre that is not concerned with the literal understanding of another's point of view: not with what another person *sees* from a given standpoint, but with what he is feeling or planning to do. (Donaldson, 1978, p. 25.)

This is a timely reminder of the relation between thought and emotion; but this relation cannot be understood in terms of a mere *decomposition* of mental life into intellectual and emotional 'abilities', then to be contrasted with one another. Seeing and feeling are not separate faculties, but two aspects of a single process.

Notes

This paper is dedicated to the late Gareth Evans, briefly Wilde Reader in Mental Philosophy at Oxford University. It was made possible by the patient support of J. S. Bruner and the Oxford University Department of Experimental Psychology, and by a Research Training Award from the Science Research Council to J. Churcher, and a Junior Research Fellowship from the Medical Research Council to M. Scaife.

1. 'Convention' here does *not* imply something set up by explicit social agreement. For brave attempts by philosophers to theorise the acquisition and modification of conventions, see Grice (1968) and Lewis (1969).
2. For a critique of this interpretation of de Saussure, see Mounoud and Guyon-Vinter (1982), who want to keep signifier and signified theoretically separate from sound-image and concept; but this is only necessary if we are dealing with an idealised sign-system (which even language fails to be, as de Saussure recognised). The move to study the 'pragmatics' of communication (linguistic or non-linguistic) entails abandoning this idealisation, and for the same reason as Piaget evidently

did in studying sensorimotor development. See also Brown (1980), for a third point of view.

3. De Saussure (1916:1974), pp. 68-9, 131-4. Culler (1976, p. 20) calls the second of these 'secondary motivation'.

4. The French is *indice* (singular), *indices* (plural); this has been variously translated as: 'indication/s' (by Cook, in 'The Origins of Intelligence'); 'indicator/s' (by Weaver, in 'The Psychology of the Child'); and 'index/indices' (by Gattegno and Hodgson, in 'Play, Dreams and Imitation in Childhood'). We have adopted the last of these, and inserted it where necessary in brackets in the quoted excerpts from Cook's translation.

5. 'Group' is used by Piaget in the mathematical sense, and in this context the elements are spatial displacements.

6. On the co-ordination of eye- and head-movement, see Carpenter (1977), p. 29. The interaction between posture and eye-movement in infants is discussed by Bullinger (1982).

7. From the work of Bower (1974) and Bullinger (1982) it seems likely that the co-ordination of saccades and smooth pursuit in subjective groups occurs between two and four or five months. (However, see Trevarthen *et al*, 1975.) The conditions for the occurrence of true smooth pursuit in early infancy are still not clear.

8. See Carpenter (1977), pp. 82-3 (on accommodation vergence), and p. 94 (on vergence and version).

9. Marr (1976) has suggested an algorithm for such constructions, in terms of finding the axis of a 'generalised cone'.

10. An interesting source of explicit statements by Piaget on this issue is his chapter on Sociology in the *Introduction a l'Epistemologie Genetique* (Piaget, 1950, Vol III, chapter 10).

Bibliography

Bates, E., Camaioni, L., and Volterra, V. 'The acquisition of performatives prior to speech.' *Merrill-Palmer Quarterly*, 1975, *21*, 205-26.

Bower, T. G. R. *Development in Infancy*, San Francisco, W. H. Freeman, 1974.

Brown, M. 'Pre-linguistic perception and the linguistic sign.' Paper presented at the annual conference of the developmental section of the British Psychological Society, Edinburgh, September 1980.

Bruner, J. S. 'From communication to language—a psychological perspective', *Cognition*, 1975a, *3*, 255-87.

Bruner, J. S., 'The ontogenesis of speech acts', *Journal of Child Language*, 1975b, *2*, 1-19.

Bullinger, A., 'Cognitive elaboration of sensorimotor behaviour', in Butterworth, G. (ed.) *Infancy and epistemology*, Brighton, Sussex, Harvester Press, 1982.

Butterworth, G., 'What minds have in common is space: a perceptual mechanism for joint reference in infancy', Paper presented at the annual conference of the developmental section of the British Psychological Society, Southampton, September 1979.

Butterworth, G., 'Object permanence and identity in Piaget's theory of infant cognition', in Butterworth, G. (ed.) *Infancy and epistemology*, Brighton, Sussex, Harvester Press, 1982.

Butterworth, G., and Cochran, E., 'Towards a mechanism of joint visual attention in human infancy', *International Journal of Behavioural Development*, 1980, *3*, 253-70.

Butterworth, G. and Jarrett, N., 'The geometry of pre-verbal communication', Paper presented at the annual meeting of the developmental section of the British Psychological Society, Edinburgh, September 1980.

Carpenter, R. H. S., *Movements of the eyes*, London, Pion, 1977.

Churcher, J., and Scaife, M., 'How infants understand spatially oriented gestures', Paper presented at the annual conference of the developmental section of the British Psychological Society, Southampton, September, 1979.

Culler, J., *Saussure*, Hassocks, Sussex, Harvester Press with Fontana, 1976.

Donaldson, M., *Children's Minds*, London, Fontana/Collins, 1978.

Grice, H. P., 'Utterer's meaning, sentence meaning, and word meaning', *Foundations of Language*, 1964, *4*, 225-42.

Lacan, J., *The four fundamental concepts of psychoanalysis*, Harmondsworth, Penguin, 1973: 1979.

Lempers, J. D., 'Production of pointing, comprehension of pointing, and understanding of looking behaviour in young children', Doctoral thesis, University of Minnesota, 1976.

Lempers, J. D., Flavell, E. R., and Flavell, J. H., 'The development in very young children of tacit knowledge concerning visual perception', *Genetic Psychology Monographs*, 1977, *95*, 3-53.

Lewis, D., *Convention: a philosophical study*, Cambridge, Mass., Harvard University Press, 1969.

Lock, A. *The guided reinvention of language*, London, Academic Press, 1980.

136   *Social Cognition*

Marr, D., 'Analysis of occluding contour', *Procedings of the Royal Society, Series B,* 1977, *197,* 441-75.

McShane, J., *Learning to talk,* Cambridge, Cambridge University Press, 1980.

Mounod P., and Guyon-Vinter, A., 'Representation and sensorimotor development', in Butterworth, G. (ed.) *Infancy and epistemology,* Brighton, Sussex, Harvester Press, 1982.

Murphy, C. M., and Messer, D. J., 'Mothers, infants and pointing: a study of gesture', in Shaffer, H. R. (ed.) *Studies in mother-infant interaction,* London, Academic Press, 1977.

Piaget, J., *The origins of intelligence in the child,* London, Routledge & Kegan Paul, 1936: 1953.

Piaget, J., *The child's construction of reality,* London, Routledge & Kegan Paul, 1937: 1955.

Piaget, J., *The child's conception of space,* London, Routledge & Kegan Paul, 1948: 1956.

Piaget, J., *Introduction a l'epistemologie genetique,* Paris, P. U. F., 1950.

Saussure, F. de, *Course in general linguistics,* New York, Philosophical Library, 1916: 1959; references are to revised edition, London, Fontana, 1974.

Scaife, M., 'Infant responses to the attention-directing signals of adults', Paper presented at the 10th International Study Group on Child Neurology and Cerebral Palsy, Oxford, 1976.

Scaife, M., and Bruner, J., 'The capacity for joint visual attention in the infant', *Nature,* 1975, *253,* 265-6.

Searle, J., *Speech acts,* Cambridge, Cambridge University Press, 1969.

Sinha, C., 'Negotiating boundaries: psychology, biology and society', in Barker, M., Birke, L., and Muir, A., *Dialectics of biology and society,* London, Allison and Busby, 1981, in press.

Strawson, P., 'On referring', reprinted in Flew, A. G. N. (ed.) *Essays in conceptual analysis,* London, Macmillan, 1950: 1956.

Trevarthen, C., Hubley, P., and Sheeran, L., 'Psychological actions in early infancy', *La Recherche,* 1975, *6,* 447-58.

Young, L. R., 'Pursuit eye-movements—what is being pursued?' in Baker, R., and Berthoz, A. (eds.) *Control of gaze by brain stem neurons.* Amsterdam, Elsevier/North Holland Biomedical Press, 1977.

7 Representational development and the structure of action

Chris Sinha

Introduction

This chapter is concerned with the development of actions directed to the achievement, or instantiation, of mentally represented goals. Theories of adult learning and functioning of motor skills emphasise the complex hierarchical structure of the plans governing their implementation (Schmidt, 1975), and suggest that the representation of such plans is best conceptualised in terms of stored schemata in which 'the specifications of an action are held in memory as descriptions of fairly general ways of initiating the action and of the expected or intended effects on the agent's body and the environment' (Morton, 1980: 58).

The development of control of even the simplest components of intentional actions is characterised by the passing of control from local, low-level to distal high-level executive centres, and the gradual functional integration of modular units into hierarchically-organised, goal-orientated action sequences (Connolly and Elliott, 1972). The growth of structural complexity of actions can be measured in terms of the degree of hierarchical embedding required for their implementation (Greenfield, 1978), and can be observed throughout infancy and early childhood. The development of organisation of action is therefore best approached in terms of the emergence and elaboration of a complex functional system (Luria, 1973).

Functional analysis of complex behavioural systems frequently reveals levels of structural and integrative complexity in humans which are without parallel in non-human species. In phylogenetic evolutionary development, it would seem, complex systems which have previously been viewed as emergent, qualitative 'faculties', are better conceptualised as resulting from co-actions between component systems, characterised by a rich interconnectedness of specialised functions. A typical pattern in such developmental processes consists of the progressive interaction between the *differentiation* and *integration* of systems and system sub-parts. An initial integrative mechanism differentiates, and the resultant functions are reintegrated at a higher level of organisation. The consequence of this process—which may be seen as both a 'goal' and an 'effect' of adaptation—is both increased specialisation and increased flexibility.

As the work of Trevarthen (this volume) has shown, this pattern is characteristic of ontogenetic as well as phylogenetic developmental processes. Nowhere is its manifestation more striking than in the development of intentional action, in whose structures and products we may discern the full complexity of human conceptual subjectivity and inter-subjectivity (Reynolds, in press). In this chapter, I explore the development of intentional actions between the ages of nine months and three years, illustrating the account with data from search tasks, imitation tasks and language comprehension tasks. The data are interpreted within a theory of the development of conceptual representation in infancy and early childhood, in which I suggest that conceptual distinctions, embodied or represented in objects and social interactions in the child's environment, are negotiated and learned by the child, and then interiorised as control systems governing constructive and communicative actions.

Concepts and Intentional Actions

In this chapter, I shall be concerned with praxic actions: that is, with actions which are intentionally orientated to the transformation of one state of affairs in the world to another state. Not all praxic actions are constructive in nature, but I shall show that elementary structures ('protoconcepts') governing non-constructive praxis are elaborated into differentiated conceptual schemata governing more or less complex constructive praxic action. I shall not directly be concerned with communicative action, in which the goal of the action is to effect a transformation, not in the external world, but in the behaviour or mental state of another person. However, not only do praxic and communicative actions develop together, drawing upon one another in development (Lock, 1980), but the conceptual structures guiding both are derived from social interactions in which infants negotiate, through co-operative action, the representational significance which should be accorded to objects and actions within particular contexts.

For Piaget (1955, 1971), the actions of the child on the world are accorded not merely a privileged, but a constitutive status in the development of intelligence (or conceptual subjectivity). Yet it seems at times as if Piaget attributes two different meanings to the notion of an 'active intelligence': the first, a specific one, consists in the definite hypothesis that cognitive development is entirely characterised by successive stages in the organisation of operative intelligence, in which 'logico-mathematical concepts presuppose a set of operations that are abstracted not from the objects perceived, but from the actions performed upon these objects' (Piaget and Inhelder, 1969: 49). The second, a more general one, sees 'intelligence as the development of an assimilatory activity . . . whose successive structures serving it as organs are elaborated by interaction between itself and the external environment.' (Piaget, 1953: 398). My suggestion is that it is unnecessary to accept the hypothesis that cognitive development consists in simply the development of the co-ordination of the logic of individual actions, in order to accept a general view which sees the development of conceptual subjectivity in terms of the functional elaboration of structures governing interactions with the environment, if one sees 'environment' as in part mediated through social-interactive structures.

Although the objects of actions only have significance in terms of their functional assimilation to the schemata governing those actions, it is equally true that these schemata must accommodate to the *particular* properties of *actual* objects in order that they may progressively approximate to the structures of developed, adult conceptual schemata. In this accommodatory process, the role of adults in indicating for children what schematic value should be accorded to the properties of objects is of at least as much importance as the role of individual, exploratory play with objects, which, as Piaget (1962) himself notes, tends in any case to be assimilatory rather than accommodatory in nature. Any particular object such as a cup, can potentially, by nature or by design, enter into a number of different action schemata. These may be simple (as in bringing the cup to the mouth, or successively banging it on a table top); or they may be complex (as in building a 'bridge' or 'arch' out of cups). Further, the action schema employed may either be congruent with the functional design features of the object (as in placing a brick *in* a cup) or incongruent with these design features (as in placing a brick *under* an inverted cup).

The canonical object-schema

Now, the 'incongruence' of the latter example does not reside in the physical features of the object, for a cup makes a perfectly good lid when inverted, and for that matter the same inverted cup will serve as an excellent supporting surface for a brick to be placed on top of. Although there are definite limits to the functional flexibility of objects—the reader might amuse herself in imagining implausible uses for cups—most common objects are potentially 'assimilable' to a variety of different schemata. Much of what is often referred to as 'creative problem-solving' consists in constructing novel assimilatory functional links between schemata and objects, or adaptively accommodating schemata to the objects to hand. Piaget's (1953) account of the development of the co-ordination of means-ends relationships in the sensorimotor stages rests upon this sort of analysis. However, artefacts such as cups, developmentally as well as by design, are most readily represented in terms of their utility in *particular* schemata. Thus, the socially standard—or *canonical—function* of a cup is to serve as a container; and the canonical *orientation* of a cup, in which it best serves that function, is that in which its cavity is upright, and thus accessible; and the canonical *spatial relation* which a cup contracts with another object in the instantiation of its canonical function, is one of containment (or enclosure).

These three aspects—function, form (orientation) and relation—of the canonical object-schema are mutually constitutive, but each has a different mode of cognitive involvement in the object-schema. The function, or use-value, of the object is specified by the spatio-temporal relations between object-parts and body-parts in the implementation of the schema (or, in the case of complex objects, such as machines, the spatial relations between object-parts and object-parts). The canonical orientation, and in general the form, of the object is specified by the most economical and appropriate means by which these spatial relations may be brought into being in a dynamic action sequence; and the canonical relation is that final state towards which the implementation of the object-schema is directed (again, the 'final state', in complex objects, may be a cyclical repetition of events, a variable state, and so on). Although the canonical object-schema is a dynamic, structural whole, it is not a decomposable one, at least for adults. For example, an object-part, such as the bottom of the cup, can act as a perceptual index for the spatial relation of *support,* independently of its involvement in a containment schema. The criteria for the recognition or production of a particular spatial relation, as Miller and Johnson-Laird (1976) have shown, can be specified as a set of perceptual predicates, and these predicative features may be decontextualised from the canonical object-schema, and recontextualised into a novel schema functionally directed to the production of a different relation.

This process of decontextualisation-recontextualisation of perceptual predicates (or features of *form)* is best thought of in terms of the different, alternative schematic *values* which may be accorded to the same perceptual information in relation to different purposes requiring the instantiation of different schemata. Any complex cognitive system, be it a human being or a computer programme, must be capable of according schematic values to perceptual data in a flexible manner, if it is to be capable of goal-directed actions or of any cognitive activity implying pattern-recognition of complex perceptual arrays. The concept of 'frame' in *Artificial Intelligence* (Minsky, 1974) is, as has frequently been pointed out, formally and functionally equivalent to an object-schema; although such frames are commonly specialised to object recognition, this constraint is not a necessary one, and frames or schemata in actual psychological processing serve constructive and communicative, as well as recognitory, functions. The flexibility of schematic valuation of perceptual information in adult humans is well illustrated by familiar illusions (figure-ground illusions, Necker cube, impossible solids etc.), and current theories of perception (Oatley, 1978) emphasise the active, structuring, schematic nature of perceptual processes and their functional interconnectedness with representational or conceptual/cognitive mechanisms.

Perception and Representation

It is instructive in this context to examine more closely the notion of 'schematic valuation' of information. First, such a process implies a definite distinction between *representation* (knowledge, concepts) and *perception,* such that representational systems are irreducible to mere agglomerations of perceptual features, albeit there exists a rich interconnection between perceptual and conceptual processes.[2] A schema-based theory is thus incompatible with hypotheses proposing a direct mapping between perceptual features of external reality and conceptual or semantic entries in the mental lexicon (Clark, 1975). Rather, conceptual or representational processes are best conceived in terms of a schematic or procedural (Johnson-Laird, 1977) system, in which schemata are represented in terms of certain functional procedures whose actual instantiation in real contexts are constrained to perceptual-featural criteria.

My proposal is thus similar to that of Olson and Bialystok (in press), who stress that 'a concept is a structural description plus a meaning', in which 'meaning' loosely translates as schema, and 'structural description' as perceptual-featural recognitory criteria. As they say (p. 13) 'we have given meaning a priority in that it is the criterion in terms of which structural descriptions are formulated'; that is, structural descriptions function so as to enable the instantiations of meanings. As they point out, the processes of assimilation and accommodation can be conceived of as processes of elaboration of, respectively, structural descriptions (predictive criteria) and meanings (schemata). Although these processes tend to complementary equilibrium, combined and uneven cognitive development may lead to desynchronisation of the processes, resulting in the phenomenon noted by Nelson (1974: 284): 'in the course of development there will emerge words without an adequate conceptual base [i.e. lexically-labelled recognitory structural descriptions with relatively impoverished schematic 'meanings'] as well as concepts without words' [i.e. schemata, with or without appropriate structural descriptions, which remain as yet unlabelled]. However, it is clear that the advent of referential language (such as, signifying acoustic sequences 'standing for' concepts) introduces a further level of complexity, for words themselves may be assimilated to either of the two aspects of the concept—schematic meaning or recognitory description.

This leads to a second issue with regard to schematic valuation of perceptual information. Earlier, I spoke of the canonical object-schema as *combining* functional, perceptual (formal, featural, recognitory) and relational information in a structural whole. In the preceding paragraph, however, I indicated that a concept should be viewed as a schema *plus* recognitory perceptual criteria. This apparent contradiction can be resolved by assuming that a *partial differentiation* occurs in development between the systems governing schematic knowledge and recognitory-criterial knowledge, respectively. It is precisely this partial differentiation, and the reintegration of the two systems at a higher level of organisation, which is the basis of the flexibility of the conceptual system in its valuations and revaluations of perceptual information, with respect to different goals and purposes, involving different schematic representations and their instantiation in actions. Insofar as the system governing recognitory-criterial knowledge tends towards the perceptual predicative criteria operative in the adult speech-community, that system will increasingly assume the form of a *semantic memory*. Insofar as the system governing schematic knowledge tends towards the representation of more complex and elaborate sequences of action and interaction, that system will increasingly assume the form of a *procedural* or *episodic memory*, representing event structures and inter-episodic relations in terms of structures similar to 'scripts' as defined by Schank and Abelson (1977).

Finally, before moving on to present the data, what precisely is the nature of the relationship between a recognitory feature (or feature constellation) and a given schema which evaluates the feature(s)? I suggest that the relationship of evaluation is one in which real world features are evaluated against mentally represented constructions, prototypic in nature, which are the basic conceptual currency of the cognitive system. Prototypes *represent* the generative link between a schema and the recognitory-criterial rules for its instantiation, thus linking instantiation rules (Bridges, Sinha and Walkerdine, 1981) for the schema with the 'lexicon' of semantic primitives constituting the developed semantic memory. A canonical object-schema is represented by a privileged prototypic representation, probably at the 'basic' level of abstraction defined by Rosch (1977), and representing, as she indicates, both perceptual and functional information. This analysis resolves the contradiction between 'functional' and 'perceptual' accounts of conceptual development (Clark, 1973; Nelson, 1974) by postulating that prototypes are *representative* structures mediating the relations between function (procedural schema) and form (recognitory featural criteria).

Complex constructive praxis necessitates the evaluation of real-world features against constructed end-state representations generated by the assemblage of the current-state features into a different configuration than that currently obtaining, and the implementation of a procedural schema permitting the transformation of current state to intended end-state. The construction of a plan is therefore equivalent to a mental representation of the action sequence (henceforth, syntagm) encoded in the schema. Simple object recognition, however, necessitates only the evaluation of the real-world features against the recognitory criteria for the canonical object-schema, a process involving the matching of real-world configuration against a prototype. Thus, in the early stages of development, object recognition is associated with the actual instantiation of the canonical object-schema; young children are often observed to act out an action syntagm (such as drinking) when they encounter an instance of the canonical object-schema (for a cup), a process of *recognitory assimilation* which is later internalised.

Complex constructive praxis necessitates the ability to *decompose* the featural complexes constituting prototypes, in order that these features may be revalued against an intended end-state. In this process, 'motor activity is controlled by simulated perceptual content that is only gradually created empirically' (Reynolds, in press: 46). The ability to engage in constructive praxis therefore has as a condition precisely the requirement enabling the gradual systematisation of semantic memory: that is, decomposition of prototypes into constituent featural 'primitives' approximating to the predicative criteria for natural language semantic categories. It is not, therefore, the case that prototypic representation should be seen as analogue *alternatives* to featural lists in memory, but as structured assemblages of features which may be broken down and recombined. However, the preceding analysis suggests that the ability to break down the prototype may be a later ontogenetic development than the initial ability to construct the prototype as a representative index of a canonical object-schema. In other words, synthesis precedes analysis, although not, perhaps, by very much in real time.

Development of Representation

Piagetian theory leads us to suppose that the capacity for 'representation' emerges only at Stage VI of sensorimotor development, usually attained between fifteen and twenty-four months of age. However, I shall now present evidence that elementary representational structures ('protoconcepts') are initially laid down in infancy, before the end of the first year of life. These protoconcepts are to be understood as canonical object-schemata, in which recognitory criteria are entirely governed by characteristics of canonical form/orientation, and in which relational information and recognitory criteria are inseparably inter-twined in the evaluation of a functional schema. Thus, we shall show that although the minimal criteria for the possession of concepts by infants are fulfilled, the criteria for evaluative flexibility are not, and that the infant's protoconceptual system is unable functionally to separate the criteria for the instantiation of a relational schema (containment) from the criteria for the instantiation of a canonical object-schema (a cup as a container). The primitive nature of the protoconcepts leads to very curious effects upon infants' performance in search tasks.

Experiment 1

Subjects: 38 infants were tested, 19 at 12 months and 19 at 15 months of age.

Apparatus: A circular white tray, 34 cm radius, on which were placed cylindrical plastic mugs with handles, measuring 10 cm high × 28 cm circumference, some coloured blue, some orange. A selection of small toys, maximum height 1½ cm.

Procedure: Testing was done in the infants' home with the mother present. After rapport had been established, the tray was set facing the infant who was supported from behind by the mother. Two blue (or orange) cups were placed on the tray, with a separation of 8 cm between them, either both upright or both inverted. A toy in which the infant had previously show interest was hidden either *in* or *under* one of the cups (cup 'A'): *in* if the cup was upright, *under* if it were inverted. The tray was pushed forward and the infant encouraged to retrieve the toy. This was repeated until the infant had successfully retrieved the object three times in succession from that cup. During this series of 'A' trials, a delay was gradually introduced between hiding and permitting search. On the final 'A' trial, the experimenter, after hiding the object, leant forward and made eye contact with the infant, saying 'Go on, you find it now.' Then the tray was pushed forward. On the 'B' trial, the object was again placed in cup 'A', and this was moved round behind (from the infant's point of view) the distractor cup, the distractor cup being simultaneously moved round to the initial 'A' position in order to transpose the cups. The procedure for the 'A' trial was repeated.

The experimenter attempted to ensure that the infant could not be guided by visual search for the object in the upright cups condition, and was assisted in this by the mother, who was asked to confirm that she could not herself see inside the cup. After a break of 5-10 minutes, the other condition was run in which the orientation of the cups was changed, as well as their colour and the side on which the 'A' trials were run. These three variables were counterbalanced.

Results: The data in Table 1 are for the cup first searched at on the 'B' trial. The cup-orientation effect (such that upright cups were easier than inverted) appears with almost equal strength in both age-groups, and

| | Upright | | Inverted | |
	√	×	√	×
12 months	13	6	3	16
(N = 19)				
15 months	13	6	6	13
(N = 19)				

Table 1: Success rate of infants aged 12 months and 15 months in retrieving an object from *in* an upright or *under* an inverted cup after transposition.

was reliable for both age-groups by a McNemar test (p .001 [younger] p .008 [older]). The effect held strongly at an individual level: 17 infants succeeded for the upright condition and failed for the inverted, while none showed the opposite pattern. The effect applied to about half the sample; there were no order effects. There was also a difference in *types* of error for the two conditions. We observed two types of error pattern for the 'B' trials: either the infants would move their hand within 2 seconds from the incorrect to the correct cup, or they would stop dead and sit back. With the inverted cups, the proportion of children showing a 'stop dead' response was .89, whilst with the upright cup, the proportion was .43 (a reliable difference at the 5 per cent level by the McNemar test for the homogeneity of proportions). Not only did the inverted cups lead to more errors, they also made the infants less willing to make an immediate correction of an erroneous response.

Discussion: These results are highly suggestive of a 'canonicality effect', such that the infant's representation of the characteristics of the spatial relation between cup and toy, in terms of the recognitory criterion (that is, the orientation of the cup) for the instantiation of the object-schema, influences the extent to which they can access rules for the praxic action of *changing the location of search in accordance with the predictable functional properties of a container.* Put more simply, the cup is not a proper container for the infants if it is inverted, and does not possess the functional property of retaining its contents over a spatial displacement. However, there are clearly multiple confoundings in the experiment, and the effect might simply be due to one or both of the following factors:

(a) the execution of the motor programme for retrieval of an object from inside a container is easier than the execution of a motor programme for retrieving an object from underneath a lid;

(b) the perceptual difference between an object presenting a cavity, and one presenting a surface, with or without associated visibility of the object.

The next experiment was designed partially to eliminate such hypotheses.

Experiment 2

Subjects: 29 infants served as subjects, 14 at 12 months and 15 at 15 months of age.

Apparatus: The same tray and toys as in Experiment 1; 2 wooden model houses whose base cavity was within 1 cm^3 of that of the cups. The apex of the roof of each house was flattened, by cutting off the top 1½ cm, so that the house could stably be set upside down.

Procedure: This was exactly as for Experiment 1.

Results:

	Upright		Inverted	
	√	×	√	×
12 months (N = 14)	4	10	7	7
15 months (N = 15)	10	5	6	9

Table 2: Success rate of infants aged 12 months and 15 months in retrieving an object from *under* an upright or *in* an inverted toy house after transposition.

Discussion: As can be seen from Table 2, the younger infants performed at chance with inverted houses, even though they had the cavity upwards, and marginally worse (though not reliably so) with upright houses. For the elder group, there was a slight advantage to the upright houses condition (that is, cavity down), though it was again not reliable. The contrast between the performance of the two age-groups on the upright house condition, however, was reliable

(χ^2 (1-tailed) = 4.35, p .05). Clearly the effect of orientation in Experiment 1 is not reducible to orientation *per se,* but it is due to the orientation of a *particular object:* indeed the tendency towards a house-upright advantage for the older group in this experiment suggests that the factor at work is the *canonical* orientation of a particular object, that is the features of form serving as a recognitory criterion for an object-schema. It is plausible to suggest that, while cups are familiar objects for very young infants, model houses are not, although a 'house-schema' is beginning to be elaborated by the older infants.

Of course, this experiment cannot serve entirely to eliminate all other hypotheses; but by extending the experimental matrix to different conditions and age-groups (Freeman, Lloyd and Sinha, 1980), we are satisfied that:

(a) the effect can properly be called a 'canonicality' effect, in that its determination is governed by the orientation of particular objects in such a way that they can most readily subserve their canonical function;

(b) it appears across a variety of search conditions and may be found in infants as young as nine months of age;

(c) it is comparable or greater in strength to other spatial and perceptuo-motor factors governing object search performance in infants.

This canonicality effect is very interesting, and deserves further analysis. Rather obviously, it casts doubt upon the Piagetian construct of 'object permanence' as a catch-all term for representational ability. Objects for infants in their sensorimotor development, do not exist merely by virtue of 'the actions of the infant upon them': rather, they are defined in terms of the *spatial and functional relations they contract with other objects in object-schemata.* A simple observation supports this suggestion: by the age of nine months or so, the play which infants spontaneously engage in with objects typically involves placing two or more objects in relation to each other, rather than assimilating *one* object to a schema focussed upon a body part. Forman, Dempsey and Kuschner (1975) analyse the development of object-object spatial positioning in infants from nine to 16 months, and as Bates, Benigni, Bretherton, Camaioni and Volterra (1980) point out, following Piaget himself, much play, at the end of the first year of life, consists in substitution routines in which different objects are successively assimilated to the same schema whose accommodatory adaptation is to another, constant object.

In our experiments, the 'constant' reference object is the hiding place, which, in terms suggested by Bruner (1975) thus acts as a 'topic' upon which the location of the toy is 'predicated' as a 'comment'. The question is, does a change in the location of the topic preserve or abolish the predicative relationship which defines the relational 'existence' (or assimilatory identity) of the hidden object? If the child has access to a primitive conceptual rule specifying that the predicative containment-relation is *preserved* over topic displacement (that is, containment is *accommodated* to location change), then the infant will pass the test. If not, the infant will search again at the last place at which the relation was instantiated. Now, we know that in fact the orientation of the topic object is totally irrelevant to the solution of the search problem; but for these infants, a necessary criterion for the containment relation to be preserved over a change in location is that the cup be upright. For the infant, the relational concept of containment is entirely inseparable from the recognitory criteria for a canonically oriented container, and that the object is incapable of fulfilling its function (preservation of the containment relation) if these criteria are not fulfilled. For this reason, although the child may properly be said to be capable of accessing representational rules—and thus has the status of a conceptual subject—these rules have not yet developed into concepts proper, and are best thought of as proto-conceptual schemata. In these schemata, functional, relational and formal information are interwoven around a canonical 'core' co-integrating them. Thus, knowledge of objects and knowledge of spatial relations do not arise from separate bases, but differentiate from a common source, whose emergence can be traced to the end of the first year of life.

Infants at this age, then, demonstrate a very definite type of evaluative inflexibility—an inability to conserve an initial evaluation over a simple spatial displacement—and a lack of differentiation of relational concepts from object schemata. Where can we seek the source of their later ability flexibly to revalue perceptual information with respect to different schemata? Earlier on, I suggested that the role of adults in indicating for children what schematic value should be accorded to perceptual information was a crucial one. The next experiment indicates how this might be so.

Experiment 3

Subjects: 12 infants, aged between 14 and 17 months, mean age 16 months ± 6 weeks served as subjects.

Apparatus: The same tray and toys as in Experiments 1 and 2; 2 sets of 10 'Ambi' Stacking and Nesting cubes, the largest having sides of 7½ cm, decreasing for the others in steps of ½ cm.

Procedure: This was similar to that for Experiments 1 and 2, but before initiating the search trials, the experimenter played either a *stacking* or a *nesting* game with the infant, enlisting his or her co-operation, as far as was possible, in building the stacks and nests. After building and rebuilding two or three times the stack/nest, the experimenter extracted the second largest cube from each of the stack/nest arrays, and employed them in the transposition task. For both the stacking and nesting condition, the cubes were oriented cavity downwards, and the object hidden *under* the 'A' cube for one set of trials, and the cubes were oriented cavity upwards, and the object hidden *in* the 'A' cube for another set of trials. After a delay of 5-10 minutes, the other condition was run; half the infants took the stacking condition first, and half the nesting condition first. Within each condition, half the infants took the *in* trials first, and half took the *under* trials first.

Results:

Hiding Place	Game Played			
	Nesting		*Stacking*	
	√	×	√	×
In/cavity up	9	3	5	7
Under/cavity down	4	8	10	2

Table 3: Success rate of infants aged 16 months in retrieving an object from *in* a cavity-upwards or *under* a cavity-downwards cube after transposition, when the cube has been employed in either a *nesting* or *stacking* game. (N = 12.)

The data show a cross-over effect, such as that playing a stacking game congruent with the cavity-down orientation of the cube enhanced performance for *under* trials and depressed it for *in* trials; and playing a nesting game congruent with the cavity-upward orientation of the cubes enhanced performance for the *in* trials and depressed it for the *under* trials. An assessment of the reliability of the effect may be made by analysing the data at the level of the individual subjects. A count was made of occasions on which subjects found the congruent condition easier, harder or of the same difficulty as the non-congruent condition for *in* and *under* trials. Thus, each individual could show 0, 1 or 2 congruent advantages or 0, 1 or 2 non-congruent advantages. The results were clearcut: 3 individuals showed no effects, 1 showed 1 congruent and 1 non-congruent advantages, 8 showed 1 or 2 congruent advantages and no non-congruent advantages, and none showed 1 or 2 non-congruent advantages and no congruent advantages. The 8-0 split is reliable (binomial p .004), and the data also indicate that the congruence effect applies to two-thirds of the sample.

Discussion: Even these rather older infants have not yet differentiated their relational knowledge from object-schema knowledge: indeed, we shall show next that this does not occur until around about the age at which Piaget claims that 'representation' or 'the semiotic function' emerges. Yet, their performance is rather differently governed from that of the infants in the previous experiments. Unlike cups, these cubes do not have a 'canonical' orientation. Like the cups, they can, in this context, perfectly well preserve the 'containment' relationship independently of the way up they are, over a simple spatial displacement. But the infants treat the problems as if the orientation of the cubes *is* criterial, just as in Experiment 1, but with one crucial difference: *the criterial orientation serving to evaluate the containment relationship is determined by the child's experience of the object in social interaction with an adult.* It is in the realm of social interactions that we should seek the origins of the evaluative flexibility of the human conceptual subject, rather than in the assimilative 'egocentric' actions of the individual organism.

To develop further the analysis of the last experiments, the cubes are the invariant 'topic' across both stacking and nesting games. But different games played with the cubes introduce different relational predicates into the cube-schema in the two conditions. In effect, the relational 'comment' upon the individual cube-schemata consists in their contextualisation or evaluative embedding (in a quite literal sense) within a larger 'stacking' or 'nesting' schema, which in this micro-situation can be seen as having the status of a *script* for evaluating perceptual information against the cube-schema. This script can be thought of as a *presuppositional context* against which the topicalised cube is perceived and evaluated by the infant.

Viewed in this way, the 'canonicality effect' in Experiment 1 can be seen as a specific, and privileged, instance of a much more general phenomenon whereby the significance of objects and events is evaluated by children according to criteria derived from joint praxic (and, of course, communicative) actions with members of the adult speech and conceptual community. Learning, as Piaget had always correctly insisted, is an active process, but it is a process of interactive exploration of a socially and intersubjectively 'signified' world. Indeed, the canonicality effect itself demonstrated this inescapably social aspect of cognitive development; for the representational rules which the infant has constructed in order to accommodate to the particular characteristics of cups, as objects, are representations of the social status of the cup as an artefact, used in certain ways in certain interactive contexts, just as much as they are representations of the physical status of the cup as an object affording 'containment', 'drinking' and so forth. Indeed, the two amount to the same thing.

To return to the developmental account, we have seen that for infants of up to about 16 months of age, representational knowledge schematically and integrally incorporates both relational and object relations: the 'protoconcept' of containment is initially inevaluable against anything other than a canonical or presuppositionally-designated containing object. Yet the differentiation of relational concepts from object concepts is precisely the condition which I have specified as a condition for the ability to engage in complex constructive praxic action, when that action involves the revaluation of perceptual information in terms of a schema for transforming an initial state to a different, intended end-state. In the previous experiments, we have seen that infants cannot evaluate an object which presents a non-canonical perceptual aspect against a relational schema canonically instantiated in the object-schema. In the next experiments, we see what happens when young children are required to evaluate an object in canonical or non-canonical orientations against a relational conceptual schema which is *not* canonically instantiated in the object-schema.

Experiment 4

Subjects: 125 children were tested, 64 boys and 61 girls, divided into four age-groups:
Group 1: 36 children, median age 18 months (range 16-20 months)
Group 2: 36 children, median age 24 months (range 22-26 months)
Group 3: 31 children, median age 30 months (range 28-32 months)
Group 4: 22 children, median age 36 months (range 34-38 months)
Apparatus: A pair of the plastic mugs as used in Experiment 1, either both blue or both orange. Two wooden coloured cubes, sides 4 cm.
Procedure: The experimenter seated himself on the floor facing the child. The two mugs, referred to as 'cups', were introduced, as were

the two blocks. The experimenter placed a cup in front of the child, saying, 'Here you are, here's yours,' and the other cup and one block in front of himself, saying, 'And here's mine.' The cups were always initially similarly oriented, either both upright (for half the subjects) or both inverted. The experimenter attempted to gain the attention of the child, and carried out one of the six actions involving the construction of *in, on* and *under* relationships between cup and block, as shown in Figure 1.

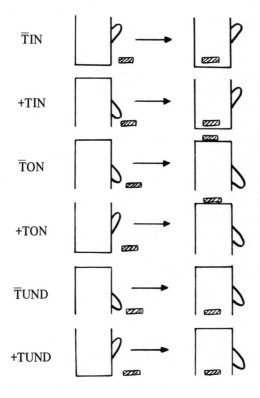

Figure 1: Trial types for Experiment 4.

The experimenter then asked the child to construct the same array, using his/her own cup, saying, 'Now it's your turn, you do it,' and handing the other block to the child. The experimenter's model was visible throughout the trial. The child's response was noted and the experimenter proceeded with the next trial, until all six trials were complete. Trial order was randomised.

Results:

	Group 1 (18 mo.) N = 25		Group 2 (24 mo.) N = 28		Group 3 (30 mo.) N = 25		Group 4 (36 mo.) N = 16	
Individual Outcomes	$\overline{T}$	+T	$\overline{T}$	+T	$\overline{T}$	+T	$\overline{T}$	+T
Both √	19	6	23	17	24	21	16	15
In √, On ×	6	14	5	6	1	2	0	0
In ×, On √	0	0	0	0	0	0	0	1
Both ×	0	5	0	5	0	2	0	0

Table 4: Non-verbal action imitating task using cups: *In* and *On* trials.

Table 4 shows the results for the *in* and *on* trials. Incorrect responses to these trials mainly involved placing the brick *in* instead of *on* the cup, or vice versa. For Groups 1 and 2, *in* placements were reliably easier than *on* placements, for both $\overline{T}$ and +T trials (G.1: p .02 $\overline{T}$, p .001 +T; G.2: p .05 $\overline{T}$, p .02 +T). This finding may be interpreted as a canonicality effect, in that the younger two groups of children find it easier to instantiate a canonical containment relationship between cup and brick than a non-canonical support relationship. The effect is not reducible to differences in motor executive complexity, since within $\overline{T}$ and +T conditions, *in* and *on* placements are of the same order of difficulty. However, the effect interacts with differences in motor complexity, specifically the need to transform orientation: for

	Group 1 (18 mo.) N = 25		Group 2 (24 mo.) N = 28		Group 3 (30 mo.) N = 25		Group 4 (36 mo.) N = 16	
Responses	$\overline{T}$	+T	$\overline{T}$	+T	$\overline{T}$	+T	$\overline{T}$	+T
Under	9	8	13	12	19	16	15	15
In	10	16	5	10	0	2	1	1
On	6	1	6	1	0	1	0	0
Beside	0	0	4	5	6	6	0	0

Table 5: Non-verbal action imitation task using cups: *Under* trials.

G.1 only, $\overline{\text{T}}$ON was reliably easier than +TON (p .002) (all tests binomial). The canonicality effect has disappeared as a reliable effect by age 30 months, and Groups 3 and 4 are both performing at or near ceiling for all trials.

Table 5 shows the results for *under* trials. Groups 1 and 2 are performing below chance, and G.1 subjects produce reliably more *in* errors than *on* errors: another canonicality effect, such that where an error is made it is likely to be of the nature of constructing an erroneous canonical end-state relation (p .002). For none of the groups is there any difference between the $\overline{\text{T}}$ and the +T versions of the *under* trials, again showing the independence of the canonicality effect from questions of motor executive complexity.

Discussion: Once again, we find that a canonicality effect is to be discerned, in particular in the results for the youngest, 18-month-old age-group. These children seem to be almost incapable of producing any other than an *in* relationship (or a canonical containment relationship) between a brick and a cup. This is not because they are in principle incapable of producing other types of spatial relationship—as everybody knows, 18-month-olds will readily imitate block-building games involving *on* relations, or hiding games involving *under* relations. Nor is it because of motor problems: the canonicality effect is distinguishable from, although it does interact with, motor complexity factors. The canonicality effect is an effect which enters into action at the level of the formation and execution of a syntagmatic *plan,* in which the spatial relationship which is the goal of the action is represented independently of the canonical function and orientation of the object which will be used in the construction of the intended end-state relation. Children at this age, it seems, cannot readily evaluate a schema for *on* or *under* relations against objects canonically associated with *in* relations, even when there is a perfectly visible model in front of them of the end-state which they are required to construct.

As has often been remarked (Greenfield, 1978), imitative ability reflects not only the general cognitive developmental level of the imitator, but also the subject's understanding of the structure of the model to be imitated. The data from this experiment demonstrate both these propositions quite clearly. The 18-month-old infant has still not acquired the ability cognitively to differentiate relational knowledge from the recognitory criteria for knowledge of objects and object classes. It is clearly not the case that the Group 1 children are responding 'preconceptually': if that were the case, they would be responding solely on the basis of the perceptual parameters of the information presented, rather than, as they do, responding to the perceptual information in terms of its schematic value. In a sense, these children are 'functionally dominated' in that their evaluation of perceptual information is constrained to the canonical function (and concomitant canonical relation) of the object which is the target of their actions, and they are incapable of evaluating that information against any other functional relational specification.

This should not, however, mislead us to suppose that the perceptual parameters of the array are 'secondary' to the functional specification of its parts: rather, there is an undifferentiable link between the two, provided by the interweaving of both functional and formal specifications around a canonical core protoconcept. However, around about the beginning of the third year of life, it seems, some partial differentiation of relational from object knowledge occurs, such that they are able to construct a spatial relation from objects that are thereby placed in a non-canonical relationship with each other, providing that a clear model of the end-state which is required is present to them. Does this mean that at the age of two years children have acquired the capacity to evaluate perceptual information against criteria for the instantiation of a semantic rule?

To answer this question, it is necessary to induce in the child an end-state representation which is not only at variance with current, perceived reality, but is not actually instantiated in a model, either of action or of an end-state. In this way, it is possible to test the extent to which the recognitory criteria for spatial relations are differentiated from those for object classes, and the extent to which the child is capable of reintegrating them in complex constructive praxis directed to a mentally represented goal. The most appropriate test for such an ability is a language comprehension task in which an end-state must be instantiated from purely linguistic input.

Experiment 5

Subjects: The subjects were the same four groups of children as participated in Experiment 1, with the addition of a fifth group, of 12 children aged between 42 and 51 months, mean age 45 months.

Apparatus and Procedure: These were similar to those employed in Experiment 4, with the difference that (a) only the child had a cup and a brick, (b) the instructions were of the form 'put the brick in/on/under the cup.'

Results:

	Group 1 (1.6 yrs) N = 24		Group 2 (2.0 yrs) N = 33		Group 3 (2.6 yrs) N = 28		Group 4 (3.0 yrs) N = 21		Group 5 (3.9 yrs) N = 12	
Individual Outcomes	$\overline{T}$	+T	$\overline{T}$	+T	$\overline{T}$	+T	$\overline{T}$	+T	$\overline{T}$	+T
Both √	15	2	22	5	27	5	19	15	12	9
In √, On ×	9	12	9	13	1	8	1	1	0	0
In ×, On √	0	0	2	2	0	1	1	2	0	0
Both ×	0	10	0	13	0	14	0	3	0	3

Table 6: Language comprehension task using cups: *In* and *On* trials.

Taking Table 6 (*in* and *on* trials) first, the canonicality effect noted in the two youngest groups of children in the imitation task also appears in this language comprehension task (G.1: p .002, $\overline{T}$; p .001, +T; G.2: p .05, $\overline{T}$; p .005, +T). It is also present, unlike in Experiment 4, for the Group 3 subjects on the +T trials only (p .02). Again, then, the canonicality effect appears to be in interaction with the task demand factor of necessary orientation transformation, which latter factor seems to be affecting the children more than it did for the imitation task, and its effects, like those of canonicality of end state, now affect the children in Group 3, who in the previous experiment were performing almost at ceiling. Only by age three years are the children performing near to ceiling on this language comprehension task, a time lag of six months over the non-linguistic imitation task.

	Group 1 (1.6 yrs) N = 24		Group 2 (2.0 yrs) N = 33		Group 3 (2.6 yrs) N = 28		Group 4 (3.0 yrs) N = 21	
Responses	$\overline{T}$	+T	$\overline{T}$	+T	$\overline{T}$	+T	$\overline{T}$	+T
Under	2	1	3	5	11	8	14	11
In	10	18	7	18	1	10	0	6
On	8	1	18	5	9	2	4	2
Beside	1	1	5	5	7	8	3	2

Table 7: Language comprehension tasks using cups: *Under* trials.

Table 7 shows the responses to the *under* trials. As can be seen, these trials were not administered to the eldest group of subjects, but again Group 4 (three-year-olds) are responding predominantly correctly. As in Experiment 4, there is no difference in difficulty between $\overline{T}$ and +T *under* trials for any age-group. Only for Group 1 subjects is there a reliable (*p* .02) canonicality effect, such that *in* errors significantly exceed *on* errors. However, we again find the overall six months delay in performance for *under* trials: whereas the majority of children were responding correctly by 2½ years on the imitation task, it is not until 3 years that correct responses predominate on the language comprehension task.

Discussion: Although the previous experiment showed that the initial differentiation of relational from object-schema recognitory criteria commences around the beginning of the third year of life, this experiment shows that its full differentiation and reintegration in a more powerful and flexible system is not complete until the end of the third year. It is no accident that it is only by three years old that the children can display an adequate comprehension of such linguistic instructions, for it is only with the institution of a structured semantic store, in which lexical items such as relational prepositions, are represented independently of their canonical instantiations, that constructive praxic action can be guided by representation evoked from a communicative input.

Another feature of interest in the data concerns the rather different response patterns for *under,* as opposed to *in* and *on* trials. For the latter, the canonicality effect, though different in its source from the variable of complexity of action (orientation transformation), did interact with it. In contrast there was never any difference in either imitation or comprehension tasks, in difficulty between $\overline{T}$ and +T *under* trials. Why should this be so? The previous analysis of the search tasks gives the clue. For both *in* and *on* trials, the cup is the invariant target of the placement; thus the child may deal first with the orientation of the cup and then with the placement. However, in order to place a brick *under* a cup, it is necessary *first* to place the brick in position, *then* to invert the cup and place it over the brick, In effect, *in* and *on* trials require a topicalisation of the cup as target, with the brick placement as a 'comment' instantiating a predicative relationship. *Under* trials, on the other hand, require that the child topicalise the brick and its placement as a comment. It is very difficult for children to achieve this predicative reversal in this particular context. A simple observation bears out this analysis: many of the children, when required to construct the *under* relationship in Experiment 4, attempted to derive it directly from an *in* relation; that is, by placing the brick in the cup, then turning the cup over. Often, of course, the brick then fell out, at which the child would often start the whole procedure over again.

Note, however, that this difficulty with differential topicalisation is entirely context-dependent. There is no intrinsic reason whatsoever why children find it difficult to place a cup over a brick, and in fact when shown how to do so they will readily play a disappearance game with a cup as a cover 'hiding' different objects. The difficulty arises not from the structure of the action *per se,* but from the way that it is schematically represented as a syntagmatic sequence linking an initial with an end state, in a context of canonical schematic representations of cup-as-topic.

In further experiments (Freeman, Sinha and Condliffe, 1981) we have examined another aspect of the contextual dependence of these different effects, one to do with the presuppositional structures governing the representation of the topicalised object. If, as in Experiment 3, one uses cubes rather than cups in imitation and comprehension tasks, after playing stacking and nesting games, one finds that the 'in' bias for these experiments is reproduced in nesting conditions, but reversed to an 'on' bias in stacking conditions.

Conclusion

Clearly, as has increasingly been recognised (Donaldson, 1978; Olson and Nickerson, 1978; Walkerdine and Sinha, 1978), young children display an extraordinary degree of sensitivity and flexibility with respect to contextual cues. However, as an analysis of the development of action demonstrates, this contextual sensitivity is a highly functional and adaptive cognitive mode, allowing for the differential represen- tation of an evaluation of perceptual information in terms of different schematic representations. As we have seen, as these schemata become more complex, enabling the development of complex, constructive praxic action, they become increasingly constrained to the criteria underlying the development of a semantic knowledge system. Equally, their internal structures may be analysed according to the same terms as those involved in the production of linguistic discourse.

The development of action, then, serves to draw our attention to the complexity of the processes underlying apparently simple phenomena such as the search for hidden objects, or the imitation of actions, and to the underlying unity of the conceptual representational systems governing both praxic and communicative action. Perhaps most importantly, it clearly demonstrates the way in which the development of concepts is a process in which the child is negotiating and learning socially-embedded, culturally significant conceptual distinctions.

Finally, we have seen how the development of representation involves both differentiation and integration of different aspects of the representational system. From about the end of the first year of life, until about the end of Piaget's sensorimotor stage VI, the representational system consists largely in a set of undifferentiated protoconceptual structures combining knowledge of objects with knowledge of relations, and evaluating information to simple canonical prototypic recognitory schemata. Thereafter, an initial differentiation of the systems governing object knowledge and relational knowledge yields to a higher-level reintegration, in which complex schematic procedures are constrained to the criteria of the semantic system of the adult speech community.

Throughout this developmental process, social-interactive episodes in which local schematic values are 'fixed' for the child, in routine formats (Bruner, 1975), play as much a crucial role as do the child's assimilative explorations. Cognitive development is both an individual and a social process, and its end product—the human conceptual subject—is a culturally specific and socially determined mode of individuality.

Notes

1. The research reported in this chapter was carried out at the University of Bristol with the assistance of the Social Science Research Council of Great Britain. I would like to thank Sharon Lloyd for her assistance in designing and executing some of the reported experiments. Norman Freeman directed the LARINCS project on which the chapter is based, and I would like to acknowledge his critical contribution to the ideas developed here, while retaining responsibility for this expression of them.

2. Both George Butterworth and Colwyn Trevarthen (personal communications) have independently pointed out to me that the notion of canonical representation has affinities with Gibson's one of *affordance*, suggesting that my arguments are not incompatible with direct perception theory. I take the point, particularly insofar as Gibsonian

theory is non-featural; but the issue is very complex, and I still would wish to draw a basic distinction between *knowledge* (involving representation and memory) and *perception*, albeit recognising the strong developmental and functional connectedness of these.

References

Bates, E., Benigni, L., Bretherton, I., Camaioni, L., and Volterra, V., *The Emergence of Symbols: Cognition and Communication in Infancy*, London, Academic Press, 1980.

Bridges, A., Sinha, C. G., and Walkerdine, V., 'The development of comprehension', in G. Wells (ed.) *Learning through Interaction: the study of language development*, Cambridge, Cambridge University Press, 1981.

Bruner, J. S., 'From communication to language: a psychological perspective', *Cognition*, 1975, *3*, 225-87.

Clark, E. V., 'Non-linguistic strategies and the acquisition of word-meanings', *Cognition*, 1973, *2*, 161-82.

Clark, E. V., 'Knowledge, context and strategy in the acquisition of word meaning', in D. P. Dato (ed.) *Georgetown University Round Table on languages and linguistics*, Washington D.C., Georgetown University Press, 1975.

Connolly, K., and Elliott. J., 'The evolution and ontogeny of hand function', in N. Blurton-Jones (ed.) *Ethnological Studies of Child Behaviour*, Cambridge, Cambridge University Press, 1972.

Donaldson, M., *Children's Minds*, Glasgow, Fontana, 1978.

Forman, G. E., Kuschner, D., and Dempsey, J., 'Transformations in manipulation and production with geometric objects: an early system of logic in young children', *Centre for Early Childhood Education*, University of Massachusetts, 1975.

Freeman, N. H., Lloyd, S., and Sinha, C. G., 'Infant search tasks reveal early concepts of containment and canonical usage of objects', *Cognition*, 1980, *8*, 243-62.

Freeman, N. H., Sinha, C. G., and Condliffe, S. J., 'Configuration and collaboration with young children in language comprehension tasks', in W. P. Robinson (ed.) *Communication in Development*, London, Academic Press, 1981.

Greenfield, P. M., 'Structural parallels between language and action', in A. Lock (ed.) *Action, Gesture and Symbol: the emergence of language*, London, Academic Press, 1978.

Johnson-Laird, P. N., 'Procedural semantics', *Cognition*, 1977, *5*, 189-214.

Lock, A., *The Guided Reinvention of Language*, London, Academic Press, 1980.

Miller, G., and Johnson-Laird, P. N., *Language and Perception,* Cambridge, Cambridge University Press, 1976.

Minsky, M., 'Frame-systems', Massachusetts Institute of Technology Artificial Intelligence Laboratory Memorandum, 1974.

Morton, A., *Frames of Mind: Constraints on the Common-Sense Conception of the Mental,* Oxford, Oxford University Press, 1980.

Nelson, K., 'Concept, word and sentence: interrelations in acquisition and development', *Psychological Review,* 1974, *81,* 267-85.

Oatley, K., *Perceptions and Representations,* London, Methuen, 1978.

Olson, D. R., and Nickerson, N., 'Language Development through the school years: learning to confine interpretation to the information in the text', in K. E. Nelson (ed.) *Children's Language,* New York, Gardner Press, 1978.

Olson, D. R., and Bialystok, E., 'Mental representations of space: the representation of objects and the representation of form', in P. van Geert and B. de Gelder (eds.) *Representation and Knowledge,* in press.

Piaget, J., *The Origin of Intelligence in the Child,* London, Routledge & Kegan Paul, 1953.

Piaget, J., *The Child's Construction of Reality,* London, Routledge & Kegan Paul, 1955.

Piaget, J., *Play, Dreams and Imitation,* London, Routledge & Kegan Paul, 1962.

Piaget, J., *Structuralism,* London, Routledge & Kegan Paul, 1971.

Piaget, J., and Inhelder, B., *The Psychology of the Child,* London, Routledge & Kegan Paul, 1969.

Reynolds, P. C., 'The primate constructional system: the theory and description of instrumental object use in humans and chimpanzees', in M. von Cronach and R. Harre (eds.) *Approaches to the Study of Goal-Directed Action,* Cambridge, Cambridge University Press, in press.

Rosch, E., 'Classification of real-world objects: origins and representations in cognition', in P. N. Johnson-Laird and P. C. Watson (eds.) *Thinking: readings in cognitive science,* Cambridge, Cambridge University Press, 1977.

Schank, R. C., and Abelson, R. P., *Scripts, Plans, Goals and Understanding: an inquiry into human knowledge structures,* Hillsdale, New Jersey, Lawrence Erlbaum, 1977.

Schmidt, R. A., 'A schema theory of discrete motor learning', *Psychological Review,* 1975, *82,* 225-60.

Walkerdine, V., and Sinha, C., 'The internal triangle: language, reasoning and the social context', in I. Markova (ed.) *The Social Context of Language,* London, Wiley, 1978.

PART III

SOCIAL COGNITION AND AFFECT

8 Cognitive factors limiting shared care arrangements for young children

Peter Smith

Introduction

One of the first social relationships which an infant usually makes, is with its mother. Indeed the concept of monotropism, advanced by Bowlby in 1958, embodies the idea that a unique social bond or attachment relationship between mother (or mother-substitute) and infant is not only natural, but essential for healthy development. A high degree of continuity in this relationship is considered important, with the implication that shared care of young children would have adverse consequences.

While Bowlby's general theory of attachment (1969) continues to be influential, this aspect of his theory now receives little support from psychologists. I shall argue that the available evidence suggests that a moderate degree of shared care in infancy is normal and harmless. However there is some evidence that extreme degrees of shared care can adversely affect socio-emotional development. This argument is based on a survey of the consequences of shared care in both preliterate and urban human societies. Primarily, relationships between adults and young children are reviewed, though child-child relationships are more briefly considered. In another paper (Smith, 1980) I have considered the biological origins of attachment relationships in primates, and in mammals generally. I argued there that from a sociobiological and evolutionary perspective, too, monotropism is an unlikely hypothesis; but that some limits on adult-child bonds would be expected.

Monotropism may be rejected in terms of empirical data, and this rejection may be consistent with evolutionary thinking; but it remains to relate this, and the viability or otherwise of moderate and extreme shared care in infancy, to developmental theory. Bowlby in fact postulated two mechanisms to curtail early social bonds, which were based on a psychodynamic view of human motivation influenced by early ethological theory. I shall argue that these two mechanisms are invalid. Recent cognitive-developmental views of early social relationships suggest other ways in which there might be constraints on early social bonds. In part, the mechanisms suggested relate to evidence already available concerning the interrelationships between cognitive and affective development; in part, they point to directions for research in the development of memory, which have not yet been well explored.

The development of early social attachments

Although critical of Bowlby's monotropism hypothesis, I shall proceed by accepting much of the general perspective of attachment theory as propounded by Bowlby (1969), Ainsworth (1973) and Sroufe and Waters (1977). That is, by around nine months of age the child is able to distinguish the appearance and behaviour of familiar and unfamiliar persons, and acts so as to maintain proximity with a familiar person. Maintenance of proximity is indicated by locomotion, and signalling as for example in separation protest at departure. Sroufe and Waters (1977) consider an attachment relationship or affective bond to have developed between an infant and another person if the organisation of infant behaviour is such as to maintain proximity with that person. The person acts as a secure base from which the infant may explore, and to which he or she can return for proximity or physical contact if distressed; if no such person is present—if the child is not in proximity to any attachment figure—then exploration will be inhibited and distress heightened.

Attachment theorists would accept that by three or four years this is no longer the case. As Marvin (1977) argues, at this age children's non-egocentric or perspective taking abilities are beginning to be manifest. Thus, a child can begin to understand the point of view of the attachment figure, and accept that the person will return following a departure. In the meantime, the child's internal representation of the attachment figure will suffice, at least for limited periods of separation. Marvin's argument brings in an explicitly cognitive-developmental view to explain the end of the proximity-maintaining attachment phase.

Weinraub and Lewis (1977), examining styles of separation in mothers and their two-year-old children, found that even this early the separation protest of the infant is influenced for example by whether the mother gives an explanation concerning her departure.

Weinraub, Brooks and Lewis (1977) also criticise the general concept of attachment. This is not so much on the basis of a cognitive-developmental view of earlier phases of social relationships, as on the argument that the child from birth is part of a wide social network, and soon engages in a variety of social relationships, with differing functions such as play, exploration/learning, nurturance, caregiving and protection.

One can accept much of the 'social network' perspective, without abandoning the attachment concept. Indeed the argument here is that applying a more cognitive view to the development of attachments will lead to an abandonment of monotropism and a clearer view of multiple caretaking. The need of young infants for security, for proximity to an attachment figure, is consistent with a cognitive-developmental view of the development of fear and security (Smith, 1979), and with the evolutionary history of attachment in mammals and especially primates (Wilson, 1975). At issue here is the number of attachment figures who can reasonably be expected to fulfil this function for a young child. If we define a caretaker to be someone with whom a child (between about nine months and three years) may be left at times alone, then the issue is one of the viability of shared care. The empirical evidence on shared care will now be considered.

Moderate degrees of shared care are common

On the basis of anthropological and sociological reports, it would appear that moderate shared care is very common in agricultural communities, and is not unusual in either hunter-gatherer communities, or modern urban societies.

Among present day hunter-gatherers, it is indeed usual for the mother to be the principal caretaker. A mother characteristically carries her baby with her while out gathering plant foods; this might happen for the first two or three years of the baby's life, until weaning occurs. Nevertheless, the baby may have considerable contact with a number of other adults in the band and in particular father-infant relationships are usually close (West and Konnor, 1976). Other women, possibly relatives, may not only help in comforting a baby but also in suckling if the mother is absent (Tindale, 1972; Turnbull, 1965).

However separations of mother and infant are much more likely in agricultural subsistence economies, where women may be engaged in arduous physical labour in the fields which effectively precludes continuous care of their infants. In a survey of 186 non-industrial societies, Weisner and Gallimore (1977) found that in only five of them was the mother the 'almost exclusive' caretaker in infancy. In forty per cent of the societies others had important caretaking roles in infancy; and in eighty per cent, important caretaking roles in early childhood.

A number of possible shared care arrangements may be typically used in such societies. For example, the grandmother may share care with the mother, as amongst the Tiara of Okinawa (Maretzi and Maretzi, 1963) or the Lesu in New Ireland (Powdermaker, 1933). Other wives may help out in polymatric societies, such as the Ganda (Ainsworth, 1967), or other female relatives and friends may be relied on, as in the Mixtecans of Mexico (Romney and Romney, 1963) or the Tarong of the Philippines (Nydegger and Nydegger, 1963). In some of these cases at least the non-maternal caretaker may share suckling with the mother; in others, the mother returns periodically to feed the baby.

In the latter case, another common option is to leave the baby with an older sibling, or a child nurse who may or may not be a relative, generally between about six to sixteen years of age. Such arrangements are, for example, found amongst the Kikuyu (Leiderman and Leiderman, 1974), the Nyansongo (LeVine and LeVine, 1963), the Ngoni (Read, 1968), the Chaga (Raum, 1940), and the Samoans (Mead, 1943).

The extent of shared care in modern industrial societies depends greatly on the extent to which mothers of young children are in outside employment, and is complicated by the existence of institutionalised arrangements as in day nurseries. It is worth noting however that even with families where the mother is not working (or at least, not many hours per week), shared care is not uncommon. In New England, Fischer and Fischer (1963) found one quarter of their mothers reporting care from the child's maternal grandmother. In Nottingham, Newson and Newson (1965) reported fifty-two per cent of fathers as 'highly participant' in the care of their one-year-old babies, and in London working-class homes, Tizard and Tizard (1971) found a mean of about four caretakers in families of mothers not working full-time, these often being both parents and two grandparents. Taking a strict definition of a caretaker as someone with whom a child may be left alone, Smith and Turner (1980) found in Sheffield that the great majority of mothers shared care with at least one or two other persons, even when they were not working, typically leaving the child for a few periods of perhaps two or three hours each week. The other caretakers were usually the father or grandparent, or else a friend, neighbour or older sibling or other relative.

Rutter (1972) has distinguished between three types of shared care. In the first, the mother is the primary caretaker and she is assisted by one or a few subsidiary caretakers. In the second, care is shared fairly equally among a few stable figures. In the third, a large number of caretakers are present and this is usually associated with discontinuous relationships and inadequate interaction. Whereas the first and second types would count as moderate shared care, the third type would be extreme shared care.

The examples above are of the first two types of shared care in Rutter's classification. Probably type one is modal both in hunter-gatherer societies, and for many families in modern industrial societies. However the modal situation in many agricultural societies, as Weisner and Gallimore's survey suggests, may be type two. Obviously the distinction between types one and two is one of degree. Perhaps the clearest example of a type two situation is that of the Israeli Kibbutz. Here, care of young children is fairly equally shared in a stable way between the two parents and one or two metaplot, and also the night nurse, although for the latter the children will usually be asleep (Faigin, 1958; Rabin, 1958; Miller, 1969).

The clearest examples of Rutter's third type of shared care have occurred in children's homes and institutions. Day care facilities and creches provide a rather different set of circumstances and will be discussed separately.

Moderate shared care does not lead to difficulties in social development

Although moderate shared care is so common, the unique importance of maternal care emphasised by Bowlby (1958) and others has had considerable influence on official attitudes and policies, and on mass media treatment of the issue. As Etaugh (1980) remarks, 'child-care books and magazine articles appearing during the last 20 years have tended to present a more negative view of nonmaternal care' than is justified on the available evidence.

Again leaving aside the day care evidence for the moment, we do have some direct evidence that infants can form attachments to several persons and that infants reared polymatrically experience normal social development.

Schaffer and Emerson's (1964) longitudinal study in Scotland, although largely based on mothers' reports, indicated that when babies first showed separation protest, twenty-nine per cent showed it to more than one person. By eighteen months of age, eighty-seven per cent did so, and thirty-one per cent showed it to five persons or more (again, fathers, grandparents, older siblings and neighbours). Using direct behavioural observations, Cohen and Campos (1976) found in a USA sample that ninety per cent of babies showed attachment to father at ten to sixteen months, and the adequacy of fathers as attachement figures is borne out by Willemson, Flaherty, Heaton and Ritchey (1976), Feldman and Ingham (1975) and Lamb (1976).

Amongst the Kikuyu, Liederman and Liederman (1976) found that those infants raised with three or four main caretakers seemed equally attached to the mother and another of the main caretakers by the time the baby was ten or twelve months of age. Marvin *et al* (1977) studied eighteen Hausa infants aged six to fourteen months, with a range of from one to ten caretakers. Social development seemed normal, and Marvin reported that 'these Hausa infants are, on the average, attached to three or four different people'. Although often one figure seemed preferred, for several infants preferences were slight or apparently absent. In the light of these two studies, the hypothesis that there is a persisting hierarchy in attachments (Rutter, 1979) seems open to question.

In the Israeli Kibbutzim also, young children seem to be attached to the metapelet as much as to their mother (Fox, 1977). Attachment to the mother is reported to develop normally (Maccoby and Feldman, 1972).

Of course, neither these studies nor many more could prove conclusively that moderate shared care does not lead to any harmful effects. However any realistic comparison is between moderate shared care, and care almost exclusively by one person. Thus onus of proof should not be on considerations of the effects of moderate shared care. As Leiderman and Leiderman (1977) put it, 'the high value placed on the exclusive maternal caretaking model by Western behavioural scientists is apparently a by-product of a cultural bias based on economic factors and the nuclear family form in our society'. Given the prevalence of shared care, one might more reasonably ask whether monomatric care has some adverse effects—what empirical evidence we have suggests slightly different emphases to social development in the child (Moore, 1975). Moreover, urban mothers alone with one or more young children are more vulnerable to psychiatric disturbance such as depression (Brown, Bhrolchain and Harris, 1975).

Extreme shared care may lead to difficulties in social development

In the examples of moderate shared care cited earlier, caretakers are relatively stable, and the number a child will experience in the first two or three years will probably not greatly exceed ten. However, neither of these things can be said for children placed in children's homes or institutions. Large size, staff rota systems, and high staff turnover can mean that caretaking will be diffused among very many more caretakers, justifying the term extreme shared care. For example, David and Appel (1961) found an average of twenty-five caretakers for infants in the Poupponniere Amyot in Paris (range, 16 to 33). Even under an Intensive Individualised Nursing Care system introduced for certain babies, the number still averaged eleven. The latter system was reported to improve the babies' social responsiveness, but generally the investigators reported that 'emotional interchange between child and nurse . . . is almost lacking or at least quite poor'. Similarly Stevens (1971) reported an average of twenty-nine caretakers over a six-month period for children at the Metera Babies Centre in Athens, with babies receiving 'mothering' from about thirteen different nurses per week. There was clear evidence that up to half of the babies observed had not developed any specific social attachments.

There have been a number of studies indicating adverse effects of this kind of institutional care for children's development, and indeed they formed part of Bowlby's argument in favour of monotropism. Casler (1961) earlier made the point that deficits of institutionalised children could be due to a general lack of stimulation, rather than any specific effects of discontinuous care. However two recent studies go some way to unconfounding the number of caretakers, and the amount and quality of general stimulation.

Tizard and Rees (1975) reported on the progress of twenty-six children in London placed in residential care before the age of four months and still there at four and a half years. These children averaged twenty-four different nurses by age two years (range, four to forty-five). By the age of four and a half they had averaged fifty different care-takers. Eighteen of the children were at that point described by staff as not caring deeply about anyone. In cognitive and linguistic development, the children performed at the same levels as controls; the institutions were 'good' ones, providing a reasonably stimulating environment. However the extreme shared care did seem to have disturbed normal attachment development. Did this matter? At a follow-up at eight years (Tizard and Hodges, 1978), although many children had left the institution, most were seen as severe problems by teachers, who described them as excessively attention-seeking, restless, unpopular and anti-social.

These findings have been independently replicated by Dixon (cited by Rutter, 1979, and personal communication), who also studied the later adjustment of children reared in institutions from the first year of life. Again, cognitive and linguistic development were roughly normal, but they were disruptive, attention-seeking and unpopular at school. This latter conclusion is based on direct observation, as well as teacher's ratings. As Rutter (1979) concludes, 'it seems probable that this inept social behaviour at school was a consequence of the children's relative lack of selective binding in infancy (due in turn to a pattern of upbringing in which each child experienced as many as 50-80 caretakers)'.

It cannot be said that this evidence is conclusive; and the early lack of relationships may not be irreversible (Clarke and Clarke, 1976). But it does seem likely that extreme shared care makes attachment relationships more difficult to form, and later social adjustments more problematic.

The evidence on day care

Day care centres, like children's homes, are an instututionalised form of substitute care in modern industrial societies. However they differ from children's homes in two important ways. Firstly, the mother (usually) provides continuity in care for an appreciable part of the child's day. Secondly, the number of caretakers at a day centre may be small and relatively stable. In high quality day care for young children, it is usual for a relatively small group of infants, probably under ten, to receive care primarily from a few main caretakers, probably less than five. In such circumstances, the amount and quality of adult-child interaction may equal or exceed that of the home (Rubenstein and Howes, 1979), and infants may show attachment behaviour to caretakers as well as mothers (Ricciutti, 1974).

Wilcox, Staff and Romaine (1980) compared the effects of individual and multiple assignment of caregivers to the development of infants in day care. In individual care, one caregiver was responsible for four infants; in multiple care, five caregivers for twenty infants. No significant differences were found in the children's contacts with adults, separation from or reunion with mother, or Bayley Mental or Motor Development scores. As the authors point out, staff turnover was low (only two changes in two years) so even with group care there was a stable core of five caregivers with whom each child could become familiar.

It would be impossible to provide an exhaustive review of the literature on day care here. However, recent reviews (Etaugh, 1980; Belsky and Steinberg, 1978) conclude that high-quality centre-based day care does not have adverse effects on the child's emotional or intellectual development. One aspect of 'high-quality' undoubtedly is that staff turnover should be low, and child-staff ratios high, thus ensuring the quality and stability of caregiver-child relationships (Anderson, 1980). In such circumstances, we have moderate shared care. More detailed research on the quality and stability of relationships in day-care is needed, but a provisional conclusion would be that the evidence on day care conforms with earlier conclusions; namely that moderate shared care is fully compatible with normal social development, while extreme shared care may not be.

Why should an increasing number of caretakers raise problems for normal attachment development? What mechanisms are involved? Bowlby (1958, 1969) postulated two ways in which there would be severe limits on the number of attachment relationships. Firstly, a critical period for attachment formation, terminated by the 'fear of strangers' phenomenon. Secondly, the inhibitory effects of a principal attachment bond on subsidiary bonds.

Is there a critical period for attachment formation?

Bowlby (1969) argued that there was a sensitive period, of maximum range six weeks to nine months, during which it was very much easier to develop attachments than subsequently. The very young baby of course was too young to discriminate particular people. After about six to nine months, it was argued, an attachment had been made to the primary caretaker but the 'fear of strangers' phenomeonon, now evident, would make new attachments almost impossible. Scott (1963) put forward a similar view.

The theoretical background to this hypothesis was partly psycho-analytic, partly ethological. The empirical evidence for a strong 'fear of strangers' at nine months seemed consistent at the time, but now has been greatly re-interpreted. Much of the fear seen was due to the artificial way the stranger behaved, and the unfamiliar laboratory conditions used for testing (Rheingold and Eckerman, 1973). Reviewing more recent work, Sroufe (1977) concluded that one could justifiably consider that infants might be wary of strangers from nine months onwards, but that affiliative responses would predominate in a familiar setting and with a friendly, responsive stranger.

Bretherton (1978) showed that infants would become more friendly with a responsive stranger (with mother present) over the course of a session, and Smith, Eaton and Hindmarch (in press) obtained similar findings over four successive sessions. Fleener (1967) compared one-year-olds' responses to a responsive caretaker who had looked after them for three 3-hour visits, and another, unfamiliar caretaker. The infants clearly showed more approach to, and distress at separation from, the more familiar caretaker. These studies show that affiliative responses develop over time with new caretakers, and suggest that new attachment bonds may develop. That new bonds do indeed develop after nine months of age is evident from studies of fostering (Robertson and Robertson, 1971) and adoption (Tizard, 1977), and from several reports that the number of attachment figures naturally increases through the first and second year (Schaffer and Emerson, 1964; Ricciutti, 1974; Leiderman and Leiderman, 1974).

Does a primary bond inhibit the development of subsidiary bonds?

Bowlby (1958) argued that the formation of a first or principal bond would in itself inhibit the formation of other, subsidiary bonds. The theoretical basis for this can be found in William James' writings on instinctual responses. The empirical evidence presented was slight, consisting mainly in the comment that in residential nurseries children tended to latch themselves on to a particular nurse.

This mechanism, which if operative would severely limit the number of bonds formed, is contra-indicated by all the evidence cited earlier showing that multiple attachments can be made. In particular, some studies have found that babies may be equally attached to two care-takers, at least in terms of the measures of attachment used (Leiderman and Leiderman, 1974; Lamb, 1976; Marvin *et al*, 1977). Also, Schaffer and Emerson (1966) found that infants who showed strong attachments to the principal caretaker also tended to show strong attachments to other caretakers, which would appear to be opposite to the effect predicted by the inhibitory mechanism.

The evidence of residential children latching themselves on to a particular nurse can be explained at a different level. Once the beginnings of a bond are formed between a nurse and a particular child, other nurses might recognise this and deliberately not form alternative bonds. Just this was reported by Stevens (1971) at the Athens Baby Centre, where: 'this happens, however, because it has become recognised by the other nurses that that baby belongs to that nurse and they will therefore leave him to her'. The inhibition is thus at the level of conscious motivation, and not the internal psychodynamic process Bowlby presumably had in mind.

A more cognitive view of attachment relationships

Over recent years a view of early social relationships has developed which puts less emphasis on psychodynamic aspects and more emphasis on links between cognitive and social-affective development. I shall sketch out the main features of this approach, and then suggest how it may provide constraints on infant attachments other than those which Bowlby had considered.

The main phenomena which cognitive-developmental theorists have usually sought to explain in early social development, have been separation anxiety, and the fear of strangers. Even if the latter has been exaggerated (Sroufe, 1977) some wariness of strangers, together with anxiety at separation from an attachment figure, typically emerge in the second half of the first year. Only by then have infants reached a stage of object/person permanence whereby they could be expected to react to an unfamiliar person, or the absence of a familiar person, in a consistent way. Schaffer (1974) argues that by eight or nine months a child has developed recall as well as recognition memory, and is able to evaluate stimuli simultaneously as well as sequentially. Cicchetti and Sroufe (1978), in a longitudinal study, have found empirical evidence that cognitive measures such as of object permanence can be related to measures of affect. Also, Lewis and Brooks-Gunn (1979) have argued that the acquisition of a concept of self is another crucial cognitive component to emotional or affective response in social situations. However all these cognitive abilities need to be linked to further postulates in order to explain why an infant's affective responses take the form they do with different people and in different situations.

A number of theoretical perspectives have been advanced to explain this. Kagan (1974) believes that with social as with non-social stimulation, a moderate degree of discrepancy can be successfully assimilated by the child and will be enjoyable, but that too much discrepancy will lead to avoidance, wariness or crying. In the early months of life discrepancy may be referred to static aspects of stimuli, but by about eight months Kagan feels that attempts at assimilation by the infant are best described in terms of the activation of hypotheses, or expectancies. At this age, babies have reached about stage 4 in the Piagetian sensorimotor series, and would have expectancies of cause-effect relations in the environment. Effects difficult to assimilate could cause distress. A slightly different emphasis is put by Sroufe, Waters and Matas (1974), who argue that novelty or incongruity leads to attention, but that the affective consequence will depend on the infant's evaluation of the context of the whole situation.

An alternative approach comes from Bower (1977), who suggests that it is the inability to communicate with a stranger which is frightening for an infant. As I have suggested elsewhere (Smith, 1979), although Bower puts the emphasis on verbal communication, his hypothesis might be strengthened if communicative ability was generalised to the ability to maintain contingent interaction sequences. Watson and Ramey (1972) and others have shown that infants enjoy situations where they can receive contingent stimulations, and react to it in positive socio-emotional ways.

This approach might be thought to be not so different from that of discrepancy theorists. If another person's behaviour is unpredictable, it would be expected to be anxiety-provoking by either theory. However whereas predictable social encounters would be expected to be pleasant or at least neutral by discrepancy theorists, this would not be so in terms of the contingency explanation unless the infant was also able to influence or exert control on the situation. Gunnar (1980) has separated out the affective consequences of predictability, and control, in an experimental situation with a toy. She found that predictability could increase fear if the situation was aversive; but that control could reduce distress, notably by twelve months of age in the conditions of her experiment.

If a situation is predictable, then this implies that children will learn from past experience the consequences of this situation. Bronson (1978) has argued that phenomena such as stranger anxiety are best explained, at least by the end of the first year of life, in terms of learnt associations or expectations based on earlier experience; in this case, earlier social interactions with strangers. This has been another alternative approach to discrepancy theories. Certainly, it would seem that as a child gets older, discrepancy or incongruity *per se* would be an increasingly less useful guide to affect and action. But what form does the learning that Bronson is arguing for, take? If it is learning of consequences irrespective of what the infant does, then this is a situation where the infant has prediction but not control; this may be typical of some social situations, and especially experimental ones, but not of the usual course of new relationships. In the latter, the infant is learning interactive sequences; not only how another person behaves, but how to influence that person's behaviour.

In summary, discrepancy-type theories seem to be increasingly inadequate as an explanation of affective responses, toward the end of the first year of life and through the second year. A more plausible perspective is that infants enjoy being able to interact contingently with others (Bower, 1977) and that the way in which learning plays a major role (Bronson, 1978) is by the infant learning how his or her behaviour affects the other person, and makes certain responses of behaviour sequences more or less probable.

The parent or older caretaker of a very young infant seems to make it easy for the infant to predict and apparently influence his or her behaviour, by 'pacing' responses so as to react contingently to the baby's signals; by the end of the first year, if not earlier, the infant is able to take a more equal role in maintaining interaction sequences and thus the overall relationship (Schaffer, 1977). By this time also a level of cognitive development has been reached at which a true attachment relationship can emerge, but the foundation for the latter will also have been laid by repeated mutually contingent interaction sequences over some period of time and in different contexts. This parental or stable caretaking relationship can be compared with the social situation of an infant either with a peer, or with an older stranger.

In the case of peers, it will be difficult for two infants to predict and influence each other's behaviour if both are still poor at this kind of ability and usually require some degree of adult pacing or 'scaffolding' in interactions. As Bronson (1973) pointed out, the learning of interpersonal contingencies does seem difficult in young children. The affective quality of peer relationships does seem to be related to cognitive development (Jakobsen, 1980). However attachment relationships between young children probably require much more time to develop than between an adult and child. There is little direct evidence for this, but strong attachment relationships between young children (promoting security, and its converse, separation anxiety) have only been reported in exceptional circumstances; notably the group of refugee children described by Freud and Dann (1951).

In the case of an older stranger, the stranger is able to pace responses to the baby, but the baby has yet to learn how to influence the stranger. The infant will need some time to learn how to do this, and regular amounts of contact so that the ability to predict and influence the other person is updated, and not forgotten. In time, a new relationship will develop. However, consider the infant in a multiple shared care situation. With too many caretakers, or too discontinuous care, the ability of the infant to learn and remember how to interact with the caretakers could be very limited, even assuming caretakers highly motivated to provide mutually contingent and satisfying interaction. This cognitive limitation on the infant's learning and memory abilities could be one source of constraint on the success of multiple shared care situations.

Consider now the caretaker in such a situation. The caretaker clearly needs some time to get to know the infant, as *vice versa*. But this process should be quicker for the caretaker than the infant, given what we know about the increase in memory capacities with age. However the pleasure or feeling of efficacy which the caretaker gets from the relationship (Goldberg, 1977) will be influenced in a way which the infant's affective response cannot be; by the knowledge of the wider context of the relationship. The caretaker will likely have some knowledge of the extent to which he or she can predict and influence the whole future course of the relationship with the infant. This may well affect that person's commitment to the relationship, and hence the degree to which that person makes the effort to respond positively, sensitively and contingently to the infant in any particular caretaking session.

Two general mechanisms have now been postulated, which might put some limits on the viability of multiple shared care. One is hypothesised to principally affect the infant, the other the caretaker. Some evidence for each will now be considered.

Time for the infant to get to know the caretaker

Observations of infants with a new (potential) caretaker show that affiliative responses become more frequent over a few sessions (Smith, Eaton and Hindmarch, in press) but it seems unlikely that a full attachment relationship can develop so rapidly. Fleener (1967) found that infants did show some attachment-type behaviour to a more familiar caretaker after three sessions, but only in comparison to a quite unfamiliar caretaker; all the infants tested preferred their mother to the familiar caretaker.

However longer-term natural studies have indicated that further attachments can develop, over a period of several months. For example Ricciutti (1974) reported that a familiar caretaker in a day care setting began to play a significant role as an attachment figure, compared to the mother, after about seven months. Leiderman and Leiderman (1974) found in their Kikuyu study that non-maternal caretakers were reacted to like strangers when the baby was seven to nine months old, but like the mother by the time the baby was ten to twelve months old. Studies of fostering (Robertson and Robertson, 1971) would also be compatible with the idea that some weeks or months of regular care-taking would be a necessary condition for an attachment bond to develop.

There is less evidence on the forgetting of relationships. Rheingold and Bayley (1959) did find that a caretaker who looked after six-month-old babies intensively for eight weeks was apparently 'forgotten' by the children one year later. It was not clear whether the babies formed an attachment to the caretaker at six months, but they certainly had distinguished her from other persons after a week or so.

Presumably, there would be some trade-off between the total length of time the infant and caretaker have known each other, and the duration and frequency of each caretaking session. At present, not enough systematic data are available to enable much estimation of how much time and how many sessions might typically be necessary to enable attachment bonds to form. Smith and Turner (1980), on the basis of maternal reports, found that mothers were happy to leave one or two-year-olds with relatives or friends, at least for periods of a few hours, even if the latter only undertook regular caretaking once or twice a month. Although the infants might in addition have spent some time with the other caretaker in the presence of the mother, this nevertheless suggests that in favourable conditions infants can feel secure even with only infrequent sessions with the caretaker. On the other hand, Cummings (1980) compared behaviour with 'stable' and 'non-stable' caregivers in day care. The stable caregivers had worked about 700 hours in the centre with the child present, the non-stable caregivers about 300 hours. In a laboratory setting the child was clearly more attached to the mother than either caregiver, but on leaving the mother at the day centre, the children usually separated without distress, and more usually so with the familiar caregiver. Thus study suggests the importance of stability, but indicates more conservative measures for the time needed for bonds to develop.

Although time and frequency of sessions are important, the environmental context, the activity of the caregiver and his or her responsiveness to the infant are also likely to affect bond formation. Even if perceptually quite familiar after a long time, an infant might not feel very secure with a caretaker whose behaviour he or she cannot readily influence. This leads us to the other factor, of the commitment of the caretaker.

Caretaker commitment to the relationship

Besides the time a caretaker is present with an infant—perceptually visible, at least—it is also important whether the caretaker is responsive to the infant's signals. A caretaker's responsiveness and general commitment to the relationship could be diluted by a number of factors.

Firstly, if the caretaker is responsible for many children, this in itself would tend to limit the care and attention which could be devoted to one child. Data on very large families could be relevant here, but in such a family a young infant would have some much older siblings who might also serve as attachment figures. In a residential setting, while attachment to same age peers may occur it is probably a longer and intrinsically more difficult process, since a same-age peer cannot pace responses to be contingent in the way that an older peer or adult can.

Secondly, the caretaker's commitment could be affected by conscious knowledge that she or he has little control over the relationship with the infant. This would be so if, for example, interaction times were inflexible, as in shift systems in children's homes; if it was known to be likely that the caretaking role might end soon (child leaves institution, caretaker finds another job) and the child possibly never be seen again; or if the child was known to have principal caretakers, such as parents, with whom the caretaker had little contact or influence (as perhaps, in some child-minding situations).

These factors would tend to be exacerbated in residential homes and situations of extreme multiple care. There is evidence that in such situations caretakers' behaviour is less contingent on the infant's behaviour (Rheingold, 1956; Provence and Lipton, 1962). Even allowing for larger numbers of children, a nurse in a residential home may not feel the sense of commitment to a relationship that would act to maximise responsiveness. As David and Appel (1961) put it, 'in routine care . . . she does not remain with the child because there is no spontaneous interest or personal need to do so'.

In moderate shared care, such factors diluting commitment need not arise. Close relatives and friends are likely to feel more spontaneous interest and involvement in a relationship with the infant. In good quality day care it seems likely that low staff turnover, high staff morale, and good staff-child ratios are conducive to responsive care and more committed relationships (Rubenstein and Howes, 1979; Anderson, 1980).

Conclusions

Two sets of mechanisms have been proposed which might, in effect, act to limit the success of extreme multiple caretaking. These are the time taken for the infant to get to know the caretaker, and the commitment felt by the caretaker given the overall context of the relationship. While the latter especially cannot be automatically assumed for moderate shared care (indeed it cannot be automatically assumed for monotropic care), conditions are argued to be much more favourable in such circumstances.

These proposed mechanisms are based on modern attachment theory, but much more empirical evidence is needed to assess their relative importance. Despite the attention given to the mother-infant relationship, and recently to father-infant relationships, other caretaker-infant relationships have been largely neglected. The literature on day care and children's homes is voluminous, but more detailed research attention to the characteristics of caretaker-infant relations within these settings may well be the key to understanding the success or otherwise of different institutions in furthering children's development.

It has been pointed out that the mechanisms suggested are more cognitive than the mechanisms suggested earlier by Bowlby (1969) which were based on psychodynamic and ethological theorising. However this is in no way in opposition to an ethological-evolutionary approach to the issue of attachment relationships, one of the most fruitful results of Bowlby's work. There are no strong evolutionary grounds to expect infants to be monotropic; there are good evolutionary grounds to expect infants to be able to make a few bonds, but to be wary of trusting themselves completely to unfamiliar adults before they have got to know them (Smith, 1980). Insofar as such developmental pathways are canalised, there is no problem in assuming that the mechanisms involved are as much 'cognitive' in operation as they are 'social' in effect.

A new direction for memory research is also suggested here. Most research on children's memory has concentrated on recognition and recall of particular stimuli; and more recently on mnemonics and metamemory (Kail, 1979). Memory for social behaviour has received little attention. In particular, factors affecting how readily infants can learn about and recall others' responsive repertoires, and how to influence them, would be of considerable relevance for the arguments adopted in this review.

References

Ainsworth, M. D. S., *Infancy in Uganda: Infant Care and Growth of Love,* Baltimore, John Hopkins University Press, 1967.

Ainsworth, M. D. S., 'The development of mother-infant attachment', in B. M. Caldwell and H. N. Ricciutti (eds.), *Review of Child Development Research, Vol. 3,* Chicago, University of Chicago Press, 1973.

Anderson, W. A., 'Attachment in daily separations: reconceptualising day care and maternal employment issues', *Child Development,* 1980, *51,* 242-5.

Belsky, J., and Steinberg, L. D., 'The effects of day care: A critical review', *Child Development,* 1978, *49,* 929-49.

Bower, T. G. R., *A Primer of Infant Development,* San Francisco, Freeman, 1977.

Bowlby, J., 'The nature of the child's tie to his mother', *International Journal of Psychoanalysis,* 1958, *39,* 350-73.

Bowlby, J., *Attachment and Loss, Vol. I: Attachment,* London, Hogarth Press, 1969.

Bretherton, I., 'Making friends with one-year-olds: an experimental study of infant-stranger interaction', *Merrill-Palmer Quarterly,* 1978, *24,* 29-51.

Bronson, G. W., 'Aversive reactions to strangers: a dual-process interpretation', *Child Development,* 1978, *48,* 495-9.

Bronson, W. C., 'Competence and the growth of personality', in K. J. Connolly and J. S. Bruner (eds.), *The Growth of Competence,* London and New York, Academic Press, 1973.

Brown, G. W., Bhrolchain, M. N., and Harris, T., 'Social class and psychiatric disturbance among women in an urban population', *Sociology*, 1975, *9*, 225-54.

Casler, L., 'Maternal deprivation: a critical review of the literature', *Monographs of the Society for Research in Child Development*, 1961, *26*, No. 2.

Cicchetti, D., and Sroufe, L. A., 'The relationship between affective and cognitive development in Down's Syndrome infants', *Child Development*, 1976, *47*, 920-9.

Clarke, A. M., and Clarke, A. D. B., *Early Experience: Myth and Evidence*, London, Open Books, 1976.

Cohen, L. J., and Campos, J. J., 'Father, mother and stranger as elicitors of attachment behaviours in infancy', *Developmental Psychology*, 1974, *10*, 146-54.

Cummings, E. M., 'Caregiver stability and day care', *Developmental Psychology*, 1980, *16*, 31-7.

David, M., and Appell, G., 'A study of nursing care and nurse-infant interaction', in B. M. Foss (ed.), *Determinants of Infant Behaviour*, London, Methuen, 1961.

Etaugh, C., 'Effects of non-maternal care on children: research evidence and popular views', *American Psychologist*, 1980, *35*, 309-19.

Faigin, H., 'Social behaviour of young children in the kibbutz', *Journal of Abnormal and Social Psychology*, 1958, *56*, 117-29.

Feldman, S. S., and Ingham, M. E., 'Attachment behaviour: a validation study in two age groups', *Child Development*, 1975, *46*, 319-30.

Fischer, J. L., and Fischer, A., 'The New Englanders of Orchard Town, U.S.A.', in B. Whiting (ed.), *Six Cultures*, New York, Wiley, 1963.

Fleener, D. A., 'Attachment formation in human infants', unpublished Ph.D. thesis, Indiana University, 1967.

Fox, N., 'Attachment of kibbutz infants to mother and metapelet', *Child Development*, 1977, *48*, 1228-39.

Freud, A., and Dann, S., 'An experiment in group upbringing', *Psychoanalytical Study of the Child*, 1961, *6*, 127-63.

Goldberg, S., 'Social competence in infancy: a model of parent-infant interaction', *Merrill-Palmer Quarterly*, 1977, *23*, 163-77.

Gunnar, M. R., 'Control, warning signals, and distress in infancy', *Developmental Psychology*, 1980, *16*, 281-9.

Jacobson, J. L., 'Cognitive determinants of wariness toward unfamiliar peers', *Developmental Psychology*, 1980, *16*, 347-54.

Kagan, J., 'Discrepancy, temperament, and infant distress', in M. Lewis and L. A. Rosenblum (eds.), *The Origins of Fear*, New York and London, Wiley, 1974.

Kail, R., *The Development of Memory in Children*, San Francisco, Freeman, 1979.

Lamb, M. E., 'The role of the father: an overview', in M. E. Lamb (ed.), *The Role of the Father in Child Development,* New York and London, Wiley, 1976.

Leiderman, P. H., and Leiderman, G. F., 'Affective and cognitive consequences of polymatric infant care in the East African Highlands', in A. D. Pick (ed.), *Minnesota Symposium on Child Psychology, Vol. 8,* Minneapolis, University of Minnesota Press, 1974.

Leiderman, P. H., and Leiderman, G. F., 'Economic change and infant care in an East African agricultural community', in P. H. Leiderman, S. R. Tulkin and A. Rosenfeld (eds.), *Culture and Infancy,* New York, Academic Press, 1977.

LeVine, R. A., and LeVine, B., 'Nyansongo: a Gusii community in Kenya', in B. Whiting (ed.), *Six Cultures,* New York, Wiley, 1963.

Lewis, M., and Brooks-Gunn, J., *Social Cognition and the Acquisition of Self,* New York and London, Plenum, 1979.

Maccoby, E. E., and Feldman, S., 'Mother-attachment and stranger-reactions in the third year of life', *Monographs of the Society for Research in Child Development,* 1972, *31,* (1, Serial No. 146).

Maretzi, T. W., and Maretzi, H., 'Taira: an Okinawa village', in B. Whiting (ed.), *Six Cultures,* New York, Wiley, 1963.

Marvin, R. S., 'An ethological-cognitive model for the attenuation of mother-child attachment behaviour', in T. Alloway, P. Pliner and L. Krames (eds.), *Attachment Behaviour,* New York, Plenum, 1977.

Marvin, R. S., VanDevander, T. L., Iwanaga, M. I., LeVine, S., and LeVine, R. A., 'Infant-caregiver attachment among the Hausa of Nigeria', in H. McGurk (ed.), *Ecological Factors in Human Development,* Amsterdam, North Holland, 1977.

Mead, M., *Coming of Age in Samoa,* Harmondsworth, Penguin, 1943.

Miller, L., 'Child rearing in the kibbutz', in J. G. Howells (ed.), *Modern Perspectives in Child Psychiatry,* London, Oliver & Boyd, 1969.

Moore, T. W., 'Exclusive early mothering and its alternatives', *Scandanavian Journal of Psychology,* 1975, *16,* 255-72.

Newson, J., and Newson, E., *Patterns of Infant Care in an Urban Community,* Harmondsworth, Penguin, 1965.

Nydegger, W. F., and Nydegger, C., 'Tarong: an Ilocos Barria in the Philippines', in B. Whiting (ed.), *Six Cultures,* New York, Wiley, 1963.

Powdermaker, H., *Life in Lesu,* London, Williams & Norgate, 1933.

Provence, S., and Lipton, R. C., *Infants in Institutions,* New York, International University Press, 1962.

Rabin, A. I., 'Behaviour research in collective settlements in Israel: 6. Infants and children under conditions of "intermittent" mothering in the kibbutz', *American Journal of Orthopsychiatry,* 1958, *28,* 577-86.

Raum, O. F., *Chaga Childhood*, Oxford, Oxford University Press, 1940.

Read, M., *Children of their Fathers: Growing up among the Ngoni of Malawi*, New York, Holt, Rinehart & Winston, 1968.

Rheingold, H. L., 'The modification of social responsiveness in institutional babies', *Monographs of the Society for Research in Child Development*, 1956, *21*.

Rheingold, H. L., and Bayley, N., 'The later effects of an experimental modification of mothering', *Child Development*, 1959, *30*, 363-72.

Rheingold, H. L., and Eckerman, C. O., 'Fear of the Stranger: a critical examination', in H. Reese (ed.), *Advances in Child Development and Behaviour, Vol. 8*, New York, Academic Press, 1973.

Ricciutti, H. N., 'Fear and the development of social attachments in the first year of life', in M. Lewis and L. A. Rosenblum (eds.), *The Origins of Fear*, New York and London, Wiley, 1974.

Robertson, J., and Robertson, J., 'Young children in brief separation: a fresh look', *Psychoanalytic Study of the Child*, 1971, *26*, 264-315.

Romney, K., and Romney, R., 'The Mixtecans of Juxtlahuaca, Mexico', in B. Whiting (ed.), *Six Cultures*, New York, Wiley, 1963.

Rubenstein, J. L., and Howes, C., 'Caregiving and infant behaviour in day care and in homes', *Developmental Psychology*, 1979, *15*, 1-24.

Rutter, M., *Maternal Deprivation Reassessed*, Harmondsworth, Penguin, 1972.

Rutter, M., 'Maternal deprivation, 1972-1978; New findings, new concepts, new approaches', *Child Development*, 1979, *50*, 283-305.

Schaffer, H. R., 'Cognitive components of the infant's response to strangers', in M. Lewis and L. A. Rosenblum (eds.), *The Origins of Fear*, New York and London, Wiley, 1974.

Schaffer, H. R., *Mothering*, London, Fontana/Open Books, 1977.

Schaffer, H. R., and Emerson, P. E., 'The development of social attachments in infancy', *Monographs of the Society for Research in Child Development*, 1964, *29*, (3, Serial No. 94).

Scott, J. P., 'The process of primary socialisation in canine and human infants', *Monographs of the Society for Research in Child Development*, 1963, *28*, (1, Serial No. 85).

Smith, P. K., 'The ontogeny of fear in children', in W. Sluckin (ed.), *Fear in Animals and Man*, New York, VanNostrand Reinhold, 1979.

Smith, P. K., 'Alternative models to monotropism', *Merrill-Palmer Quarterly*, 1980.

Smith, P. K., Eaton, L., and Hindmarch, A., 'How one-year-olds respond to strangers: a two person situation', *Journal of Genetic Psychology*, (in press).

Smith, P. K., and Turner, J., 'Substitute care in a sample of non-working mothers', unpublished manuscript, University of Sheffield, 1980.

Sroufe, L. A., 'Wariness of strangers and the study of infant development', *Child Development*, 1977, *48*, 731-46.

Sroufe, L. A., and Waters, E., 'Attachment as an organisational construct', *Child Development*, 1977, 48, 1184-99.

Sroufe, L. A., Waters, E., and Matas, L., 'Contextual determinants of infants' affective response', in M. Lewis and L. A. Rosenblum (eds.), *The Origin of Fear*, New York and London, Wiley, 1974.

Stevens, A. G., 'Attachment behaviour, separation anxiety, and stranger anxiety', in H. R. Schaffer (ed.), *The Origins of Human Social Relations*, London and New York, Academic Press, 1971.

Tizard, B., *Adoption: A Second Chance*, London, Open Books, 1977.

Tizard, B., and Hodges, J., 'The effect of early institutionsl rearing on the development of eight-year-old children', *Journal of Child Psychology and Psychiatry*, 1978, *19*, 99-118.

Tizard, B., and Rees, J., 'The effects of early institutional rearing on the behavioural problems and affectional relationships of four-year-old children', *Journal of Child Psychology and Psychiatry*, 1975, *16*, 61-73.

Tizard, J., and Tizard, B., 'The social development of two-year-old children in residential nurseries', in H. R. Schaffer (ed.), *The Origins of Human Social Relations*, London and New York, Academic Press, 1971.

Tindale, N. B., 'The Pitjandjara', in M. G. Biacchieri (ed.), *Hunters and Gatherers Today*, New York, Holt, Rinehart & Winston, 1972.

Turnbull, C., 'The Mbuti Pygmies of the Congo', in J. L. Gibbs (ed.), *People of Africa*, New York, Holt, Rinehart & Winston, 1965.

Watson, J. S., and Ramey, C. T., 'Reactions to response-contingent stimulation in early infancy', *Merrill-Palmer Quarterly*, 1972, *18*, 219-27.

Weinraub, M., and Lewis, M., 'The determinants of children's responses to separation', *Monographs of the Society for Research in Child Development*, 1977, *42*, No. 4.

Weinraub, M., Brooks, J., and Lewis, M., 'The social network: A reconsideration of the concept of attachment', *Human Development*, 1977, *20*, 31-47.

Weisner, T. S., and Gallimore, R. 'My brother's keeper: child and sibling caretaking', *Current Anthropology*, 1977, *18*, 169-90.

West, M. M., and Konnor, M. J., 'The role of the father: an anthropological perspective', in M. E. Lamb (ed.), *The Role of the Father in Child Development*, New York and London, Wiley, 1976.

Wilcox, B. M., Staff, P., and Romaine, M. F., 'A comparison of individual with multiple assignment of caregivers to infants in day care', *Merrill-Palmer Quarterly*, 1980, *26*, 53-62.

Willemsen, E., Flaherty, D., Heaton, C., and Ritchey, G., 'Attachment behaviour of one-year-olds as a function of mother vs. father, sex of child, session, and toys', *Genetic Psychology Monographs,* 1974, *90,* 305-24.

Wilson, E. O., *Sociobiology: The New Synthesis,* Cambridge, Belknap Press, 1975.

9 The child's concept of emotion

Paul Harris and Tjeert Olthof

Emotion and Metacognition

If we look at the history of developmental psychology over the last twenty years, it is clear that our view of cognitive development has been dominated, under the influence of Piaget, by research on the child's understanding of the physical world. We know a great deal about the child's understanding of fundamental physical concepts such as the conservation of matter, or the reversibility of various spatial trans- formations. We know much less about the child's understanding of psychological concepts. Recent research on the development of memory has begun to redress the balance, and the following picture has emerged: the young child tends to be both unaware of the limitations of his memory and unduly passive in the encoding of materials which are difficult to remember. This is not altogether surprising since the child's memory normally functions in a trouble-free fashion, particularly for material which is meaningful. Nevertheless, in the course of develop- ment the child develops insights into those limitations which do exist, the remedial strategies which may be adopted to bypass those limitations, and also the inner mental states which signal the smooth or disrupted functioning of the child's own mnemonic machinery (Flavell and Wellman, 1977; Harris, 1978).

In this chapter, we shall describe a similar type of development with respect to emotion. The youngest children that we have tested, namely six-year-olds conceive of emotions in a simple S-R fashion, where S stands for some familiar emotion-eliciting situation and R, the set of behavioural and physiological reactions to that situation. At this age, children typically eschew references to mental states that mediate between the situation and the reactions that it arouses. In contrast, eleven-year-old children adopt a more complex three-factor theory. Although still aware of the links between particular situations and emotional reactions, they also refer to intervening mental states. This age-change has ramifications for the way in which children conceive of various key aspects of emotion: the cues and the reliability with which emotion can be identified, the strategies which may be deployed to regulate the intensity or the display of emotion, the effects of emotion on other psychological domains such as thinking and social attitudes, and finally the time-course of an emotional reaction. These ramifications are explored below.

Identification

One of the enduring questions in the psychology of emotion has been how the subject comes to identify his or her emotions. This question exercised James (1980), Cannon (1929), Freud (1937) and Schacter (1975) and their answers are by no means the same. Crudely, we may say that the subject might attend to three classes of cue. First, emotion is typically (though not always) induced by an encounter with a particular situation, often social in nature. Second, emotion is frequently accompanied by a set of behavioural and physiological reactions on the part of the subject. Third, and perhaps more controversial from a scientific point of view, is the possibility that emotion is accompanied by a set of distinctive conscious states.

The layman is inclined, we think, to claim that he identifies his emotions by an introspective examination of those conscious states, rather than the situation which gave rise to them or the behavioural and physiological reactions which accompany them. Take, for example, the celebrated episode at the beginning of Proust's *'A la recherche du temps perdu'*. Proust, in a semi-invalid state, is given some tea and a madeline cake. As he tastes the cake dipped in the tea a feeling of extreme happiness suffuses him, a feeling which is out of all proportion to the simple sensory experience that has just passed. By an active process of reconstruction, Proust traces the emotion back through the experience of dipping the cake infused with tea to a similar experience from years before, associated in his mind with the security of childhood. This emotional suffusion was not accompanied by any specific behavioural or physiological reaction and was seemingly unconnected with, or at least out of all proportion to the precipitating action, namely drinking tea and eating cake. The fact that Proust was still able to identify his emotional state as one of extreme happiness is inexplicable unless we are prepared to postulate the existence of distinct conscious states, associated with the various emotions which we identify in the language. Such a postulate is, as we have claimed above, something which the layman is quite prepared to make.

The classical psychologies of emotion have, in contrast, tended to discount the role of conscious experience, or at least to see it as a by-product of the process of identification, rather than a pre-condition. Instead, they have argued that behavioural and psychological states (James, 1980) or a combination of physiological arousal and situational appraisal (Schachter, 1975) provide the bases for the subject's identification of his own emotion.

Our own investigations have indicated that by the age of eleven years, conscious mental states are cited as the primary cue for the identification of one's own emotion, whereas younger children focus on the emotion-arousing situation. In order to find out the cues that children believe they use, we (Harris, Olthof and Meerum Terwogt, in press) interviewed three age-groups of children, of six, eleven and fifteen years, about their concept of one positive emotion (happiness) and one negative emotion (anger, for half the children; fear, for the other half). We asked children initially how they knew what emotion they felt, if for example they are feeling happy or afraid. The replies could be classified as referring either to a situation giving rise to such an emotion (I'm happy when it's my birthday), behavioural (If I'm angry, I bang the table or something), physiological reactions (I get a headache when I'm afraid), or finally a mental state (If you're happy, then you think everything is fine). Looking at the distribution of replies from the three age-groups across these categories, two changes were visible. Citation of situational factors was very frequent among the six-year-old children but rare among the eleven- and fifteen-year-olds. Citation of a mental state followed precisely the opposite pattern, being rare among the six-year-olds but common in the two older groups. The other two categories (behavioural and physiological reactions), were cited with equal frequency across all three age-groups.

This particular age-change provides the first piece of evidence for the shift from a two-factor S-R model, to a three-factor mentalistic model as outlined in the introduction. The youngest children conceive of emotions as a set of behavioural and physiological reactions to some external situation. They rarely refer to any mental state mediating or accompanying these various reactions. That young children are aware of such S-R links is also clear from the work of other investigators. Borke (1971), for example, has shown that from the age of four years, children can identify which of several facial expressions (happy, sad, angry, afraid) would be an appropriate reaction to various episodes (attending a birthday party; losing a pet, and so on) described in a story format. Even when young children do not fully understand an emotion their remarks suggest that they still tie it to a particular situation. For example, Harter (1979) reports that one five-year-old defined proud as, 'It's when I'm doing much of something good, like building.' When asked the meaning of ashamed, he replied, 'I'm not sure, but I think it's when someone doesn't have a friend.' By the age of eleven years, on the other hand, children, although still presumably aware of the link between particular situations and emotional reactions, do specify intervening mental states to the point where these are regarded as the primary cue for their own emotion.

This age-change in the conceptualisation of emotion implies that the two age-groups will differ in their notions about the accuracy with which emotion can be identified. If an inner mental component is not attributed to emotion by the younger children, they will be less concerned about misidentifying another's emotion. For example, we asked children if they might not realise sometimes that their mother or father were angry or happy. Although a minority of the younger children agreed that this could happen it was because they might not be in the right place ('I'm always with my mother but if I'm with a friend, then I don't know') or might not attend ('I don't look at them very often'). In contrast, the older children were sensitive to the fact that the visibility of the emotion depended not only on the observer but also on the observed since the latter might not reveal his or her emotion: 'Then they've got it inside them and you can't see it,' as one eleven-year-old put it.

The assumption of the six-year-old children that a particular emotion is tied to a particular situation has an additional implication which Harter (1979) has examined in detail: younger children find it difficult to conceive of a situation giving rise to two distinct and even opposing emotions. To take a prosaic example, a young child may find it difficult to admit that he is happy because he very much wanted a bike, but also sad because he wanted the more expensive, flashier model.

Harter investigated four emotions, happy, sad, angry and afraid, and found that for all four emotions, a straightforward age-linked progression could be found. Prior to six to seven years, children could not conceive of two synchronous emotions at all. At around six to seven years, they began to conceive of two emotions, but only as the product of two sequential situations. Finally at around nine years, children could conceive of two emotions arising not just successively but also simultaneously. To illustrate this distinction between successive and simultaneous, contrast the following two examples: 'I was *mad* when my brother got into my stuff and wrecked it—very mad—and then I was very *happy* when Peter put the stuff back into shape.' 'When I went horse-back riding by myself I was *glad* 'cause it was good to be away from my brothers and sisters, but I was *lonesome* all by myself 'cause there was no-one to talk to.'

Thus, we have two age-changes which take place at approximately the same time. Children of six to seven years identify emotion primarily by reference to the precipitating situation and link situations to emotions in a one-to-one fashion. Children of nine to eleven years identify emotion primarily by reference to an inner mental state and link situations to emotions in a one-to-more-than-one fashion. It is tempting to conclude that these two age-changes are related. One intriguing possibility is that synchronous emotions, particularly synchronous and conflicting emotions, are the engine for, rather than the product of, the acknowledgement of an inner mental component. Thus to the extent that the child responds with two distinct emotions to the same situation, he or she is forced to acknowledge that it is not the situation *per se* which elicits an emotion but his or her appraisal of it.

The child's dilemma is analogous to what we experience in viewing an ambiguous perceptual figure. When the stimulus remains constant we are forced to acknowledge the role played by our own perceptual processes. To the extent that the child observes himself displaying conflicting emotions in the same situation he will be forced to acknowledge the contribution to his own mental processes in the interpretation of that situation. The question of how a child's acknowledgement of the inner mental component of emotion comes about is a key issue in the development of knowledge about emotion, since it underpins many of the changes that we shall describe. Accordingly, we shall return to it again later for further discussion.

Strategies

In the previous section, we discussed the child's insight into the accuracy with which another's emotional state can be identified, an issue which introduces the notion of display rules regarding emotion. Children's understanding of these display rules was examined in a more direct fashion with questions such as the following, 'Imagine that you've had a quarrel with a friend. Could you act as if you were not really angry?' Most of the younger children agreed that such a pretence was possible, provided one acted in ways that would not normally be associated with a quarrel, by looking cheerful or smiling, for example. Thus, for the younger children, pretence amounted to a deliberately created mismatch between situation and response. The older children agreed with this but frequently added a further consideration. Instead of seeing pretence merely as a mismatch between situation and response, like the younger children, they acknowledged the possibility of a mismatch between one's behaviour and one's inner mental experience. Thus, some talked about how one's inner emotion might nonetheless reveal itself. 'I think that I try to hide it, but I think that it still goes through me,' as one child put it. Alternatively, they focussed on the redirection of the inner mental experience: 'You mustn't think about it any more, otherwise you'll be unhappy again.'

Saarni (1979) also looked at children's knowledge of display rules. Children of six, eight and ten years were told simple stories about situations in which a socially approved display rule might be invoked. For example, one story was about a child receiving a disappointing gift, in which case an appropriate display rule would be to smile despite the disappointment. Subjects were asked at the end of each story to pick out a photo depicting the appropriate facial expression and to justify their response. Across several types of stories, there was a clear age-change, with the ten-year-olds, in particular, offering more spontaneous display rules than either the six- or eight-year-olds. Saarni (1979) also tried to discover whether the children would offer display rules in response to the prompt question: 'Could he (she) look another way?' While this led to a marginal increase in the tendency of younger children to offer a display rule, its main effect was to tempt the oldest children to revoke the display rule they had initially offered and to say that the child in the story might look the way he or she actually felt. Thus younger children seemed to have little insight into the applicability of display rules as compared to the more knowledgeable ten-year-olds. Taylor and Harris (1980a) investigated knowledge of display rules in boys of seven to eight and ten to eleven years, using a similar format to Saarni (1979). They found a sharp increase with age in the spontaneous use of a display rule, confirming Saarni's results and they also found that the developmental trend was considerably retarded among maladjusted children of comparable ages to the normal group.

Thus for normal children, there is consistent evidence from three studies of a marked increase between six and eleven years in awareness of the possible discrepancy between felt emotion and outer display. Why should older children invoke display rules more often? One possibility is that younger children cannot conceive of a pretence at all. This explanation seems unlikely given the results of Harris *et al.* (in press): younger children know how to pretend by behaving differently from normal relative to a particular situation. A more plausible explanation is that by virtue of their acknowledgement of an inner mental component, the older children have a different notion of pretence. For them it appears to involve hiding one's inner mental state from others. The younger children regard emotion as a more or less publicly observable state, so that they may also regard pretence as a publicly observable deviation from normal behaviour. Certainly, the standard form of pretence among children of around six years is pretend play, which is a collective make-believe. In short, younger children may know what constitutes a deviation without knowing how to be deliberately devious.

Strategic control may be directed not simply at the outward display of emotion but at the experience itself. In order to probe children's knowledge of such strategies, we asked them whether one could change the way one really felt and if so, how. For example, if you had come back from a wonderful holiday and you were unhappy, could you do anything to stop feeling unhappy, or if you had just quarrelled with your friend, could you do anything to stop feeling angry? Several children in all three age-groups mentioned the simple strategy of altering the situation. For example, to make oneself happy again, one should call up one's friends and play with them. The use of mentalistic strategies on the other hand was found almost exclusively among children in the two older groups, particularly as a way of making oneself happy. A mentalistic strategy involved altering one's inner state without necessarily changing one's external situation. For example, one fifteen-year-old suggested, 'Think about something nice, happy memories.'

These age-changes in strategic intervention fit in with the age-changes noted for the identification of emotion. If the younger children think of emotion as a response which is elicited by an external situation, it is quite appropriate that their 'therapeutic' efforts should be directed at that situation. If, on the other hand, the older children think of emotion as being provoked by an external situation but also mediated by an inner mental state, it is reasonable that their therapeutic efforts be directed at both the provoking situation and/or the inner mental state.

The effects and the time-course of emotion

The arousal of emotion has an effect on other psychological processes. For example, happiness tends to encourage altruistic behaviour towards other people, while negative emotion tends to depress it (Underwood, Froming and Moore, 1977). Happiness also tends to promote performance on a cognitive task, while negative emotion impedes it (Masters, Barden and Ford, 1979). Finally, an emotional reaction, be it positive or negative, toward an episode makes it more memorable than a neutral reaction (Bartlett and Santrock, 1979). Our research shows that children know about these effects of emotion from a relatively young age. Thus, the majority of children in the six-year-old group studied by Harris *et al.* (in press) claimed that happiness would make one well disposed, and negative emotion badly disposed towards others. Similarly, the majority of the same age-group claimed that happiness would make it easier to do a drawing at school, while a negative emotion would make it harder. Finally, Taylor and Harris (1980b) found that the majority of the seven- to eight-year-old boys they questioned thought that children who reacted either with glee or anger to being capsised into the water, on a boat trip, would be more likely to remember the episode later than children who reacted neutrally.

Despite the early availability of knowledge about these effects of emotion, Harris *et al.* (in press) found that the youngest group were rarely able to offer any explanation for such links. For example, asked to explain why happiness might help one to draw better, most of the youngest children either said that they didn't know or failed to make any reply. In contrast, many of the older children explained that happiness would help one to fantasise while a negative emotion would be distracting. Thus, the younger children but not the older children again tended to eschew references to inner mental events in their 'theorising' about emotion.

An emotional reaction, and its associated effects, has a fairly uniform time-course: it wanes with temporal distance from the eliciting situation. Taylor and Harris (1980b) examined whether seven- to eight- and ten- to eleven-year-old boys would know about this decline. They showed subjects a set of pictures depicting a boy who had just been beaten in a fight, and the same boy at various points after the fight—at morning assembly, at lunch, at afternoon break and so forth. The pictures were lined up in a row and the child's task was to pick an appropriate facial expression (from a set of six) to go with each picture. Taylor and Harris (1980b) found that boys in both age-groups produced a similar pattern: a strongly negative facial expression was deemed appropriate just after the fight, but as the day wore on, increasingly neutral or even positive facial expressions were chosen.

In a follow-up question, Taylor and Harris (1980b) described a more complicated episode: two boys, Tom and Bill had both been turned down for the football team; Tom was very, very upset because football is the only sport he can play, but Bill was less upset because he can try for another sport. As in the previous question, a set of pictures was employed to depict the boys mentioned in the episode at various points thereafter: taking off their football clothes, eating lunch, having tea and so forth. Again, subjects were asked to pick out a facial expression for each picture in the set, once for Bill and once for Tom. The results showed that each age group knew that the boys' emotional reaction would decline over time. Moreover, they also knew that at each subsequent point in time, Tom's reaction would be more negative than Bill's.

One additional finding was somewhat unexpected. The group of normal boys aged ten to eleven years produced a fairly smooth downward slope for the emotional reaction of Tom and Bill. In contrast, the groups of normal boys aged seven to eight years and also both groups of maladjusted boys produced slopes, which declined overall, but which contained one noticeable 'bump'. The fourth picture in the series depicted Tom and Bill brushing their teeth before bedtime, and all three groups selected a relatively negative facial expression to go with this picture, more negative than the preceding picture showing Tom and Bill having tea. Why should there be this clear departure from the overall decline in negative effect? Two possibilities suggest themselves. First, it could be that bedtime is thought of as a time for introspection, for reviewing the events of the day so that the failure to get into the team is recalled and the emotion which is associated with it is reviewed. Second, and more simply, it could be that brushing one's teeth and/or going to bed are regarded as unpleasant, so that a negative facial expression is called for. All of the results presented so far would favour the second interpretation rather than the first. Specifically, the less mature child is likely to think of emotion as tied to a given situation so that bedtime is associated with a particular emotional reaction. He is not likely to think of emotion in mentalistic terms such that a particular time of day is likely to permit one to dwell on some emotion, quite independent of the situation which first gave rise to it.

Some recent research carried out in Amsterdam examined this issue more directly (van Eck, 1980; Olthof, van Eck and Meerum Terwogt, 1980). Based on the findings of Harris *et al.* (in press), it was anticipated that six-year-olds would expect one's emotional state to be dictated by the current situation, at least where that situation was emotionally charged. In contrast, since older children conceive of emotion as a mental state which is not tied to a specific situation, they would be more likely to regard one's emotional state as a melange of reactions, both to current and past situations.

To check these predictions, subjects were asked to indicate how they would feel in a target situation by choosing a schematic facial expression; the target situation was preceded by one of two other situations, either an emotionally neutral situation in the control condition or an emotionally coloured situation in the experimental condition. It was predicted that eleven-year-olds, particularly those in the experimental condition, would be influenced by the initial situation in making a choice of facial expression for the ensuing target situation, whereas the six-year-olds would choose a facial expression to correspond to the target situation regardless of the affective colour of the initial situation. For example, in choosing a facial expression appropriate for doing a jig-saw puzzle in their bedroom, older children would be more likely than younger children to be influenced by the knowledge that the preceding situation involved a reprimand from their mother. The results provided strong support for these predictions. The younger children were dominated by the target situation in making their choice of facial expression to a much greater extent than the older children; moreover, as expected, this age-change was especially marked for the experimental condition, where the initial situation was emotionally coloured and therefore likely to impinge on subsequent encounters.

These findings suggest that the deviation from a smooth decline in negative affect, which was observed by Taylor and Harris (1980b), is probably due to the assumption of the younger children that emotion is dictated by the current situation, in this case the negative affect associated with going to bed. More generally, the findings provide clear support for a prediction derived from the initial interview study of Harris *et al.* (in press) that older children, given their mentalistic conception of emotion, would be more likely than younger children to imagine the transfer of an emotional reaction into a later situation having a different emotional valence.

Nevertheless, the findings obtained by Taylor and Harris (1980b), by van Eck (1980), and by Olthof *et al.* (1980) leave several important questions unanswered. Chief among these is the issue of what we might dub 'the arithmetic of emotion'. To the extent that the older child acknowledges that an earlier emotional reaction influences a later reaction, how exactly is this influence conceptualised? One simple possibility is that emotion is conceived along a scale running from very negative, through neutral, to very positive. The current emotional state of an individual might then be regarded as the average of the two points on that scale, one point being the individual's 'base-line' state, that is, the state he brings to a particular situation, and the second point being specified by his emotional reaction to that particular situation itself. An alternative arithmetic would involve deletion and replacement. More specifically, an individual's emotional state might be regarded as being equivalent to either that point on the scale which he brings to a particular situation, or alternatively equivalent to that point on the scale elicited by the particular situation, whichever point on the scale constitutes a greater deviation from neutral. Thus an individual's emotional state would be a direct function of his reaction to some previous situation, until he encountered a situation with an emotional colouring sufficiently extreme to delete and replace that prior reaction. Of course, given the existence of some type of endogenous habituation, the chances of deletion and replacement would increase over time.

The issue of emotional arithmetic resembles in many ways the questions raised by Anderson and his colleagues (Anderson, 1978) in their research on so-called cognitive algebra. Anderson has asked how the human subject, given two or more pieces of information upon which to make a judgement, integrates those pieces of information so as to reach that judgement. For example, if the subject knows that a particular person has a given amount of ability and makes a given amount of effort, how does the subject combine those two pieces of information so as to estimate the person's achievement? Alternatively, if a person is both warm and practical, how likely is he to be judged as friendly? Although Anderson (1978) has claimed that subjects frequently combine two pieces of information by averaging their respective values, Harris and Hampson (1980) have obtained support for the use of a deletion and replacement rule in judging another's personality. Whatever the generality of the averaging rule, it is clear that the general method of attack outlined by Anderson (1978) can be addressed to the question of emotional arithmetic.

One final comment on the issue of emotional arithmetic also deserves to be made. Hitherto, I have concentrated on the child's judgement about how two emotional reactions are integrated. An equally important area for research concerns, not the child's judgement, but the actual process of integration. Recent research on the microstructure of facial expression suggests that blends of more than one basic facial expression are frequently found in adults (Eckman and Oster, 1979). It is not clear at present how such blends are generated. Should they be seen as one type of averaging across two disparate facial expressions, or alternatively as the simultaneous activation of two facial expressions? Whatever the answer to this question, the existence of such blends indicates that a pure form of the deletion and replacement model, although a potentially viable model for the way in which emotional integration is judged to take place, particularly among six-year-olds, cannot be a fully accurate model of the way that emotional integration actually does take place.

The above remarks have indicated the direction in which further work on the child's knowledge of emotion might proceed. In the next section, a brief overview of the picture so far obtained will be given. Finally, the factors which may alter the child's concept of emotion are discussed.

General Conclusions

The results that we have obtained, and also the results obtained by other investigators, are compatible with the claim that younger children have a relatively simple S-R theory of emotion in which the S stands for various frequently occurring situations such as receiving a gift, or having a toy removed, and the R refers to a set of non-mental responses, including facial expressions, and various behavioural and physiological reactions. The older children insert an extra term into this simple theory, namely an inner mental experience; the addition of this mental component leads the older children to somewhat different conclusions regarding the identification, regulation and effects of emotion.

The older children regard the identification of another's emotion as more problematic since it may or may not be revealed in overt behaviour. Admittedly, the younger children can conceive of situations where one might be unaware of another's emotion, but only because of the location or inattentiveness of the observer, not the opacity of the observed. Moreover, for the older children emotion is less closely linked in a one-to-one fashion with a particular eliciting situation. First, other psychological processes, particularly one's thought process, can redirect the course of an emotional experience; second, certain situations may simultaneously elicit more than one emotion, and third, one's emotional reaction to a current situation may be coloured by a previously aroused emotion. Finally, although younger children know the effects of emotion on cognitive and social dispositions, it is only the older children who interpret these effects in mentalistic terms.

The increasing attentiveness of older children to inner psychological processes is not, it should be stressed, peculiar to the child's understanding of emotion. Livesley and Bromley (1973) asked children of seven to fifteen years to write a free description of themselves and a range of other people. The results indicated that the proportion of psychological statements increased markedly between seven and a half and eight and a half years. The seven-year-olds tended to concentrate on non-psychological qualities such as appearances and possessions, although they had been instructed not to.

A similar result was obtained by Flapan (1968) who presented six- to twelve-year-old children with a filmed interaction to describe and interpret. The greatest age-changes occurred in the age-interval between six and nine years and typically involved a shift away from interpretation based on situational factors to interpretations based on psychological factors including thoughts, feelings and perceptions of others.

How are we to explain the child's increasingly mentalistic conception of emotion? I believe that there are at least three plausible developmental models; to sharpen the difference between these three models, I shall refer to them as the solipsistic, the behaviourist, and the sociocentric models.

Three models for developmental change

The solipsistic model assumes that the child's knowledge about emotion is primarily based on self-observation. At first, the child would notice certain correlations between situations on the one hand and his behavioural and physiological reactions on the other. Gradually the child might also become aware of certain conscious states that accompany such reactions. As noted earlier, such introspective awareness might be facilitated by those situations which provoke conflicting emotions. Alternatively, introspective awareness might be facilitated to the extent that the child found himself brooding about some past situation, and possibly still displaying some of the behavioural and physiological reactions. In the absence of the situation itself, the child might be increasingly inclined to attribute such reactions, not to the original situation but to his ensuing mental state. According to the solipsistic model, then, the shift from an S-R model to a more mentalistic model of emotion is brought about by the child's observation that his own reactions are specified more accurately by his actual or supposed mental states than by the particular situation that he is in.

The behaviouristic model is similar in certain respects to the solipsistic model. It supposes that the child is actively engaged in explaining behaviour. However, it differs from the solipsistic model in stressing that the primary source of data is the behaviour of other people rather than the child's own behaviour. We may suppose that the child initially comes to notice certain correlations between particular situations and the reactions of other people to those situations. Gradually, the child might notice that such reactions occur in the absence of a provoking situation or well after it is over. For example, his father continues to display anger long after the school report has been opened, or his younger brother continues to look fearful long after the large dog has disappeared. In such cases, the child might be increasingly tempted to attribute reactions not to the eliciting situation as such but to some persisting mental state.

The sociocentric model focusses on the community, particularly the verbal community, as a source of data or ideas about emotion. The verbal community will offer the child explanations of his or her own behaviour and that of others in terms of verbal references to emotion. At first, the child might be led to construe such remarks as referring to the non-mental accompaniments of emotion, the behavioural and physiological reactions that he or she might be displaying, or the precipitating situation. Gradually, however, the child would encounter such references being made in the absence of any overt reactions and away from the situation which may have given rise to the emotion. Thus a parent might explain some piece of behaviour to the child in terms of his or her ongoing anxiety or sadness, even though the child might be unaware of the situation that provoked it, and unaware of any overt signs of anxiety or sadness in the parent. Similarly, adults might attribute emotion to the child on the basis of some previous situation that the child was in or on the basis of subtle behavioural indices of which the child might be unaware. In this way, the verbal community could, as Skinner (1971) has suggested, draw the child's attention to the inner mental aspect of emotion and such references might occur in the absence of situational and behavioural accompaniments to that mental component. Gradually, then, under the teaching of the verbal community, the child's conception of emotion would focus on its mental aspect.

How can we distinguish between these various models? I believe that there are two sources of evidence that will help. On the one hand, we may examine the extent to which the three models allow us to explain other aspects of the child's developing knowledge as a psychologist. Such evidence is, however, not definitive since it is quite feasible that the child's understanding of different domains of psychological knowledge proceeds in different ways. The second source of evidence is cross-cultural observation. Regrettably very few cross-cultural studies of emotional development have ever been carried out. Below, I shall indicate how such evidence might, in principle, throw light on the developmental models described.

Taking up the developmental evidence first, we may note that although the child begins to adopt a more mentalistic interpretation of both emotion and personality at approximately seven to eight years, there is evidence of much more precocious understanding of mental states in other domains. Perhaps the clearest evidence comes from studies on the child's understanding of visual perception. Flavell, Flavell, Green and Wilcox (1980) found that most of the four-and-a-half-year-olds they tested knew that the clarity with which an object can be seen depends on the distance of the observer from the object. The ability to judge whether an object would be visible or occluded for a particular observer emerges at an even earlier age, by approximately two and a half to three and a half years (Flavell, Shipstead and Croft, 1978).

If we ask how the child has come to know these psychological facts at such a young age, it seems unlikely that it can be explained in terms of explicit verbal instruction from adults. Conceivably, adults might have offered some indirect instruction, for example, by calling the child closer in order to look at something. However, such experiences seem unlikely to help the child grasp the relationship between clarity and distance, unless the object actually does become clearer as the child moves toward it. This amounts to saying, in line with the solipsistic model, that the child can introspect about his mental states and can detect an inverse correlation between clarity and distance.

The two other models, the behaviouristic and the sociocentric models do not really offer a plausible explanation of such precocious knowledge. For example, it seems unlikely that the child could work out the relationship between distance and clarity by simply watching other people's behaviour. Equally, it is not clear how the utterances of the verbal community could help the child, unless, as we saw above, he has some understanding based on his own experience with which to interpret those utterances.

The solipsistic model also suggests an explanation for the precocity of the child's understanding of visual perception relative to other domains. Psychological states are differently available to consciousness, so that, for example, we are typically unaware of the mental processes involved in mnemonic association but we are easily aware of what we are looking at and whether or not we can see it clearly or with difficulty. In line with these observations, the developmental evidence indicates that although the two- to four-year-old shows insight into the effects of distance and occlusion on visibility (Flavell, *et al.,* 1980; Flavell *et al.,* 1978) the development of understanding about memory retrieval by means of association (Flavell and Wellman, 1977) emerges much later.

Thus, the solipsistic model allows us to explain how the child comes to understand certain basic facts about visual perception which it would be difficult to infer from other people's behaviour or the utterances of the verbal community. If we also assume that certain mental states are differentially available to consciousness, we can explain why the child comes to grasp certain psychological facts more rapidly than others. The solipsistic model provides, therefore, an attractive explanation of the shift to a mentalistic conception of emotion because of the way in which such a model can be plausibly extended to other psychological domains.

Nevertheless, as noted above, it might be argued that knowledge about emotion is not necessarily acquired in the same way as knowledge about visual perception or memory retrieval. Indeed, such an argument becomes especially plausible when it is borne in mind that the situations which elicit emotion, the rules for the display of emotion, the way in which emotion is talked about and, possibly, the way in which emotion is experienced all show marked cross-cultural variation. Thus emotional states may not offer the same regularities to conscious awareness as, for example, perceptual states. In order to gain some appreciation of the range of cross-cultural variation, we may examine two recent ethnographies which present a striking contrast.

Rosaldo (1980) describes a small settlement of Ilingots who inhabit a forested area about 100 miles north of Manila in the Philippines. The

Ilingots are hunters and horticulturalists with no dependence for subsistence goods on trade. About 1,500 miles to the south-west, across the South China Sea in the tropical rain forests of Peninsular Malaysia, live the Chewong, described by Howell (1981) as a small aboriginal group of shifting cultivators and hunter-gatherers. The two groups are quite similar, therefore, in terms of their ecology and basic economy.

The Ilingots were, but so far as is known are no longer, headhunters. Indeed, headhunting appears to have been a central aspect of Ilingot culture until the early 1970s, when encroachments by the outside world in the twin forms of military government and missionary zeal led to the abondonment of the practice. Rossaldo (1980) interprets head-hunting in terms of a wider set of Ilingot attitudes towards emotion and towards anger in particular.

For the Ilingot, to *si liget,* or 'have anger' connotes not simply the existence of a fleeting mental state but a more enduring potentiality. *Liget* or anger is associated with potency, energy, and vitality. Although for the Ilingot, anger is provoked as it is among us, by insults and disappointments, such incidents serve almost as an incidental justifica-tion for, rather than the true provocation of, the anger which leads to headhunting. *Liget* and the vitality which goes with it is primarily associated with men, and with young unmarried men in particular.

Headhunting is organised in terms of a collaboration between two mutually dependent groups. On the one hand, young bachelors are thought to have the necessary *liget,* the angry vitality, which turns men into killers. On the other hand, they are thought to lack the knowledge to plan and organise a raid. This they can acquire under the guidance of their elders who have taken heads before them. Reciprocally, they can infuse their elders once again with the lost vitality of their youth, as the two age-groups collaborate on a successful raid, in which the final act of killing constitutes a focus and a potential outlet for *liget.* These brief remarks can only provide a hint of the cultural pattern than Rosaldo (1980) claims to have discerned. Nevertheless, they indicate that *liget* occupies a central role in Ilingot culture, given its association with the activity of headhunting. Indeed, the community celebrates those who possess *liget* and the most dramatic manifestation of that *liget,* the successful headhunting raid.

The Chewong provide an example of a culture where most forms of emotional display are suppressed. Howell (1981) notes that in addition to their having an impoverished vocabulary for referring to inner states, 'They rarely use gestures of any kind, and their faces register little change as they speak and listen. The outsider is constantly struck by their restrained behaviour, even at meetings and partings, and the fact that they seem never to "lose control".' Even more important for the contrast with the Ilingot, is the constant use by the Chewong of rules, typically associated with a single word, for the suppression of various emotional states. For example, *punen* is associated with several rules, one being that a pleasurable event, such as a good meal at the end of a day's hunting, must not be anticipated verbally. *Punen* is used to refer both to the actual transgression, that is, verbal anticipation, and also to the consequences of transgression, which typically involve some super-natural intervention that can lead to disease or mishap. Similarly, *tola* is to show disrespect, by being overly intimate or by laughing and the offending person will suffer swellings of the hips and lower abdomen.

Howell (1981) describes how adults use these words as a means of socialisation. If, for example, a child is becoming boisterous, an adult might rebuke him or her by calling out *tola!* For the Chewong, the display of emotion appears to be not an occasion for celebration but fraught with danger. They refer less to the mental states which accompany emotion and its display than to the need for emotional suppression, on pain of disease and misfortune.

We might sum up the difference between the Ilingot and the Chewong by saying that the Ilingot celebrate the display of emotion while the Chewong admire its suppression. However, this is something of an over-simplification. Howell (1981) acknowledges one cause of pride among adult Chewong: a fearful, shy child. Apparently, fear and shyness are not suppressed but positively encouraged by adults who taunt children with tales of a Malay who might come to take them away, or a tiger who is waiting for them. On the other hand, although Rosaldo (1980) does not discuss the matter in detail, it is the fearful young man who is taunted by the Ilingot. Thus the Ilingot and the Chewong differ not so much in their emphasis on suppression versus display, but in the nature of the emotions that they select for suppression and display. For the Ilingot, passion and particularly anger is displayed and fear suppressed; for the Chewong, the reverse appears to be true.

What impact might such cultural variation have on the developing child's understanding of emotion in these two cultures? Needless to say, no systematic evidence is available. However, on the basis of the three models described earlier we would be led to make certain mutually exclusive predictions. The solipsistic model, it will be recalled, assumes that the child uses his own psychological states as the primary data for reaching conclusions about emotion. To the extent that the Chewong and Ilingot differ only in their display rules, children within these two cultures ought to acquire a mentalistic conception of emotion at approximately the same rate. Presumably in both cultures children would experience anger and fear, however they might be expected to handle the display of those emotions. Moreover, they might experience both emotions in the same situation or either emotion after the pre-cipitating situation has disappeared. Thus we would expect the child's understanding of both emotions to develop at approximately the same rate in each culture. The one possible source of variation concerns the child's differential experience of a mismatch between inner state and outer display in the two cultures. Among the Ilingot such a mismatch would be more frequent for fear than anger, while the reverse would be the case among the Chewong. Accordingly, we might also expect Ilingot children to attain a mentalistic conception of fear in advance of anger, while the reverse order would hold for the Chewong.

The behaviouristic model assumes that the child uses other people's behaviour as the primary data source for constructing a theory of emotion. To the extent that the child is led to adopt a mentalistic theory as a result of seeing emotional reactions outside of the original precipitating situation, we would expect display rules to have a marked impact on the child's conclusions. Among the Ilingot, the child would frequently see anger being displayed long after the original provoking circumstances were over, or even in the absence of any true provocation. In contrast, among the Chewong the child would be confronted with fearful reactions to animals and other taboo objects apparently out of all proportion to the existing situation. Thus the Ilingot child would arrive at a mentalistic conception of emotion for anger before arriving at the same conception for fear, whereas the Chewong child would progress in the reverse order. These two predictions are, of course, precisely contrary to the possibilities outlined above regarding the impact of display rules on a child operating according to the solipsistic model.

What predictions would the sociocentric model make? At first glance, it might appear that it would make predictions similar to those of the behaviourist model. Specifically, it would draw the child's attention to those occasions in which emotion was being displayed outside of the precipitating situation. This would be particularly true for anger among the Ilingot and for fear among the Chewong. However, it will be recalled that the sociocentric model explained the acquisition of a mentalistic conception of emotion by postulating that the child would be exposed to references to emotion in the absence of both a precipitating situation and behavioural indices of the emotion itself. Only in this fashion, could the child come to regard emotion words as referring to an inner mental component, as opposed to the situational factors and behavioural and physiological reactions that normally but not always accompany such inner mental states. An examination of the ethnographies of Howell (1981) and Rosaldo (1980) suggests that emotion words in these cultures may never acquire such a purely mentalistic flavour. Indeed, Leff (1977) has presented evidence suggesting that Indo-European languages may be distinctive in making reference to the cognitive experience of emotion, rather than to behavioural or physiological reactions. To the extent that the languages of the Ilingot and the Chewong refer not to inner mental states but to visible indices of emotion, we would expect the children in both of these cultures to be slow to adopt a mentalistic theory of emotion with regard to either anger or fear.

In conclusion, we have presented evidence for a change in the way that children—or at least children in England and Holland—conceive of emotion. Somewhere between six and eleven years, such children adopt a mentalistic conception of emotion. However, as in other areas of developmental psychology it is considerably easier to describe the changes which occur than to establish how they are brought about. An examination of two markedly different cultures suggests that the psychologist may have to collaborate with the anthropologist in order to find out how such a change is brought about and indeed whether it occurs at all outside of the Indo-European linguistic community.

References

The authors would like to thank Charlotte Hardman and Paul Heelas for their comments on the manuscript of this chapter, and for calling their attention to the ethnographic data.

Anderson, N., 'Cognitive algebra: integration theory applied to social attribution', in L. Berkowitz (ed.) *Cognitive Theories in Social Psychology*, New York, Academic Press, 1978.

Bartlett, J. C., and Santrock, J. W., 'Affect dependent episodic memory in young children', *Child Development*, 1979, *50*, 513-8.

Borke, H., 'Interpersonal perception of young children: egocentrism or empathy?', *Developmental Psychology*, 1971, *5*, 263-9.

Cannon, W. B., *Bodily Changes in Pain, Hunger, Fear and Rage*, 2nd edn., New York, Appleton, 1929.

Eck, O. van, 'Ontwikkeling van kognitie over emotie', Internal report, Free University, Amsterdam, 1980.

Ekman, P., and Oster, H., 'Facial expression of emotion', *Annual Review of Psychology*, 1979, *30*, 527-54.

Flapan, D., *Children's Understanding of Social Interaction*, New York, Teacher's College Press, 1968.

Flavell, J. H., Flavell, E. R., Green, F. L., and Wilcox, S. A., 'Young children's knowledge about visual perception: effects of observer distance from target on perceptual clarity of target', *Developmental Psychology*, 1980, *16*, 10-2.

Flavell, J. H., Shipstead, S. G., and Croft, K., 'Young children's knowledge about visual perception: hiding objects from others', *Child Development*, 1978, *49*, 1208-11.

Flavell, J. H., and Wellman, H., 'Metamemory', in R. V. Hail and J. W. Hagen (eds.) *Perspectives on the Development of Memory and Cognition*, Lawrence Erlbaum Associates, 1977.

Freud, S., *Ego and Mechanisms of Defence*, London, Hogarth, 1937.

Harris, P. L., 'Developmental aspects of children's memory', in M. M. Gruneberg and P. Morris (eds.) *Aspects of Memory*, London, Methuen, 1978.

Harris, P. L., and Hampson, S. E., 'Processing information within implicit personality theory', *British Journal of Social and Clinical Psychology*, 1980, *19*, 235-42.

Harris, P. L., Olthof, T., and Meerum Terwogt, M., 'Children's knowledge of emotion', *Journal of Child Psychology and Psychiatry*, in press.

Harter, S., 'Children's understanding of multiple emotions: a cognitive developmental approach', *Address to the Ninth Annual Symposium of the Jean Piaget Society*, May 31-June 2, 1979, Philadelphia, Pennsylvania.

Howell, S., 'Rules not words', in P. Heelas and A. Lock (eds.) *Indigenous Psychologies*, London, Academic Press, 1981.

James, W., *The Principles of Psychology*, New York, Holt, 1980.

Leff, J., 'The cross-cultural study of emotions', *Culture Medicine and Psychiatry*, 1977, *1*, 317-50.

Livesley, W., J., and Bromley, D. B., *Person Perception in Childhood and Adolescence*, London, Wiley, 1973.

Masters, J. C., Barden, R. C., and Ford, M. E., 'Affective states, expressive behaviour, and learning in children', *Journal of Personality and Social Psychology*, 1979, *37*, 380-90.

Olthof, T., Eck, O. van, and Meerum Terwogt, M., 'Assessment of children's knowledge of emotion without requiring active language use', Internal report, Free University, Amsterdam, 1980.

Rosaldo, M. Z., *Knowledge and Passion*, Cambridge, Cambridge University Press, 1980.

Saarni, C., 'Children's understanding of display rules for expressive behaviour', *Developmental Psychology*, 1979, *15*, 424-9.

Schachter, S., 'Cognition and peripheralist-centralist controversies in motivation and emotion', in M. S. Gazzaniga and C. Blakemore (eds.) *Handbook of Psychobiology*, London, Academic Press, 1975.

Skinner, B. F., *Beyond Freedom and Dignity*, New York, Knopf, 1971.

Taylor, D., and Harris, P. L., 'Knowledge of control strategies for emotion among normal and emotionally-maladjusted boys', Internal report, Department of Social Psychology, London School of Economics, 1980a.

Taylor, D., and Harris, P. L., 'Knowledge of the relations between emotion and memory in normal and emotionally-maladjusted boys', Internal report, Department of Social Psychology, London School of Economics, 1980b.

Underwood, B., Froming, W. J., and Moore, B. S., 'Mood, attention and altruism: a search for mediating variables', *Developmental Psychology*, 1977, *13*, 541-2.

PART IV

SOCIAL COGNITION AND INTELLECT

10 Cognitive tasks as interactional settings

Irene Nielson and Julie Dockrell

Introduction

It is generally accepted that the two essential ingredients of a theory of development are a clear description of *what* is developing backed by an appropriate understanding of *how* it is developing (Flavell and Wohlwill, 1969). The former ingredient is viewed as being logically prior to the latter insofar as it constrains the set of possible descriptions of the latter. Thus, despite a sympathy with the criticism that acceptance of the above logic can lead to an over-static view of the nature of development (McCall, 1977), this chapter wil focus predominantly on the *what* of development. Specifically it is concerned with the Piagetian model of cognitive development, and the thorny problems surrounding the diagnosis of cognitive structures (for example, Dasen, 1977). In particular, the chapter focuses on recent claims that neglect of the features of the interactional setting in which the child's knowledge is assessed in traditional Piagetian research has led to an underestimation of the child's—particularly the pre-schooler's cognitive abilities. Donaldson (1978) has, in fact, suggested that the achievements of the concrete operational stage are as much a reflection of the child's increasing independence from features of the interactional setting as they are evidence of the development of a logical competence.

Claims that the Piagetian tasks underestimate the child's cognitive abilities are not new (Braine, 1959, 1962; Gruen, 1966; Brainerd, 1973). Since the publication of Piaget's original works in English (Piaget, 1950), research interest has focused on the young school-aged child—the concrete operational stage of development. Paradoxically the methods used by Piaget to investigate development during this period place considerable language production/comprehension demands on the child. It would thus have been surprising if theorists had not attempted to argue that such methods lead to an underestimation of the child's cognitive structures, by failing to offer a paradigm within which task difficulty as a function of linguistic immaturity is differentiated from that which is a function of conceptual immaturity. Numerous investigations and accusations of Type II errors in Piagetian research have stemmed from this point since its original statement and investigation by Braine (1959), though none would appear to have yielded unambiguous findings (Miller, 1976).

Similarly, given that the tasks used by Piaget to examine the child's cognitive structures often require the child to possess certain other skills before success in the task is assured (Carey, 1974), failure to perform appropriately in such tasks has likewise been attributed to variables other than those of interest to Piaget. Insofar as tasks like the conservation task, as Gelman (1969) puts it, 'are at a minimum a task for logical capacity, the control of attention, correct semantics and estimation skills' then processing limitations such as memory capacity (Bryant, 1974) or task inappropriate perceptual strategies (Mehler and Bever, 1967) may lead to the child failing to reveal his true cognitive competence in performance. Lack of due consideration of such accessory skills has been argued to result in an underestimation of the young child's cognitive abilities—a prevalence of Type II errors. Such research has also, unfortunately, proved to be inconclusive—with failures to replicate results (Achenback, 1969; LaPointe and O'Donnell, 1974) and alternative explanations of 'proofs' of the young child's logical competence (McGonigle and Chalmers, 1977; Katz and Berlin, 1976) hampering any attempt at substantive modification of the Piagetian edifice. Few attempts have been made to generate an alternative structure and paradigm for developmental research from such findings, perhaps because much of the research in this area appears to have been primarily motivated by questions of *when* children have such and such an ability with implicit acceptance of the Piagetian description of *what* is developing.

Against this background of nearly two decades of inconclusive research into the probability and significance of Type II errors in Piagetian research, the renewed and enthusiastic attention paid to this question since the publication of Donaldson's small but seminal book *Children's Minds,* at first glance, seems surprising. This book, and supporting research papers such as that of Rose and Blank (1974), may be seen as delineating a hitherto neglected source of Type II errors in Piagetian research methodology, namely the neglect within this paradigm to consider problem-solving situations as interactions between people. Failure to consider the social, inter-personal demands of such contexts has thus been seen to lead to failure to appreciate that uncertainty as to the rules of the game, on the child's part, may lead him to perform well below his level of cognitive competence with consequent under-estimation of his cognitive abilities.

A second point of emphasis is the distinction between utterance meaning and speaker's meaning (for example, Grice, 1968), with the latter being viewed as the primary concern of adult and child alike in any communicative act. Thus Type II errors are now no longer viewed as resulting from lexical difficulty *per se* but rather from the processes of interpretation—linguistic, cognitive, social, contextual—that the child brings to bear in determining the meaning of the task context and what therefore is expected of him. In any cognitive task that involves verbal interaction, the child is seen as actively seeking to match the speaker's utterance to the ongoing activity in such a way as to reconstruct the intended meaning of the speaker within the extra linguistic context. Inappropriate matching through over-reliance on contextual information is seen to lead the child to misinterpret the speaker's intentions and consequently to fail to perform appropriately in that task.

However, current concern with how the test situation as a whole affects the child's performance in a given 'cognitive task' should probably not be viewed as simply as renewed interest in refining developmental methodology—its intent being solely to add a new class of interactional variables to the accessory variables that must be controlled in the investigation and diagnosis of cognitive structures. Behind the methodological issues lie the more fundamental conceptual issues. If, as the work of Donaldson and her co-workers suggest, the pre-school child is much more cognitively competent than we supposed, then we are faced with the problem of defining the nature of that competence and in determining whether a quantitative or qualitative difference exists between that competence and that required for success in the traditional Piagetian tasks.

A major question is whether it is possible to reject the Piagetian methodology that led to the initial picture of incompetence in the pre-schooler, while at the same time retaining Piagetian descriptions of the nature of the competence required for success in the traditional tasks and applying that model to the description of the competence that underlies successful performance in the modified tasks. Alternatively, the rejection of the methodology may be seen not only to provoke a need to develop new, more ecologically valid, situations in which to assess the child's reasoning powers but also to necessitate a fundamental reconstruction of our models of children's thinking processes. Acknowledgement that the pre-schooler may be more cognitively competent than hitherto suspected, does not negate the need to explain the origins of that competence and the differences between the pre-schooler and school-aged child. Explanations of such differences may simply have to be sought elsewhere. However, such differences now become harder to define, not because they do not exist, but rather because of a lack of appropriate research tools at our disposal with which to investigate them and a noticeable lack of any conceptual framework within which to interpret them. To acknowledge cognitive competence in the pre-schooler, is to acknowledge that cognitive structures must not be defined in terms of the ability to express the operations of such structures verbally and that cognitive development is in some sense independent of language. Certainly the use of language as a tool to probe the child's thinking is recognised as extremely problematic and the more so the younger the child. However, total exclusion of language variables, as in the employment of non-verbal conditioning techniques to explore cognitive function (Braine, 1962), may run the risk of obliterating differences in the various levels at which a concept is understood, confusing behavioural representation with conceptual representation (Piaget, 1955; Campbell, 1979). Further, as Campbell (personal communication) points out, the use of such techniques does not of itself guarantee that the task presented corresponds to the task perceived.

Despite the importance of the aforementioned conceptual issues, they have received little attention. In general, the argument that the child's failure in many Piagetian tasks at a certain stage of development reflects a failure of understanding rather than of reasoning, has received widespread acceptance, the theoretical implication of doing so being restricted to the conclusion that young children are simply brighter than we have hitherto believed.

In this chapter, then, we shall seek to explore in detail the validity of the methodological claim and the theoretical consequences of accepting it. The first section is primarily concerned with presentation of the evidence—empirical and theoretical—in support of the methodological claim. The second section is devoted to an evaluation of this evidence and to consideration of its theoretical consequences.

Failure of understanding as a source of Type II errors in studies of children's thinking

One of the major problems in the past that faced theorists interested in demonstrating that difficulty in the Piagetian tasks of cognitive function stemmed more from linguistic as opposed to cognitive confusion on the part of the child, was the fact that the child appeared capable of using and interpreting the crucial words that were argued to be causing him difficulty with great ease in other tasks (Inhelder, Sinclair and Bovet, 1974). Such evidence would appear to support the argument that the child's difficulty in the Piagetian tasks is primarily a cognitive rather than linguistic one. Such a conclusion, however, is only warranted if comprehension in one context implies comprehension in all contexts, that is that clear evidence of understanding in one context shows that the child has acquired a stable meaning for the expression concerned. Recent evidence, however, indicates that during the process of language acquisition, it is common at certain times in the development of word-meaning for the child's understanding of a given term to vary across contexts. For example, that the child's interpretation of the locatives in/on/under is constrained at certain points by the canonical relationships of the objects he is required to manipulate, is well documented (Wilcox and Palermo, 1974; Hoogenraad, Grieve, Baldwin and Campbell, 1978). Similarly, Gordon (1977) offers fascinating data which suggests that children's interpretation of 'more' may vary as a function of the number of feature differences between the two sets of objects being compared.

Such work indicates that apparent understanding of word-meaning in one context cannot be interpreted as directly indicating that the child will not experience problems in interpreting the appropriate meaning of that word in another context. Likewise, apparent understanding of word-meaning in a given context can be generated where none exists, through the context being highly specific as to the number of alternative responses the child can make (Schatz, 1978), or through a 'natural response bias' of the child happening to correlate with the adult's verbal instructions (cf. Carey, 1978; Grieve and Stanley, 1980). Furthermore, insofar as word-meanings develop, understanding of a word in one context can simply reflect the fact that the level of development of word-meaning to date is appropriate to the demands of that context but not to another. Uncertainty as to word-meaning in combination with the child's characteristic reluctance to admit lack of comprehension (Grieve and Stanley, 1980; Ironsmith and Whitehurst,

1978), may lead to the use of various strategies such as focusing on non-linguistic elements, in order to interpret those linguistic structures they do not understand.

Even adult interpretation of word-meaning does not occur in isolation from the normal rules of discourse. Expectations as to speaker's intentions and knowledge of the state of world affairs (be they present or absent) also influences the interpretation of the meaning of an utterance by the adult (Bransford and McCarrell, 1972; Ziff, 1972). However, the child's use of such sources of information in the interpretation of speaker's meaning is likely to be more pervasive than that of the adult, as is the relative value given to such information in the process of interpretation, given the heuristic value of such strategies in the process of language acquisition (Macnamara, 1972).

That such sources of information as to speaker's meaning are greatly valued by the child and do appear capable of dominating textual analysis of word-meaning, has been demonstrated in several studies to date; in the case of quantifiers (Donaldson and Lloyd, 1974; Donaldson and McGarrigle, 1974), in the case of relational terms (Donaldson and Balfour, 1968; Carey, 1976), and in the case of prepositions (Clark, 1973; Hoogenraad, Grieve, Baldwin and Campbell, 1978).

In their study on quantifiers Donaldson and Lloyd, for example, found that the child's interpretation of the meaning of the quantifier 'all' was dominated by an expectation that the sets of objects under discussion should be paired with each other. In this study children were asked to judge the truth or falsity of two statements. Statement A 'All the cars are in the garage' and Statement B 'All the garages have cars in them.' The study was so designed that if Statement A was true, Statement B was false and *vice versa.* This was achieved by varying the number of cars relative to the number of garages, such that these respective sets of objects never stood in a one-to-one relation with each other. However, the child's judgement of the truth or falsity of Statements A and B was found to be constrained, not by their actual truth or falsity, but rather by whether each garage in the array in front of him could be appropriately paired with a car. Thus, for a set of four garages and five cars, Statements A and B were both judged true. The saliency of an aspect of the physical situation—the fullness of the garages—appeared to dominate the child's interpretation of the linguistic form of the sentence, even though the children had clearly indicated an understanding of that term in other tasks.

Although the studies and examples cited above indicate the importance of non-linguistic information in the interpretation of speaker's meaning in contexts which are not designed to tap aspects of the child's cognitive structures, the very fact that such information can dominate the child's response when relatively simple cognitive demands are being made of him indicates its potency. There would, however, appear to be a considerable amount of evidence that such variables are operative in the tasks traditionally used to investigate children's cognitive abilities.

One such format would appear to be the setting in which the child's understanding of class/sub-class relations is assessed. A typical example of this is the presentation to the child of twenty wooden beads (A), seventeen of which are brown (A1) and three of which are white (A2). The child is asked whether 'he could make a longer necklace' with the brown beads or with the wooden beads (Piaget, 1952). Typically the six-year-old child wrongly asserts that brown beads would make a longer necklace 'because there are only three white ones'. Such behaviour has classically been interpreted as reflecting lack of reversibility and associativity in the child's cognitive structures, with a consequent inability to reason about class/sub-class relations simultaneously and resulting domination by the perceptual features of the array. Once more, however, such an interpretation of the child's difficulty is not the only possible one.

To answer the class inclusion question appropriately, the child must possess a considerable number of accessory skills (see Trabasso, Isen, Delecki, McClanahan, Riley and Tucker, 1977). Even an adult is often forced to pause and reflect on the exact meaning of the class inclusion question before being able to answer it correctly. The whole bias of the test situation is towards creating an expectation in the child that a question will be asked about the relative numerosity of the two sub-classes marked and rendered salient by perceptual contrast. This expectation must be overcome before an appropriate answer can be given. However, to overcome such an expectation, greater weight must be given to linguistic analysis in the interpretation of speaker's meaning.

As mentioned earlier the general rule used by the child at this age would appear to be 'when in doubt go by contextual analysis.' It is thus possible that the child fails to reason appropriately in this task situation because he fails to understand what is expected of him. He misinterprets the question asked of him. Several sources of evidence may be cited in support of this analysis. Firstly, the above argument would lead to the prediction that if the child could be made to give greater weighting to linguistic analysis of the question, then he might demonstrate an ability to reason simultaneously about class/sub-class relations. McGarrigle,

Grieve and Hughes (1978) showed this to be the case in a study that closely paralleled Piaget's bead task in its format, but involved black cows and white cows which were placed on their side in front of the child. The physical features of their class inclusion task still afforded perceptual contrast between sub-classes but these authors changed the wording of the class inclusion questions to give greater emphasis to the total class, 'Are there more black cows or more *sleeping* cows?' As predicted, change in the salience of the verbal specification of referent classes led to an increase in the percentage of subjects answering correctly. Findings complementary to this study have also been reported by Kalil, Youssef and Lerner (1974), Markman and Siebert (1976), Jennings (1970), Winer and Kronberg (1974), Wohlwill (1968).

The second source of evidence in favour of the above analysis comes from the fact that in cognitively simpler tasks that do not involve class/sub-class comparisons, children are observed to make similar errors to those observed in the class inclusion task. For example, McGarrigle, Grieve and Hughes (1978) presented four- to six-year-olds with an array of eight animals, four horses and four cows facing each other aligned in a one-to-one relation on either side of a wall. Two of the cows were black, two were white. By contrast, three of the horses were black, only one being white. The children were then asked, 'Are there more cows or more black horses?' Only fourteen per cent of the children studied answered this question correctly. The child's difficulty in this task situation cannot be explained in terms of an inability to reason about class/sub-class relations simultaneously, as this study did not involve such relations. Rather, their difficulty in this task situation, and thus by analogy in the Piagetian class inclusion tasks, would appear to stem from a tendency to interpret referentially asymmetric questions as symmetric with a consequent misinterpretation of the experimenter's question. Further support for such an analysis is also to be found in Grieve and Garton's detailed study of class inclusion (Grieve and Garton, 1980) Such studies, as the authors point out,

> by indicating that the child's difficulty in comparing sets and sub-sets consists of successfully locating the intended referent of a set term in a referentially asymmetric question . . . suggest that instances of failure to answer asymmetric questions correctly are more concerned with a lack of effective communication between adult and child, than a lack of ability on the child's part.
>
> (Grieve and Garton, 1980, p. 20)

It has also been argued that inappropriate interpretation of the experimenter's question is responsible—at a certain stage of development—for children's failure in traditional Piagetian conservation tasks (McGarrigle and Donaldson, 1975). Once again, it would appear to be the weighting the child gives to behavioural and contextual information in the analysis of speaker's meaning that misleads him. The evidence for such a statement comes from McGarrigle and Donaldson's (1975) conservation study. In this study, the children's conservation abilities were studied under two conditions: the traditional Piagetian format in which transformation of the array was affected intentionally by the experimenter, and a modified format in which transformation was effected by the actions of a naughty teddy bear. The resulting misleading perceptual configuration of the array was the same in each case. However, the incidence of conservation response in four- to five-year-olds was observed to rise from sixteen per cent in the standard condition, to sixty-three per cent in the modified condition. Such a result is not at all consonant with Piagetian explanations of the child's difficulty at this stage of development in this task.

It is, however, totally predictable from McGarrigle and Donaldson's argument, that intentional manipulation of the array by the experimenter in the traditional task format leads the child to expect a question about that aspect of the array which has changed. Such an expectation is appropriate to the world of everyday discourse where we normally comment on that which has changed rather than that which is static (Macnamara, 1972). It is unfortunately inappropriate to the conservation task and in this context is seen to lead the child to misinterpret the reference of the experimenter's post-transformational question, behavioural specification of reference dominating linguistic specification. Destruction of the relevance of the transformation of the array to the interpretation of the experimenter's post-transformational question, by making the former the result of the extraneous activities of a naughty teddy, as in the modified condition, thus facilitates the revelation of true competence in performance.

So far we have discussed only one way in which the young child's comprehension strategies pose problems for the inference from task performance to cognitive competence. Another kind of pragmatic explanation of the child's difficulty in the traditional Piagetian conservation task is to be found in the work of Rose and Blank (1974). These authors note that in the conservation task the experimenter asks the same question twice of the child, within a very short period of time.

Repetition of a question, particularly when an asymmetric power relation exists between participants in a dialogue, is, in the absence of change in an event relative to the interpretation of the question, arguably a very powerful cue that the original answer to the question has been wrong. This repetition of the question in the traditional conservation task post-transformationally may lead the child to construe his original answer to the question as wrong, or to view the repetition of the question as indicating that the transformation of the array had, after all, affected the validity of his original judgement and to change his judgement accordingly (Rose and Blank, 1974).

Whilst informal observations in the literature do indicate that such rules of discourse affect the children's performance (Smedslund, 1969), Rose and Blank provided experimental evidence that such a factor was operative in the Piagetian conservation task. They showed that the incidence of conservation rose significantly from that observed in the standard Piagetian task in an otherwise identical task, in which the conservation question was asked once only, post-transformationally. Further, experience of this one judgement situation was found to facilitate the children's performance on a standard conservation task given a week later. Such rapid facilitation effects thus provide the sort of evidence that Dasen (1977) argues is necessary for demonstrating that original difficulty in the standard task was performance rather than competence determined.

If repeating a question has such a strong effect on the child's responses, then we may also expect requests for justifications of responses to be interpreted in more than one way. The use of such requests, arising from the desire to know the grounds of a judgement may, however, be construed as challenging the child's answer with consequent inhibition of future successful performance. That pragmatic rules of discourse and/or asymmetry in the power relation between participants in an interaction affect the child's performance in tasks of cognitive function, has been clearly demonstrated.

Lloyd (1975), for example, has observed that children's justifications of their responses in a given task were found to be more elaborate and more cognitively complex when they were explaining the reasons for their responses to a somewhat dim teddy bear, as opposed to an adult experimenter. In this case, not only was the child placed in control of the situation but also the reason for having to justify his response was comprehensible—he was the one with the greater knowledge. Similarly, Blank (1974) demonstrated how the children's justification responses in traditional Piagetian conservation task were socially regulated—

justifications were found to vary as a function of whether both participants in the interaction were able to view the array. Where a shared perspective on the event was not possible, the child's verbalisations became correspondingly more complex. A similar finding has been observed with younger children by Maratos (1973). That the child's current verbal performance is not necessarily a good indicator of his competence is also indicated by Slobin and Welsh (1973), finding that young children are unable to imitate their previously recorded spontaneous utterances.

Such findings clearly illustrate the importance of pragmatic features of the interaction to the child's understanding of an event and the extent to which he makes his reasoning verbally explicit. The use of justifications in making inferences about cognitive competence has probably, through neglect of the aforementioned factors, led to an underestimation of the child's competence, particularly insofar as the meaning of such justifications to the child has never been empirically investigated. (But see, now, Beveridge, 1979). Given the socially anomalous situations in which requests for justification are made, it is more than possible that responses to such requests reflect 'the need to say something' to the adult examiner. Certainly the significance of such responses remains unclear. A striking recent example of readiness to offer inappropriate justifications is afforded by Hughes and Grieve (1980). Judgements of bizarre propositions such, 'Is milk bigger than water?' were supported by absurd justifications such as 'Milk is bigger 'cos it's got colour.'

Is failure to understand a sufficient account of children's difficulty in reasoning tasks?

Does evidence of the above type provide sufficient grounds for concluding that young children are more cognitively competent than has been hitherto suspected?

As Reese and Schack (1974), Larsen (1977) and Light, Buckingham and Robbins (1979) point out, there is a paradox surrounding the sort of work just described. While these authors claim to have demonstrated a new source Type II errors in Genevan research, the modified procedures that they implemented in order to do so are open to the accusation that they increase the probability of Type I error. The obvious candidates for such a criticism are McGarrigle and Donaldson (1975) and Rose and Blank (1974). In their studies of conservation, children were not requested to justify their responses. Failure to request such justifications is thought by Genevan researchers to increase the probability of false positives in the diagnosis of cognitive structures (Piaget, 1962). However, the validity of this and other criticisms of the modified procedures can only, as Brainerd (1973) points out, be resolved through the consideration of conceptual issues. In the above case we need to consider the definition of conservation and the epistemological status of these judgements to the child. Thus, any evaluation of the findings cited in the first section, requires examination of the methodology of these studies in the context of the nature of the conceptual competence they purport to demonstrate in the child. In general the claim has been that such studies demonstrate the same type of competence that is attributed only to older children in Genevan research. We turn now to examine these criticisms and their validity in greater detail.

At least five types of criticism may be made of the studies we have mentioned. Firstly, the changed procedures may be criticised for omitting some essential aspect of the original Piagetian format—a case in point is the omission of requests for justifications just discussed. Insofar as the essence of the conservation task as an index of the child's concrete operational structures lies in the conservation judgement being felt as logically necessary, failure to request justifications is seen to negate the value of the task as a diagnostic tool as the 'logical necessity' of the judgement to the child, cannot be assessed from whether his response was correct or not. Countering this criticism, however, are the points that the requests for justification may be misconstrued by the child, that what the child does and what he says he does in a given task do not necessarily correspond (Karmiloff-Smith, 1978) and that, although the logical necessity of the judgement to the child can only be assessed by reference to his ability to articulate the premises of his reasoning, failure to give adequate grounds for a judgement does not entail that the judgement is inadequately grounded.

The respective value of each of these arguments is difficult to assess. There is however some evidence to suggest that requesting justification *per se* does not necessarily inhibit performance. Neilson, Dockrell and McKechnie (1980) studied children's conservation abilities in the traditional and in McGarrigle and Donaldson's modified task. Within each task, half of the children had to justify their judgements, half did not. In neither task was the request for justification found to significantly reduce the observed proportion of correct responses. However, few of the children diagnosed as conservers according to a 'correct judgement only' criterion in McGarrigle and Donaldson's modified task, could justify their correct judgements in a manner which would be acceptable by Genevan criteria for conservation (see Inhelder *et al.,* 1974). Whether such children should be viewed as only 'pseudo conservers' remains dependent on future clarification of the epistemological status of these judgements.

The second criticism of the modified tasks is that their procedures promote successful performance by offering the child greater opportunity to solve the task through inappropriate means such as guessing, use of response biases, direct perception, and so on (see Smedslund, 1969). A case in point is again McGarrigle and Donaldson's study of length and number conservation. As Dockrell, Neilson and Campbell (1980) point out, this study had a number of methodological defects. The small number of counters used, the variations in the questions asked, the fact that in the unequal conditions the more numerous, distant row was always the one transformed, each provide an opportunity for the child to succeed in the conservation task by direct perception or subitising, by agreeing with the last thing the experimenter said or by consistently selecting the row furthest from himself. Utilisation of these cues, more effectively in the modified as opposed to the traditional task, may simply be seen to reflect realignment of the child's attention due to excitement at teddy's appearance. Alternatively, facilitation could simply have been due to the teddy bear acting as a distractor—a screen (see Frank, 1966)—leading the child to ignore the transformed array and to repeat his original (correct) judgement in response to the post-transformation question. In response to such criticisms, however, Dockrell, Neilson and Campbell (1980) have shown that, although control of such experimental artefacts reduces the overall rate of conservation in four- to six-year-olds, it does not eradicate the difference between the modified and traditional task. Further, no attentional differences were observed in their study between the modified and traditional procedure, suggesting that teddy's role cannot simply be explained as that of a distractor.

Further support for McGarrigle and Donaldson's interactional analysis came from a supplementary study. Children, who had been tested in the McGarrigle and Donaldson's modified conservation task, were then given a 'colour conservation' task in which they had to judge the sameness of colour of two identical red hexagonal blocks, before and after the shape of one of the hexagons had been changed through rotation of its component parts by the experimenter. One-third of the subjects were observed to change their judgements. Since these children showed no preference for choosing the altered block as redder, such a result cannot be explained by supposing that 'redder' was taken to refer to the 'greater area' of the transformed hexagon. Rather, such results would appear to support McGarrigle and Donaldson's argument that intentional change of a property is seen by the child as indicating that the experimenter is going to talk about that property.

Light *et al.* (1979) have shown that the principle underlying McGarrigle and Donaldson's argument is generalisable to other tasks. Children were given a traditional and a modified conservation of discontinuous quantity task. The material used was beakers containing pasta shells. In the modified task, transformation of the pasta shells from one beaker to another of different shape was seen to be necessitated by the fact that the first beaker was chipped. Success rates in the two conditions were five per cent and seventy per cent respectively. Clearly it may be argued that this facilitation is due to the children's perception of the transformation as having nothing to do with the judgement sought as in the McGarrigle and Donaldson argument.

Given the replicability of McGarrigle and Donaldson's study (Light *et al.*, 1979; Neilson *et al.*, 1979), the persistence of the result when more careful controls were applied (Dockrell *et al.*, 1980), and the generalisability of the argument (Light *et al.*, Dockrell *et al.*, 1980), McGarrigle and Donaldson's claim that Piagetian tasks underestimate the child's cognitive ability appears a strong one. However, the results which are seen to support McGarrigle and Donaldson's findings are not without their own ambiguity—nor is McGarrigle and Donaldson's explanation of the success of their modified procedure. For example, if children who give wrong judgements in traditional conservation tasks do so because of misleading interactional cues, then these same children should change their judgements in other analogous tasks. But in the Dockrell *et al.* colour conservation task, for example, no correlation was observed between the child's susceptibility to change of judgement in *this* task and in the traditional number and length conservation tasks. Further, whilst the colour conservation study supports McGarrigle and Donaldson's argument of the potency of intentional transformation of an array in the specification of the linguistic reference of future conversation about the array, the work of Murray and Tyler (1978) indicate that the *type* of transformation effected is also of importance. Murray and Tyler presented tests of conservation, verbally and observed, that only certain types of transformation evoked a shift of judgement. What such work possibly indicates is that particular attention to the actions of the experimenter in interpreting the reference of the post-transformational question is only given when the child is having basic conceptual difficulty with the task at hand, a point that will be returned to.

The notion that it is intentional transformation of the array by the adult that *in and of itself* provides problems in the traditional conservation tasks at a certain stage of development, is also called into question by the results of Rose and Blank. While these results support the general principle of the importance of interactional variables in concept assessment, the facilitation of correct responses in their one judgement condition should not have occurred, according to McGarrigle and Donaldson's arguments. In that task, the child is still faced with an intentional transformation of the array and this should have led to a misinterpretation of the experimenter's post-transformational question. That it did not, suggests the need to modify the McGarrigle and Donaldson's argument. It is, in fact, possible that teddy facilitated conservation in McGarrigle and Donaldson's study because he provided a reason in the child's eyes for the experimenter asking the same question twice, thus preventing the child from misconstruing the reason for repetition of the question (Neilson, Dockrell and Campbell, 1979).

However, whether or not McGarrigle and Donaldson's findings can be assimilated to those of Rose and Blank's, the significance of the child's sensitivity to features of the interactional setting in the conservation task, still remains relatively unclear. This sensitivity may be seen merely to inhibit, in certain *contexts,* the manifestation of competence in performance. In addition, such sensitivity may interfere with judgement only at certain critical periods in development.

This point is at the heart of the third criticism which can be made of the claim that the modified procedures described in the first section of the chapter clearly demonstrate that the young child is far more competent than hitherto supposed. To show that a variable or variables affects performance in a given task, is not to show that these variables are the sole or even primary reason for the difficulty normally experienced in that task. Thus, for example, while McGarrigle's modified class inclusion procedures show that features of the physical situation in interaction with the language used by the experimenter affect the child's interpretation of what he is required to do, it may be argued that they do so only by virtue of the nature of the child's cognitive competence: that variables of this nature come to dominate the child's performance, not because he does not know what is being requested, but rather because he does not have the cognitive competence to carry out the task. He thus resorts to the use of familiar heuristic systems or strategies such as reliance on the rules of discourse for deciding between alternative responses, or allows his choice between such responses to be dominated by the perceptual salience of the distinguishing variables.

Thus it may be argued that to put special emphasis on the super-set by linguistic means (as in McGarrigle's black and white sleeping cows class inclusion study) may promote correct responses, not because it helps the child to understand better what is expected of him, but rather because such a change involves making the super-set more perceptually salient. Black cows are not logically a sub-set of sleeping cows; their contingent status as a sub-set of sleeping cows had therefore to be made perceptually evident in McGarrigle's study. The children's correct response to the question, 'Are there more black cows or more sleeping cows?' could thus have been determined by the fact that the class of sleeping cows was more perceptually salient to them and that this perceptual salience was also reinforced linguistically—the adjective 'sleeping'—drawing the child's attention to the unusual state of these cows and thus to the more numerous set. Attributing failure to 'interpretational difficulty' may be seen to carry with it the same problems as attributing failure to 'attentional difficulties' (see Gelman, 1969), namely that these terms describe behaviours that *require* explaining, rather than explaining them (Larsen, 1977). Such mechanisms can produce spurious successes just as readily as misleading failures.

A similar criticism can be made of the claim that the type of reasoning children engage in in real life situations (Donaldson, 1978), and their comprehension of certain aspects of natural language (Macnamara, Baker and Olson, 1976; Macnamara, 1977), demonstrates the child's capacity for deductive reasoning at an age when their performance in Piagetian tasks would lead one to conclude that they were incapable of such reasoning. Again, while Donaldson's and Macnamara *et al*'s observations may be described as if they were governed by logical principles, it does not follow that they were (see Papert, 1977). The apparent logical nature of children's utterances are as likely to be generated by the application of real world knowledge of probable relations between events or objects. Which interpretation of children's utterances is the more appropriate would appear to depend on the future design of contextually appropriate tools for this age-group, in which plausible conclusions from factual premises are differentiated from necessarily true conclusions (see Bereiter and Hidi, 1977; Hidi and Hildgard, 1978).

The fourth methodological/conceptual criticism to be made of the evidence for the claim that Piagetian tasks underestimate the child's cognitive capacity is perhaps the most important one. Namely, that in modifying testing procedures so as to demonstrate competence in the younger child, inadequate attention may have been paid to the distinctions in Piagetian theory among the various ways in which conceptual structures may be said to underlie behaviour. Insofar as such structures evolve, they are in a sense always present. However, Piaget (1950, 1977) draws a distinction between the various states of development of such structures and thus between the various levels at which a concept may be understood or represented.

Here it may be argued that several of the inferences made about the child from his behaviour in the modified tasks, by failing to acknowledge such distinctions, confuse a low-level competence with that of a higher level. Once such distinctions are acknowledged, the competence underlying the young child's behaviour can be seen as not equivalent to that of the older child. Such studies may be seen to clarify the nature of the young child's infra-logical system, rather than demonstrate that it is really concrete-operational. The clearest example of this (see Robinson, 1978) would appear to be the claims made for Maratos (1973), and Shatz and Gelman's (1973) demonstration that the child can adapt his utterances to the state of the listener. Such behaviour (as well as that demonstrated in other studies such as that of Hughes, 1975), has been taken as evidence that the young child is not as egocentric as Piaget believed him to be, his failure to perform appropriately in Piaget's tasks being once more attributable to performance variables —such as failure to understand what was expected of him (Donaldson, 1978)—and to processing limitations (Asher and Oden, 1976; Bearison and Levey, 1977).

But egocentricity for Piaget does not simply refer to the child's behaviour not being adapted to the perspective of another, but also to the child not *understanding* that for communication to be successful the message must meet the listener's requirements. The child must know not only *how* to do something effectively (knowledge of which may be represented at a purely sensorimotor level) but *why* he does it that way.

In the first place neither the child's social egocentrism nor the egocentrism of his knowledge of the physical world is a quality which can be observed within his selfconsciousness or by watching his external behaviour. Social egocentrism as much as

> purely intellectual egocentrism is an epistemic attitude: it is a
> way of understanding others just as egocentrism in general is a
> way of looking at things.
>
> (Piaget, 1959)

Thus observation of the child's behaviour—as in Maratos' study—
cannot without supplementation be used to demonstrate that the child
is non-egocentric in the sense in which the term is used by Piaget.
Behaviour alone cannot inform one of the child's awareness of the
perspective of others and the requirements of good communication. If
we equate appropriate behaviour with awareness of the principles
underlying that behaviour, then we run the risk of confusing different
levels of representation of knowledge in cognitive development. (Studies
such as that of Maratos may nevertheless be seen to question the
developmental significance that Piaget has in the past ascribed to
egocentrism. [Piaget, 1950; see Donaldson, 1978]).

These criticisms focus on the *what* of development, on the claim
that the pre-school child possesses the type of conceptual competence
that Piaget reserves for his description of the older child's mental
capacity. The last criticism that we will make of the studies presented
in the first section centres on their failure to deal with the *how* of
development. Even if one grants these studies their claim to have
demonstrated the Piagetian type of competence in the pre-schooler—a
competence that is hidden from display by various performance factors
—one is faced with the paradox that (given the child's sensitivity to
extraneous contextual information) it becomes very difficult to understand how that competence could have developed in the first place, and
how it finally comes to be generalised and reflected in performance
across a wide variety of situations. None of the studies reported in the
first section appear to recognise these new problems their research
poses.

Conclusion

This chapter has sought to review various sources of evidence that
suggest that Piagetian tasks underestimate the child's cognitive
competence by neglecting various biassing features of the interactional
setting. Whether this is the case would appear to depend on (a) how
that competence is defined, (b) what model of the relation of competence to performance is proposed, and (c) how the origins of that

competence are explained. If the studies presented in the first section are taken to provide sufficient evidence to demonstrate a type of cognitive competence in the pre-schooler that is reserved in Piagetian theory for the older child, then the criticisms reviewed in the second section of this chapter suggest that such a claim—in the context of the currently available evidence—is too strong. Rather, the pre-schooler's extreme sensitivity to contextual variables may illustrate further the figurative and pre-operational nature of his thinking during this period. Performance which fluctuates between analogous situations (for example, the coloured block task and the conservation task) or within tasks, is not sufficiently stable to count as the logical competence which Piaget describes when he discusses concrete operational thought. It is precisely these unstable types of behaviour which Genevans (for example, Inhelder *et al.,* 1974) are apt to take as indicators of transitional or incomplete development of the principles of concrete operational thought.

In reaching such a conclusion, however, we do not deny the importance of recent experimental findings reported in the second section, nor do we deny the possibility hinted at in Donaldson's notion of 'embedded thought processes' (Donaldson, 1978), that the lasting effect of these studies will be to necessitate a complete revision of current notions about the nature of cognitive development; that the currently dominant Piagetian mode of characterising cognitive competence with its emphasis on the contextually independent nature of the structure of thought, is fundamentally wrong to whatever level of cognitive development it is applied. However, since none of the authors cited in the first section offer an alternative conceptual framework in which to place their findings, we cannot evaluate this possibility.

Any premature attempt to develop such a framework carries with it the danger that undue attention to task variables which can explain *failure*, may make us blind to the basic problem of defining the nature of the competence required for *success* in the task. Currently we know too little about the world of the pre-schooler to make radical claims about his abilities. The studies reported in this chapter may be seen as highlighting the need for further research into the world of the pre-schooler, to be undertaken in a positive fashion with the aim of providing a richer characterisation of the nature of his thinking (see Grieve and Garton, 1980), rather than simply attempting to characterise his thinking as logical or non-logical.

By emphasising the communication problems and the contextual sensitivity associated with performance in this age-group, such studies also draw attention to the methodological problems which any such investigation would face (see Campbell, 1979). Resolution of such problems does not appear easy and certainly should not be made—as indicated in the latter part of this chapter—at the expense of ignoring important distinctions among various levels at which an event may be said to be known. For the moment, the only prescription for future research that such studies would appear to offer is in the promotion of 'profile analysis' of the child's performance across a variety of 'contextualised' and 'decontextualised' situations (see Grieve and Garton, 1980; Kamura and Easley, 1977; Braine, 1959), and in the promotion of the albeit limited techniques of situational variation (Cole *et al.,* 1971; Greenfield, 1976), structural analysis (Kimura and Easley, 1977) and training methods (Bovet, 1974; Dasen, Lavellee and Retschitzki, 1978) in the inference of competence from performance.

We would like to thank Margaret Donaldson, Bill Barnes-Gutteridge and Robin Campbell for comments on the original version of this chapter. We are particularly grateful to Robin Campbell whose many comments served to sharpen our thinking and our literary style. We also thank our typist, Cath Brown.

References

Achenbach, T. M., ' "Conservation" below age three: fact or artefact?', Proceedings of the 77th Annual Convention of the American Psychological Association, 1969, *4,* 275-6.

Asher, S. R., and Oden, S. L., 'Children's failure to communicate: an assessment of comparison and egocentrism explanations', *Developmental Psychology,* 1976, *12,* 132-9.

Bearison, D. J., and Levey, L. M., 'Children's comprehension of referential communication: decoding ambiguous messages', *Child Development,* 1977, *48,* 716-20.

Bereiter, C., and Hidi, S., 'Biconditional vs factual reasoning in children', Toronto O.I.S.E. (E.R.I.C. Document Reproduction Service Number ED138 351), 1977.

Beveridge, M., 'Making sense of nonsense', paper read at the British Psychology Society—Developmental Section—Symposium, University of Southampton, 1979.

Blank, M., 'Cognitive functions of language in the pre-school years', *Developmental Psychology,* 1974, *10,* 229-45.

Bovet, M. C., 'Cognitive process among illiterate children and adults', in J. W. Berry and P. R. Dasen (eds.) *Culture and Cognition,* London, Methuen, 1974, 311-34.

Braine, M. D. S., 'The ontogeny of certain logical operations: Piaget's formulations examined by non-verbal methods', *Psychological Monographs,* 1959, *73,* 5.

Braine, M. D. S., 'Piaget on reasoning: a methodological critique and alternative proposals', in W. Kessen and C. Kuhlman (eds.) *Thought in the Young Child,* Monographs of the Society for Research on Child Development, 27, 1962.

Brainerd, C. J., 'Judgements and explanations as criteria for cognitive structures', *Psychological Bulletin,* 1973, *79*.3, 172-9.

Brainerd, C. J., 'Postmortem on judgements, explanations and Piagetian cognitive structures', *Psychological Bulletin,* 1974, *81*.1, 70-1.

Bransford, J. D., and McCarrall, N. S., 'A sketch of a cognitive approach to comprehension: some thoughts about understanding what it means to comprehend', in P. N. Johnson-Laird and P. C. Watson (eds.) *Thinking. Readings in Cognitive Science,* Cambridge University Press, 1977.

Bryant, P. *Perception and Understanding in Young Children,* London, Methuen, 1974.

Campbell, R. N., and Bowe, T., 'Functional asymmetry in early language understanding', in G. Crachman (ed.) *Salzburger Beitrage zur Linquistik III* (Salsburg papers in Linguistics, Vol. III), Tubingen, Gunter Narr, 1977.

Campbell, R., 'Cognitive development and child language', in P. Fletcher and M. Garman (eds.) *Language Acquisition,* Cambridge University Press, 1979, 419-36.

Carey, S., 'Cognitive Competence', in K. Conolly and J. Bruner (eds.) *The Growth of Competence,* London, Academic Press, 1974.

Carey, S., 'Less may never mean more', in R. N. Campbell and P. T. Smith (eds.) *Recent Advances in the Psychology of Language. Vol. I: Language development and mother-child interaction,* London, Plenum Press, 1976.

Carey, S., 'The child as a word learner', in M. Halle, G. Miller and J. Bresnan (eds.) *Linguistic theory and psychological reality,* Cambridge, M.I.T. Press, 1977.

Clark, E., 'Non-linguistic strategies and the development of word meaning', *Cognition,* 1973, *2,* 161-82.

Cole, M., Gay, J., Glick, J., Sharp, D. W., 'The cultural context of learning and thinking', New York, Basic Books, 1971.

Dasen, P., (ed.) *Piagetian Psychology: Cross-cultural contributions,* New York, Gardner Press, 1977.

Dasen, P. R., Nglini, L., and Lavellee, M., 'Cross-cultural training studies of concrete operations', paper presented at the 4th International Association for Cross-Cultural Psychology, Munich, July 28-August 5, 1978.

Dasen, P. R., Lavellee, M., and Retschitzki, J., 'Training conservation of quantity (liquids) in West African (Baoule) children', *International Journal of Psychology*, 1979, *14*, 57-68.

Dockrell, J., Neilson, I., and Campbell, R., 'Conservation accidents revisited', *International Journal of Behavioural Development*, (in press, 1980).

Donaldson, M. C., and Balfour, G., 'Less is more: a study of language comprehension in children', *British Journal of Psychology*, 1968, *59*, 461-72.

Donaldson, M., and Lloyd, P., 'Sentences and situations: children's judgements of match and mismatch', in F. Bresson (ed.) *Problemes actueles en psycholinguistics*, Paris, C.N.R.S., 1974.

Donaldson, M., and McGarrigle, J., 'Some clues as to the nature of semantic development', *Journal of Child Language*, 1974, *1*, 185-94.

Donaldson, M., *Children's Minds*, London, Fontana, 1978.

Flavell, J. J., and Wohlwill, J. F., 'Formal and functional aspects of cognitive development', in D. Elkind and J. H. Flavell (eds.) *Studies in Cognitive Development: Essays in honour of Jean Piaget*, London and New York, Oxford University Press, 1969, 67-120.

Gelman, R., 'Conservation acquisitions: a problem of learning to attend to relevant attributes', *Journal of Experimental Child Psychology*, 1969, *7*, 67-8.

Gordon, P., 'Partial lexical entry and the semantic development of more and less', unpublished BSc Thesis, Stirling University, 1977.

Grice, H. P., 'Utterer's meaning, sentence meaning and word meaning', *Foundations of Language*, 1968, *4*, 225-42.

Greenfield, P. M., 'Cross-cultural research and Piagetian theory: paradox and progress', in K. Riegel and J. Meacham (eds.) *The Developing Individuals in a Changing World*, The Hague, Mouton, 1976.

Grieve, R., and Stanley, S., 'Less obscure? Pragmatics and 3-4 year old children's semantics 1980', unpublished manuscript, Department of Psychology, University of Western Australia, Australia.

Grieve, R., and Garton, A., 'On the young child's comparisons of sets', unpublished manuscript 1980, Department of Psychology, University of Western Australia, Australia.

Gruen, G. E., 'Note on conservation: methodological and definitional considerations', *Child Development*, 1966, *37*, 977-83.

Hidi, S., and Hildyard, A., 'Four-year-old's understanding of pretend and forget: no evidence for propositional reasoning', *Journal of Child Language*, 1978, *6*, 493-510.

Hoogenraad, R., Grieve, R., Baldwin, P., and Campbell, R., 'Comprehension as an interactive process', in R. N. Campbell and P. T. Smith (eds.) *Recent Advances in the Psychology of Language,* New York, Plenum Press, 1978.

Hughes, M., 'Egocentrism in preschool children', unpublished Doctoral thesis, University of Edinburgh, 1975.

Hughes, M., and Grieve, R., 'On asking children bizarre questions', *First Language, 1,* 1980.

Inhelder, B., Sinclair, H., and Bovet, M., *Learning and the Development of Cognition,* London, Routledge & Kegan Paul, 1974.

Ironsmith, M., and Whitehurst, G. J., 'The development of listener abilities in communication: how children deal with ambiguous information', *Child Development,* 1978, *49,* 348-52.

Jennings, J. R., 'The effect of verbal and pictorial presentation on class-inclusion competence and performance', *Psychonomic Science,* 1970, *20,* 357-8.

Kalil, K., Youssef, Z., and Lerner, R. M., 'Class inclusion failure: cognitive deficit or misleading reference', *Child Development,* 1974, *45,* 1122-5.

Kamura, A. I., and Easley, J. A., 'Is the rate of development uniform across cultures? A methodological critique with new evidence from Themne children', in P. R. Dasen (ed.) *Piagetian Psychology Cross-Cultural Contributions,* New York, Gardner Press, 1977, 26-63.

Karmiloff-Smith, A., 'The interplay between syntax, semantics and phonology in language acquisition processes', in R. N. Campbell and P. T. Smith (eds.) *Recent Advances in the Psychology of Language,* New York, Plenum Press, 1978.

Katz, H., and Beilin, H., 'A test of Bryant's claims concerning the young child's understanding of quantitative invariance', *Child Development,* 1976, *47,* 877-80.

Light, P. H., Buckingham, N., and Robbins, A. H., 'The conservation task as an interactional setting', *British Journal of Educational Psychology,* 1979, *49,* 304-10.

Lloyd, P., 'Communication in preschool children', unpublished Doctoral thesis, University of Edinburgh, 1975.

LaPointe, K., and O'Donnell, J. P., 'Number conservation in children below age six: its relationship to age, perceptual dimensions and language comprehension', *Developmental Psychology,* 1974, *10,* 422-8.

Larsen, G., 'Methodology in developmental Psychology: an examination of research on Piagetian theory', *Child Development,* 1977, *48,* 1160-6.

Maratos, M. P., 'Non-egocentric communication abilities in preschool children', *Child Development,* 1973, *44,* 697-700.

Markman, E. M., and Siebert, J., 'Class and collections: internal organisation and resulting holistic properties', *Cognitive Psychology*, 1976, *8*, 561-77.

Mehler, J., and Bever, T. G., 'Cognitive capacity of very young children', *Science*, 1967, *158*, 140-2.

Miller, S. A., 'Nonverbal assessment of Piagetian concepts', *Psychological Bulletin*, 1976, *83*, 405-30.

Murray, F. B., and Tyler, S. J., 'Semantic characteristics of the conservation transformation', *Psychological Reports*, 1978, *42*, 1051-4.

McCall, R. B., 'Towards an epigenetic conception of mental development in the first three years of life', in M. Lewis (ed.) *Origins of Intelligence*, Plenum Press, 1976, 97-122.

McGarrigle, J., and Donaldson, M., 'Conservation accidents', *Cognition*, 1975, *3*, 341-50.

McGarrigle, J., Grieve, R., and Hughes, M., 'Interpreting inclusion: a contribution to the study of the child's cognitive and linguistic development', *Journal of Experimental Child Psychology*, 1978, *26*, 528-50.

McGonigle, B., and Chalmers, M., 'Are monkeys logical?' *Nature*, 1977, *267*, 694-6.

Macnamara, J., 'Cognitive basis of language learning in infants', *Psychological Review*, 1972, *79*, 1-13.

Macnamara, J., 'Children's command of the logic of conversation', in J. Macnamara (ed.) *Language Learning and Thought*, New York, Academic Press Inc, 1977, 261-86.

Neilson, I., Dockrell, J., and Campbell, R., 'Conservation accidents revisited', paper presented at the British Psychology Society—Developmental Section—Symposium, University of Southampton, 1979.

Neilson, I., Dockrell, J., and McKechnie, J., *Context and Cognition*, in preparation, 1980.

Papert, S., 'Testing for propositional logic', in J. Macnamara (ed.) *Language Learning and Thought*, Academic Press Inc, 1977, 289-91.

Piaget, J., *The Language and Thought of the Child*, London, Routledge & Kegan Paul, 1926, 3rd Edn. 1959.

Piaget, J., *The Origins of Intelligence in the Child*, New York, International Universities Press, 1950.

Piaget, J., 'The stages of intellectual development in childhood and adolescence', in H. E. Gruber and J. J. Voneche (eds.) *The Essential Piaget*, London, Routledge & Kegan Paul, 1977.

Reese, H. W., and Schack, M. L., 'Comment on Brainerd's criteria for cognitive structures', *Psychological Bulletin*, 1974, *81*, 67-9.

Robinson, E. J., 'The child's understanding of inadequate messages and communication failure: a problem of ignorance or egocentrism?' Paper presented at Wisconsin Conference on Children's Oral Communication Skills, Madison, Wisconsin, 1978.

Rose, S. A., and Blank, M., 'The potency of context in children's cognition: an illustration through conservation', *Child Development*, 1974, *45*, 499-502.

Shatz, M., and Gelman, R., 'The development of communication skills: modification in the speech of young children as a function of listener', Monograph of the Society for Research in Child Development, No. 152, 1973.

Shatz, M., 'On the development of communicative understandings: an early strategy for interpreting and responding to messages', *Cognitive Psychology*, 1978, *10*, 271-301.

Slobin, D. I., and Welsh, C. A., 'Elicited imitation as a research tool in developmental psycholinguistics', in C. A. Ferguson and D. I. Slobin (eds.) *Studies in Child Language Development*, New York, Holt, Rinehart and Winston, 1973.

Smedslund, J., 'Psychological diagnostics', *Psychological Bulletin*, 1969, *71*, 234-48.

Trabasso, T., Isen, A. M., Dolecki, P., McClanahan, A. G., Riley, C. A., and Tucker, T., 'How do children solve class inclusion problems?' Paper presented at the 13th Annual Carnegie Symposium on Cognition, Colorado, U.S.A., 1977.

Wales, R. J., 'Children's sentences make sense of the world', in F. Bresson (ed.) *Problemes actuels en psycholinguistics*, Paris, Editions de C.N.R.S., 1974.

Wilcox, S., and Palermo, D. "'In', 'on' and 'under' revisited", *Cognition*, 1974, *3/3*, 245-54.

Winer, G. A., and Kronberg, D. D., 'Children's responses to verbally and pictorially presented class inclusion problems and to a task of number conservation', *Journal of Genetic Psychology*, 1974, *125*, 141-52.

Wohlwill, J. F., 'Responses to class inclusion questions for verbally and pictorially presented items', *Child Development*, 1968, *39*, 449-65.

Ziff, P., *Understanding Understanding*, Ithaca, New York, Cornell University Press, 1972.

11 Peer interaction and learning: can two wrongs make a right?

Martin Glachan and Paul Light

> Cognitive conflict created by social interaction is the locus at which the power driving intellectual development is generated.
>
> (Perret-Clermont, 1980)

The importance of a child's interactions with his age peers as an influence upon the development of his social behaviour has long been acknowledged (for example, Parten and Newhall, 1943; Campbell, 1964; Hartup, 1970). The idea that peer interaction might have a special part to play in cognitive development also has a long history, but has received little systematic attention from psychologists. In this chapter we shall provide some account of the background to this topic from a cognitive developmental perspective, and then present some new findings on the efficacy of peer interaction as a facilitator of learning.

Our starting point is with some specific suggestions regarding peer interaction and cognitive development made by Piaget half a century ago, but we must preface our consideration of them by a brief resume of Piaget's concept of egocentrism, which embodies his attempt to link social and individual aspects of development.

In his account of preoperational thinking, Piaget suggests that it depends for its properties on the unifying feature of egocentrism. Preoperational thinking is centred on the objects of the child's interest or activity, and upon the child's own point of view. Such centration involves neglect of other features of situations, and of alternative points of view, with the result that reasoning is distorted and genuine social behaviour limited.

The transition to operational thinking involves the replacement of this egocentrism by a system of reversible operations, relations and classes which are decentred with respect to self. In the intellectual field the child becomes able to attend to multiple features of situations, and his thinking begins to show flexibility. Similarly in the social field, the child becomes able to move freely from one perspective to another, so that social co-operation and communication becomes possible. Thus a close parallel exists between individual cognitive development on the one hand, and social development on the other.

This assertion of a parallelism between individual and social aspects of development has been a consistent feature of Piaget's writings, but his views have apparently changed over the years as to the nature of the relationships involved. Is it the case, for example, that social decentration is a by-product of an intellectual decentration achieved through individual (impersonal) experience? Or, to take the opposite view, is social decentration achieved through social experience, bringing intellectual decentration in its train? In his early writings, Piaget argued the latter case, thereby giving a critical role to social experience in the achievement of operational thinking (for example, Piaget, 1928, 1932, 1950). He argued that consciousness of one's own reasoning processes arises from the disposition to prove and justify to others what one has asserted, and that to do this one must reflect critically upon one's own reasoning with the eyes of an outside observer:

> The social need to share the thought of others and to communicate our own with success is at the root of our need for verification. Logical reasoning is an argument which we have with ourselves, and which reproduces internally the features of a real argument.
>
> (Piaget, 1928, p. 204)

It was in this connection that Piaget suggested a special role for the child's interactions with his peers. He characterised adult-child interactions as fundamentally asymmetrical, being ultimately dependent upon relations of authority. Only with his peers, Piaget argued, could the child begin to resolve the apparent contradictions between different viewpoints since: 'Criticism is born of discussion, and discussion is only possible among equals' (Piaget, 1932, p. 409).

Such an emphasis on child-child interactions as a major facilitator of learning has obvious practical implications. Piaget commented that the strictly individual work which he saw as characteristic of traditional schools ran contrary to the most obvious requirements of intellectual development (1932, p. 412). While this point has been reiterated by psychologists concerned with the application of Piagetian theory to education (for example, Sigel, 1969; Ginsberg and Opper, 1969; Elkind, 1976), it seems to have received little critical attention. This may be because Piaget, far from developing and elaborating this issue empirically, appears subsequently to have abandoned it completely. In his more recent work the question of the causal role of social experience in individual cognitive development is treated as being simply inappropriate, on the grounds that the distinction between social and the individual is artificial, and that operational thinking and directed social behaviour are in any case just two aspects of a single reality (Piaget, 1965; Piaget and Inhelder, 1969a).

Such a position leaves a number of obviously important questions about the impact of particular kinds of experience upon individual cognitive development hanging, apparently unaskable. Not surprisingly, this has led to some dissatisfaction. Zazzo (1960), for example, suggested that in his desire to avoid compartmentalising social and other factors in development, Piaget was falling instead into a confused globalism. Others have pointed out that it is not so much a matter of which questions are askable, but of which questions Piaget himself is trying to answer. Barker and Newson (1979) perhaps come to the heart of the matter when they distinguish between epistemological and psychological questions:

> Piaget's theory of operative development describes and analyses the emergence of the structural aspects of thinking, and while certain areas may be more influenced by discussion with peers, and development in others most encouraged by the manipulation of objects and the prediction of results, this is not the epistemological question to which the author addressed himself ... In fact it is not really an epistemological issue of any great significance at all (p. 240).

However, they continue:

> Psychologists, immersed in the contingency of fact ... cannot be satisfied with philosophical theory, and are led to ask different sorts of questions (p. 241).

The same point is made by Hamlyn (this volume) when he says of the conditions facilitative of learning that: 'Such considerations are in a genuine sense psychological, and are not part of genetic epistemology.'

The psychologist, then, may be excused for ignoring Piaget's recent reticence on these matters, and for turning back to issues raised by his earlier work. Just such a return has been advocated by Smedslund (1966b) and more recently by Damon (1979), who urges the need to breathe new life into the early work: 'in which social co-operation and conflict were cited as the prime instigators of development' (p. 209).

Piaget's original observations concerning the significance of peer interactions were made in the context of discussions of perspective-taking and moral judgement, so that it is not surprising to find recent reference to his thesis in these fields of study. Flavell (1968), for example, in his study of the development of perspective-taking, discusses the idea that peer interaction has a distinctive influence on this process, but concludes that there are no good grounds for emphasising the importance of child-child as against adult-child interactions. Likewise Kohlberg (1969), discussing moral judgement, considers peer interactions but concludes that there is little evidence that such interactions play any critical or unique role in moral development.

Both in the field of moral development (for example, Hoffman, 1970) and in the field of perspective-taking (for example, Light, 1979) recent attention has focused primarily upon parent-child relationships as an influence upon development. Piaget's emphasis upon reciprocity, and his claim that this could only arise between individuals 'considering themselves as equals' have not been rejected, but emphasis has been laid upon the capacity of the parent to interact with the child on the basis of a more or less consciously *constructed* equality.

Experimental studies

Our present concern is with the impact of child-child interaction upon cognitive development. One empirical approach to this issue has involved correlational studies designed to look at long-term effects of exposure to differing amounts of peer interaction. Thus Hollos and Cowan (1973; Hollos, 1975) studied children in towns, small villages and isolated farms, while other studies have been conducted with city, moshav and kibbutz children in Israel (West, 1974; Nahir and Yussen, 1977). Apart from their somewhat inconsistent results, the main problem with such studies is that these different social environments of child-rearing clearly differ in a host of ways, and not simply in amount of opportunity for peer interaction.

The obvious alternative approach is through experimental studies of short-term effects on problem-solving of exposure to different social contexts. A considerable number of studies have been reported in which aspects of social context have been manipulated as an independent variable, with some form of problem-solving as the dependent variable. We shall refer to these as learning-studies. Specific attention to peer interaction is a relatively recent development, and it will be necessary to provide some background before focusing on such studies.

In recent years a number of learning-studies have been conducted by Genevan researchers (for example, Inhelder, Sinclair and Bovet, 1974), and Piaget's tasks, especially the conservation tasks, have been widely used in studies conducted elsewhere. However, Piaget has stressed the assimilatory aspect of learning:

> 'In fact both social and educational influences and physical experience are on the same footing in this respect, they can have some effect on the subject only if he is capable of assimilating them (1970, p. 721).

He rejects any role for 'imposed transmission' in the acquisition of operational thinking (Piaget and Inhelder, 1969b), and this includes a rejection of any major role for verbal training.

Bruner's (1964) claims for the importance of language were answered by Sinclair's (1967) verbal training studies, which dismissed the idea that the child needs only to understand the correct use of certain expressions to understand conservation and seriation. Both parties showed a concern with semantic and syntactic features of language. In the last decade, however, psychologists interested in language have come to concentrate much more on its communicative functions (for example, Ryan, 1974; Bruner, 1975). Heber's (1977, 1978) replication and extension of Sinclair's work reflects this shift, in that attention is no longer solely given to the words used, but also to the form of discourse between adult and child. Children were found to progress as a result of 'discussion' methods, while direct instruction was ineffective. Such results are consistent with the Genevan view that training is a matter of creating disturbances which the child may resolve in a way which promotes cognitive development (Inhelder *et al.*, 1974), but also reflect a positive concern to establish the best way of creating such 'disturbances'.

Smedslund, in a long series of studies (for example, 1961, 1964, 1966a) investigated the effects of creating conflicts for the child in his interactions with objects, but concluded (1966b) that the limited impact achieved reflected the lack of *social* conflict involved. He suggested that cognitive decentration would be facilitated above all by a confrontation of differing points of view between children, thus effectively restating Piaget's early view. While learning-studies focusing on the child's interaction with objects have proved more successful in the hands of others than in Smedslund's (see Brown and Desforges, 1979), Smedslund's *volte face* was influential as a stimulus to the study of the effects of peer interaction.

Learning-studies involving child-child interaction are not numerous, perhaps because of the obvious difficulties of precise experimental control involved, but the number of studies in this area has grown considerably in recent years. In most cases the experimental design has involved individual pre-testing, some form of social 'intervention' and then individual post-testing. Comparisons may be made with controls not given the social intervention, or they may be made between different forms of social intervention. The majority of studies have employed Piaget's concrete operations tasks, conservation tasks being the most popular. The studies fall into three main categories; those which involve the subject watching the performance of a more advanced child, those which involve the subject actively interacting with a more advanced child, and those which involve interaction between children of approximately equal levels of competence. Studies in the last two categories, which are not entirely distinct from one another, have mostly arisen within the Piagetian framework. Studies in the first category, which we shall term modelling-studies, have arisen within the framework of social learning theory.

Modelling studies

The modelling hypothesis, badly stated, is that peer interaction will enhance a child's subsequent performance just insofar as it provides the child with an opportunity to observe and model himself upon the behaviour of a more able child. The hypothesis thus predicts that any intervention which allows a preoperational child to observe another child's operational response to a task will lead to progress. There need be no interaction at all, so that the 'social intervention' might consist in a child watching the performance of another on a videotape. A number of such modelling-studies have been conducted (Waghorn and Sullivan, 1970; Kuhn, 1972; Rosenthal and Zimmerman, 1972; Zimmerman,

1974; Murray, 1974) and these have typically found that such experience does enhance subsequent performance on the observed task.

From a Piagetian standpoint, imitation might be expected to have some local and immediate effect on behaviour but, being purely accomodatory, would not promote any genuine cognitive acquisition. Thus the criterion problem raises its ugly head. The Genevan demand for explanations in support of judgements on conservation tasks has been criticised on a number of counts (Brown and Desforges, 1979). If it is to be insisted on in the present case, there is the additional problem that if a modelled explanation is subsequently offered by the child in support of his judgement, it may be discounted as purely imitative. Thus only novel explanations will suffice. Evidence for the production of novel conservation explanations not heard during the intervention has not been found, at least in cases where the subject was exposed only to conserving judgements. Some evidence of generalisation of acquired conservation has been provided (Rosenthal and Zimmerman, 1972; Zimmerman, 1974; Murray, 1974) but the extent and nature of generalisation needed to establish operational conservation is open to dispute. The only evidence on durability of acquired responses comes from a study using adult models by Kuhn (1972), who showed that gains on a classification task were maintained one week later.

A simple modelling hypothesis is anathema to Piaget because it takes no account of the assimilatory aspect of cognitive growth. Kuhn (1972) has gone some way towards bridging the gap by analysing the effectiveness of different models in relation to the subject's initial cognitive level. She proposed an optimal mismatch hypothesis according to which the best model for inducing cognitive change is one which reflects a stage of development just beyond the child's own, since under these conditions the child is most likely to perceive the discrepancy with his own thinking. She assessed children's classification ability according to Inhelder and Piaget's (1964) six stages of classifactory development and then allocated them to modelling conditions in which the model performed at one stage below the subject's own (-1), at the same level (0), or at one or two stages above (+1 or +2). In each case the model gave appropriate explanations. Little change followed observations of 0 and -1 models, while +1 and +2 models induced change which was almost always to the +1 level. Some support for these findings is provided by Murray (1974) in relation to a conservation task, although regression following observations of an inferior model has been seen in some cases (Rosenthal and Zimmerman, 1972).

Kuhn's study strongly suggested that, while observing another person doing the task may be an effective agent of behaviour change, some models are more effective than others, and that the effectiveness of a particular model is a function of the child's own cognitive processes. The subject's role may appear to be a passive one, but as Inhelder *et al.* (1974) observe, a child may be mentally active while not actually conversing or physically manipulating materials. Thus the success of modelling procedures need not be interpreted in terms of passive imitation, and can even be seen as a kind of 'tacit interaction' between subject and model.

Botvin and Murray (1975) conducted a study in which some children were in active interaction with one another, while others were merely spectators. The interaction groups consisted of three conservers and two non-conservers as measured by pre-test performance. The groups were instructed that they had to reach a consensus on six conservation problems. Subjects in the 'modelling' condition were all non-conservers, who watched the experimenter elicit a judgement and an explanation from each member of an interaction group before and after each consensus was achieved. A 'no treatment' control group was used. At post-test, non-conservers in both the interaction and the modelling condition showed significant gains compared to controls, there being no difference between the two conditions. These results suggest to Botvin and Murray that any social interaction effects may be attributed most parsimoniously to a modelling process. However, this study differs from the earlier modelling-studies in that several models were observed who expressed and defended differing viewpoints. The presentation of conflicting judgements and explanations may have had an important role both for participants and spectators. In subsequent studies (Murray, Ames and Botvin, 1977) these authors have placed more emphasis on cognitive dissonance than on modelling. Using counter-attitudinal role play they showed that non-conserving (and transitional) subjects who gave conserving judgements and reasons in role play made large and significant gains. This effect was not reversible, however: conservers who role-played non-conservation did not regress.

Interaction-studies

Studies involving actual interaction between conserving and non-conserving children have provided rather firmer evidence of cognitive gains than have studies involving observation of conservers by non-conservers. Silverman and Stone (1972), Murray (1972), Silverman and Geiringer (1973), Miller and Brownell (1975) and Doise, Mugny and Perret-Clermont (1975) have all found evidence that in active encounters non-conservers yield to conservers' arguments significantly more than vice-versa, and will produce conserving responses at individual post-testing. These changes appear to be relatively secure and lasting. Conserving responses acquired through interaction have been shown to generalise to new and parallel conservation problems (Murray, 1972; Silverman and Stone, 1972; Silverman and Geiringer, 1973). Further post-testing a month after interaction shows retention of acquired conservation (Silverman and Stone, 1972; Silverman and Geiringer, 1973; Doise, Mugny and Perret-Clermont, 1975). Perret-Clermont also observed that over sixty per cent of children who acquired conservation through interaction introduced novel arguments (Doise, Mugny and Perret-Clermont, 1975).

Miller and Brownell (1975) have investigated the question of why non-conservers are more likely to yield to conservers than vice-versa. In order to establish whether the conservers were generally more socially dominant they asked pairs of children a variety of control questions unrelated to conservation. Conservers 'won' forty-one arguments and non-conservers thirty-eight. However, on conservation questions conservers won fifty-nine arguments and non-conservers only eight. On the conservation questions the conservers were likely to assert their answers, produce counter-arguments, and manipulate the stimulus materials. In contrast, non-conservers appeared to be limited to a restatement of their original response. Miller and Brownell propose that conservers exert a stronger social influence during conservation arguments because a belief in conservation is typically held more firmly than a belief in non-conservation. Support for this was provided by Miller, Brownell and Zukier (1977), who found greater confidence in operational than in non-operational answers.

In the interaction-studies so far described, the non-conserving child has been confronted with a partner who (a) disagrees with him and (b) offers an operational solution. An important issue is how far *the fact of disagreement* can promote cognitive restructuring, quite apart from the provision of an operational solution. Miller and Brownell (1975), for instance, suggest that the mere presentation of a contradiction seemed to be a major element in the efficacy of peer interaction. This brings us back fully to the spirit of Piaget's early views on peer interaction, which, as we have seen, emphasised the resolution of contradiction.

Recent support for this position has come from the work of Willem Doise and his colleagues.

Doise, Mugny and Perret-Clermont (1976) found that children progressed on a conservation-of-length task as a result of being presented (by an adult) with a verbal solution which contradicted the child's own, whether or not the solution presented was the correct one. Mugny and Doise (1978) obtained supportive results using a spatial transformation task. Interaction with another child who offered a conflicting solution led to improved performance even if the other child was less capable than the subject. Clearly such findings cannot be interpreted in terms of a modelling hypothesis. Doise follows Piaget in suggesting that the pre-operational child 'centres' on particular features or aspects of a task, so that two pre-operational children may offer conflicting responses as a result of differing centrations. Social interaction then provides a conflict of centrations which, it is proposed, acts as a powerful stimulus to the children who co-ordinate the various centrations in an operational solution (Doise, Mugny and Perret-Clermont, 1975; Mugny and Doise, 1978).

In support of this view, Doise and Mugny (1978) found using a spatial transformation task that pairs of non-conserving children manifesting different centrations progressed, whereas pairs using the same inferior strategy did not. However, progress could be induced in pairs of the latter type if the task was arranged so that they physically approached the situation from opposite viewpoints, thus inducing conflict (Doise and Mugny, 1979).

Children were divided by Doise and Mugny (1978) into non-conservers, partial conservers and total conservers. Contrary to the findings of other studies mentioned earlier, they found that non-conservers paired with total conservers made little or no lasting progress. This they attribute to the fact that the conserver dominated the situation to the virtual exclusion of the non-conserver, something which may be particularly likely to happen with tasks involving physical manipulation of materials. Further evidence that dominance can be disruptive was obtained using a motor co-ordination task (Doise, 1978). The introduction of status differences ('leaders') reduced the progress made amongst the younger and less able children. In the same study Doise found that if subjects were not allowed to speak to one another performance was disrupted and they made little progress, an observation which reinforced his emphasis on the vital role of verbal communication.

Conflict and resolution

We have distinguished modelling-studies from interaction-studies, and within the latter category have distinguished those which are concerned specifically with the effects on a child of interaction with a more advanced partner from those which are concerned with the effects on both parthers of more symmetrical interaction. In all three cases subjects are exposed to a conflicting viewpoint. The hypotheses advanced by researchers have largely been concerned with the mode of transmission and perception of this conflicting view; whether it is sufficient for the child to passively observe a conflicting view expressed, whether verbal expression of the conflict is necessary, and so on. Less attention has been given to the question of how conflicts are resolved, and why experience of conflicting views should facilitate learning and cognitive growth. It has been variously suggested that the child succumbs to the greater conviction with which the 'operatonal' view is held (Miller and Brownell, 1975), that the subject's tendency to model himself on the other produces a cognitive dissonance resulting in cognitive growth (Botvin and Murray, 1975), or that socially perceived conflicts between different centrations lead to co-ordination of those centrations (Doise *et al.*, 1975).

Two elements suggest themselves as important in the resolution of conflicts: verbal reasons and explanations on the one hand, and active hypothesis testing with concrete materials on the other. The importance of explanations is clearest in the cases of asymmetrical interaction (for example, between a conserver and a non-conserver). There is evidence, as we have seen, that conservers are likely to give reasons and to produce counter-arguments, and indeed Doise, Mugny and Perret-Clermont (1975) found that the cases where this occurred were those most likely to result in gains by the non-conserver. Doise (1978) also emphasises verbal interactions, but seems to see their role more in terms of the presentation of conflict than in terms of resolution.

While the conservation task is a matter of judgements and explanations, some of the other tasks used in peer interaction learning-studies have involved the children in manipulating materials (for example, Doise, 1978). In these cases it is possible for the child to engage in hypothesis testing and to resolve conflicts of opinion through action. Thus the means of resolution of conflict may be task-dependent. This fact may account for some of the contradictory results obtained in this field. For example, we noted earlier that Doise found, using a task involving manipulation of materials rather than verbal explanations, that pairings between children with very low and very high pre-test scores resulted in little progress, a fact which was attributed to domination of the task by the more able child. Such dominance, preventing the less able child from practical resolution of perceived conflict, may indeed prevent his making gains on such a task. But on a conservation task, where the 'dominating' conserver provides verbal explanations of his judgements the non-conserver may profit, as numerous studies have testified. Thus social dominance will have a different meaning and different consequences according to the nature of the task involved.

Results of a recent study by Russell (1979) are perhaps interpretable in this light. Using a conservation-of-length task he found significantly greater progress for non-conserving subjects paired with a conserver than for those paired with a another non-conserver. Examination of the

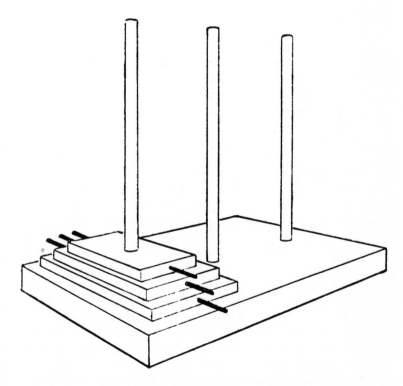

Figure 1: The Tower of Hanoi, apparatus.

verbal exchanges showed that conflict did occur in the non-conserver pairs, leading Russell to argue that cognitive conflict is not sufficient to ensure cognitive progress, and that exposure to the correct answer is also needed. However, from the point of view of resolution of conflicts, it may be important that little or no manipulation of materials seems to have occurred. Conflicts were thus likely to be resolved only through clear verbal reasoning, something more likely to be found in the presence of a conserver. Had the task involved more active manipulation of materials and a chance to test out the conflicting viewpoints, results might have been different.

An emphasis on conflict resolution also suggests the need for an extended interaction, rather than a very brief encounter. Adequate time is important, whether it be for the development of arguments and counter-arguments, or for the testing of hypotheses through action.

The Tower of Hanoi: first study

Having examined the theoretical and empirical background to the topic, we now move to presentation of two previously unpublished studies of peer interaction and learning. These were designed to take into account some of the issues raised in earlier sections of this chapter. The Tower of Hanoi is the name of a traditional game which we used in both studies. It is a game which involves physical manipulation of materials, and which does not lend itself to ready explanation in verbal terms. The apparatus is shown in figure 1, and consists of a baseboard with three (differently coloured) vertical pegs together with a number of tiles. Each of the tiles is square, with two handles on opposite sides and a hole through the centre. The tiles vary regularly in size and at the outset of the game are placed on one of the pegs in seriated order, the largest at the bottom (figure 1). The problem is to move all the tiles to another (specified) peg under the constraints that only one tile may be moved at a time, and that a larger tile may never be placed on top of a smaller one.

The problem has a natural decomposition into nested sub-problems (Luger, 1978), so that if three tiles are to be transferred the player must go through a 'two-tile routine' to shift the two smaller tiles to the spare peg, then transfer the largest tile to the specified peg, then go through the two-tile routine again to complete the task.

The first study to be described was simply concerned with establishing whether peer interaction on such a task would lead to better post-test performance than would individual experience on the task. The design thus involved individual pre-testing and post-testing separated by a period of practice with the game, in which some children again worked alone while others worked in pairs. Twenty-eight children aged between seven years and eleven months, and nine years exactly participated, twelve being assigned to the individual condition, the remainder being arbitrarity paired together. All children were pre-tested individually. After being put at their ease they were introduced to the Tower of Hanoi. When the rules had been explained they were given a sequence of three trials involving two tile problems as a 'warm up', and then three trials with three tiles. Pre-test scores were derived from the three tile problems, which all began with the tiles on one of the outer pegs.

The 'intervention' session occurred two weeks later. Children, whether as individuals or pairs, were given eight trials, all with three tiles and all beginning from the centre peg, the 'goal' peg alternating from trial to trial. They were told to try to find the best solution to the problem, and that it could be dome in seven moves. Children working in pairs were told that they had always to pick up the tiles together, using the handles, as an attempt to ensure that both children remained involved in the game. Individual post-tests, identical to the pre-tests, followed two weeks later.

The obvious criterion measure for performance on this task is the number of moves taken to solve the problem. However, an additional criterion was suggested by the observation that children used a number of distinct strategies to solve the problem. The optimal strategy, as we have noted, takes seven moves and is made up of two two-tile sub-problems (three moves each) separated by the move of the largest tile. Another frequently occurring pattern took nine moves. This involved an incorrect first move resulting in the first two-tile sub-problem taking five moves instead of three. Another strategy involved three complete two-tile sub-problems with two moves of the largest tile, taking eleven moves. If this was combined with a wrong first move, as in the nine-move sequence, the result was a thirteen-move sequence. Where children took eight, ten, twelve or fourteen moves, they had almost always followed one of the sequences outlined above but at some stage made a false move and corrected it, thus adding one to the total. Solutions taking more moves than this typically showed no clear strategy and contained apparently random moves. Above twenty moves was regarded as a failure. Children could thus be classified at pre-test according to their predominant level of performance (two out of three

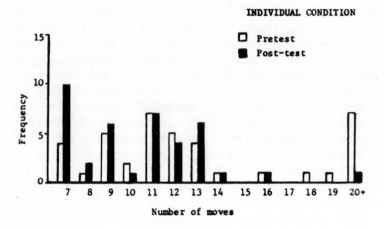

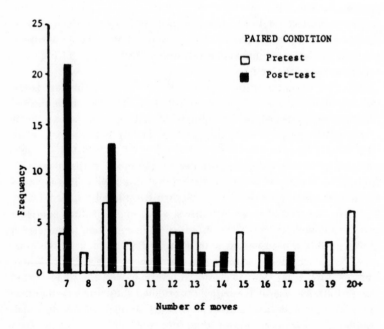

Figure 2: Pre-test and post-test score distributions for the two conditions.

trials) as: failures, non-strategists, or thirteen-, eleven-, nine- or seven-move strategists.

Pre-test and post-test score distributions for individual and paired conditions are shown in figure 2. It is clear that the paired condition produced more gains from pre- to post-test, with seven- and nine-move strategies being the most prevalent. The improvement in terms of number of moves shown by subjects in the paired condition was statistically significant, while that shown by subjects in the individual condition was not. The difference in performance between conditions at post-test did not reach significance when treated in terms of number of moves, but was statistically significant when expressed in terms of predominant strategy, reflecting the more consistent performance of subjects who had experienced the paired intervention. Closer analysis indicated that subjects who at pre-test had been 'non-strategists' tended to improve their performance regardless of the intervention condition, the difference between the conditions showing itself only for those children who showed some systematic approach to the task at the outset.

Pairs formed for this experiment will inevitably have been asymmetrical to some extent, in the sense that the children will in most cases have shown differing levels of performance at pre-test. It was therefore of interest to see whether the greater improvement shown in the pairs condition entirely reflected improvements made by the poorer members of the pairs, or whether the more able members of the pairs also profited from the interaction. The more able members of each pair (judged by pre-test performance) were matched with children in the individual condition who showed similar pre-test performance. Those in the pairs showed significantly more improvement than those in the individual condition. Thus the superiority of the pairs condition cannot readily be explained in terms of a simple modelling effect.

The Tower of Hanoi: second study

The second study was designed to investigate in more detail the conditions under which interaction would be facilitative. Individual pre-testing and post-testing was the same as that in the first study except that all six possible three tile problems were used at post-test. Three conditions were used, all involving pairs of children working together in the intervention session. The first condition (structured interaction) was identical with that used for pairs in the first study.

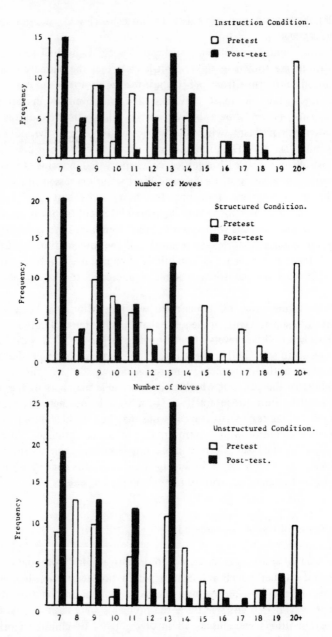

Figure 3: Second study: score distributions for the three trials used at both pre-test and post-test for the three conditions.

The second condition (unstructured interaction) was the same except that the requirement that the children jointly move the tiles was not introduced. Interest here was in the question of dominance, raised earlier. In the third (instruction) condition the children were in effect provided with the right answer by the experimenter, who verbally guided each pair through the optimal seven-move sequence for each of the eight trials. The children moved the tiles jointly. Although they were told that this was the best way to solve the problem, the children were not given rules or explanations.

Subjects were eighty children aged between seven years and eleven months, and eight years and ten months. They were randomly allocated to pairs, so that any asymmetry within pairs was the same for all conditions, and could not in itself account for differences in outcome between conditions. Frequency distributions of scores at pre-test and post-test are shown in figure 3.

It is evident that the number of non-strategists (and failures) was reduced from pre-test to post-test in every condition, as in the first experiment. It would appear that children possessed of no clear strategy at pre-test are likely to improve their performance irrespective of the intervention condition. The structured interaction condition produced at post-test a clear pattern of peaks and troughs corresponding to the various strategies, with a high frequency of seven-move and nine-move solutions. The unstructured interaction condition also produced a clear pattern of strategies, but here the less efficient strategies, especially that involving thirteen moves, were common. The instruction condition did not result in so clear a pattern of strategies at post-test, and generally showed the poorest outcome.

Three of the post-test trials were identical with the three used at pre-test, so that a within-subject statistical comparison of pre- and post-test performance was possible for each condition. Such comparison, using mean number of moves as the performance measure, showed significant improvement only in the structured interaction condition.

Between-subject comparisons could be made using all the six post-test trials. As noted, almost all children classified at pre-test as non-strategists or failures improved in all conditions. This is reflected in the fact that for such children statistical comparisons of post-test performance showed no differences between conditions. However, for the initially more able children the structured interaction condition revealed itself to be significantly more effective than either of the other conditions. Further analysis revealed that no conditions difference was shown on the two post-test trials starting from the centre peg, which were the ones also used in the intervention session. All three conditions produced equally good performance on these trials, but only children who had experienced the structured interaction condition were able to demonstrate extension of their learning to the other related problems.

What can we conclude from these results? The superiority of the structured interaction condition over the others was shown only by children who had adopted some systematic approach to the problem at pre-test. For those who at pre-test performed largely at random, all three conditions tended to produce improvement. This suggests a general practice effect for such subjects, but also suggests that the differences between the intervention conditions in terms of perception of (or opportunity to resolve) conflict are irrelevant to them. We would argue that since such subjects do not initially adopt any coherent approach to the task, they do not have a viewpoint from which to experience conflict. For such a child to enter into and experience conflict with another on this task, he must be pursuing some kind of plan or strategy of his own.

Turning to the more able subjects, the instruction situation proved itself marginally the least effective in terms of post-test performance. The opportunity to experience conflict was present, in that the children were being taken repeatedly through a solution sequence which in almost all cases differed from that which they had themselves used at pre-test. However, no opportunity was given for subjects to experiment with different ideas, nor were any rules or explanations given. Thus the children had little chance of resolving any conflict experienced.

Opportunities for resolution of conflict were present in both the structured and the unstructured interaction conditions, but significant gains were only apparent for the former. In this experiment videotapes were made of an intervention session and an inspection of these tapes provides some insight into the disparity of outcome. The verbal exchanges which occurred were unpredictive of post-test performance. Generally there were few task-related verbal exchanges, and virtually none of these involved explanations or rules defending a particular approach to the problem. As remarked earlier, the task is not one which lends itself readily to verbal explanation. What does seem to have been of importance is the nature of the decision-making process which emerged in these different situations. Judgements of whether a move was determined by one child or both were made from the tape, and the inter-observer reliability of such judgements proved to be satisfactory. In the structured interaction condition, although both children held the tiles while they were moved, it was judged that some twenty-five per cent of moves were determined by one child, with the other passively following. However, in the unstructured interaction situation almost ninety per cent of moves were judged to be determined (and often carried out) by one child only. Thus the joint decision-making process which operated most of the time in the structured condition was largely absent in the unstructured condition. The results, then, are consistent with the view that on a task which does not depend heavily on verbal judgements and explanations, the degree of mutual collaboration is an important factor in determining the productivity of an interaction.

Not only were most of the moves in the unstructured condition determined by one or other child as opposed to being determined jointly, but in many cases the same child determined nearly all of the moves. In over fifty per cent of the pairs one child determined at least twice as many moves as the other, and accounted for a clear majority of all moves. This never occurred in the structured situation. During unstructured interactions the dominant individual rarely took notice of his partner's viewpoint and thus would have experienced little conflict. The submissive partner was, in effect, passively observing a conflicting viewpoint in action, but was permitted little opportunity to resolve the conflict through his own activity. Encounters characterised by this kind of dominance between individuals who had displayed some form of strategy at pre-test never led to progress by either party. On a task of this kind, then, it is clear that domination by one child is a hindrance to productive interaction.

The results of this experiment reinforce the view that merely perceiving a conflicting viewpoint is insufficient to induce learning and that opportunity to resolve the conflict is also important. They suggest that such resolution can occur through practical activity in the absence of verbal explanations, but that for this to occur some degree of shared involvement in that task is vital.

Concluding comments

Results from the instruction condition in this second experiment demonstrate that neither pairing the children together nor providing them with the right answer will guarantee that they learn anything. Moreover, results from the structured interaction conditions in both experiments suggest that presentation of a 'correct' solution is not an essential element in a profitable interaction. Both members of a pair appear to profit from the interaction. It would seem that interaction between inferior strategies can lead to superior strategies or, in other words, two wrongs *can* make a right.

Further detailed analysis of this question is obviously needed, but it seems likely that the profit in interaction accrues from the fact that the differing strategies being pursued by the two children lead to the making of moves inconsistent with those strategies. The child is thus led to (jointly) make moves which he would never otherwise have made, so that established inefficient strategies are disrupted. As a consequence of this disruption one or both of the children may see possibilities for better strategies. Interaction is thus envisaged as a destabilising influence.

Such an interpretation accords well with Piaget's original suggestions concerning the value of peer interactions, and with the work of Doise and colleagues reviewed earlier. If the present studies have placed less emphasis on verbal discussion than these authors have done, it is not because such discussion is seen as irrelevant to the value of peer interaction. It is rather that we see the importance of verbal as against practical interaction as very much dependent upon the nature of the task involved. Either or both may contribute to the perception and resolution of conflict.

The obvious task dependence of any detailed analysis of peer interaction situations presents both a difficulty and a challenge to the researcher. If this field of study is to be productive, either of new insights into the process of development or of findings of educational value, some kind of typology will be needed both for types of interaction and for types of task. A framework is needed which will both describe and enable prediction of the consequences of particular types of interaction in relation to particular types of task. In the course of research directed towards this goal, the conflicting viewpoints of researchers as to the mechanisms and processes involved may well find resolution.

References

Barker, W., and Newson, L., 'The development of social cognition: definition and location', in S. Mogdil and C. Mogdil (eds.) *Toward a Theory of Psychological Development*, Windsor, N.F.E.R., 1979.
Botvin, G., and Murray, F., 'The efficacy of peer modelling acquisition of conservation', *Child Development*, 1975, *46*, 796-9.

Brown, G., and Desforges, C., *Piaget's Theory: a Psychological Critique,* London, Routledge & Kegan Paul, 1979.

Bruner, J., 'The course of cognition development', *American Psychologist,* 1964, *19,* 1-15.

Bruner, J., 'The ontogenesis of speech acts', *Journal of Child Language,* 1975, *2,* 1-19.

Campbell, J., 'Peer relations in childhood', in M. Hoffman and L. Hoffman (eds.) *Review of Child Development Research,* Vol 1, New York, Russell Sage Foundation, 1964.

Damon, W., 'Why study social-cognitive development?' *Human Development,* 1979, *22,* 206-11.

Doise, W., *Groups and Individuals,* Cambridge, Cambridge University Press, 1978.

Doise, W., Mugny, G., and Perret-Clermont, A-N., 'Social interaction and the development of logical operations', *European Journal of Social Psychology,* 1975, *5,* 367-83.

Doise, W., Mugny, G., and Perret-Clermont, A-N., 'Social interaction and cognitive development: further evidence', *European Journal of Social Psychology,* 1976, *6,* 245-7.

Doise, W., and Mugny, G., 'Individual and collective conflicts of centrations in cognitive development', *European Journal of Social Psychology,* 1979, *9,* 105-9.

Elkind, D., *Child Development and Education: a Piagetian Perspective,* New York, Oxford University Press, 1976.

Flavell, J.,(in collaboration with Botkin, P., Fry, C., Wright, J., and Jarvis, P.), *The Development of Role-Taking and Communication Skills in Children,* New York, Wiley, 1968.

Ginsburg, H., and Opper, S., *Piaget's Theory of Intellectual Development, an Introduction,* New Jersey, Prentice Hall, 1969.

Hartup, W., 'Peer interaction and social organisation', in P. Mussen (ed.) *Carmichael's Manual of Child Psychology,* Vol. 2, New York, Wiley, 1970.

Heber, M., 'The influence of language training on seriation of 5-6 year old children initially at different levels of descriptive competence', *British Journal of Psychology,* 1977, *68,* 85-95.

Heber, M., *The Role of Language in Cognitive Development: Speech and Seriation in Children of 5-6 Years,* unpublished Ph.D. thesis, University of Southampton, 1978.

Hoffman, M., 'Moral development', in P. Mussen (ed.) *Carmichael's Manual of Child Psychology,* Vol 2, New York, Wiley, 1970.

Hollos, M., 'Logical operations and role-taking abilities in two cultures: Norway and Hungary', *Child Development,* 1975, *46,* 638-49.

Hollos, M., and Cowan, P., 'Social isolation and cognitive development: logical operations and role-taking abilities in three Norwegian social settings', *Child Development,* 1973, *44,* 630-41.

Inhelder, B., and Piaget, J., *The Early Growth of Logic in the Child*, London, Routledge & Kegan Paul, 1964.

Inhelder, B., Sinclair, H., and Bovet, M., *Learning and the Development of Cognition*, London, Routledge & Kegan Paul, 1974.

Kohlberg, L., 'Stage and sequence: the cognitive developmental approach to socialisation', in D. Goslin (ed.) *Handbook of Socialisation: Theory and Research*, New York, Rand McNally, 1969.

Kuhn, D., 'Mechanisms of change in the development of cognitive structures', *Child Development*, 1972, *43*, 833-44.

Light, P., *The Development of Social Sensitivity*, Cambridge, Cambridge University Press, 1979.

Luger, G., 'Using the state space to record the behavioural effects of symmetry in the Tower of Hanoi problem and an isomorph', paper presented to the *Conference of the British Psychological Society*, London, December, 1978.

Miller, S., and Brownell, C., 'Peers, persuasion and Piaget: dyadic interaction between conservers and non-conservers', *Child Development*, 1975, *46*, 992-7.

Miller, S., Brownell, C., and Zukier, H., 'Cognitive certainty in children: effects of concept, developmental level, and method of assessment', *Developmental Psychology*, 1977, *13*, 236-43.

Mugny, G., and Doise, W., 'Socio-cognitive conflict and structure of individual and collective performances', *European Journal of Social Psychology*, 1978, *8*, 181-92.

Murray, F., 'Acquisition of conservation through social interaction', *Developmental Psychology*, 1972, *6*, 1-6.

Murray, F., Ames, G., and Botvin, G., 'Acquisition of conservation through cognitive dissonance', *Journal of Educational Psychology*, 1977, *69*, 519-27.

Murray, J., 'Social learning and cognitive development: modelling effects on children's understanding of conservation', *British Journal of Psychology*, 1974, *65*, 151-60.

Nahir, H. and Yussen, S., 'The performance of Kibbutz and city reared Israeli children on two role-taking tasks', *Developmental Psychology*, 1977, *13*, 450-5.

Parten, M., and Newhall, S., 'Social behaviour of preschool children', in R. Barker, J. Kounin, and M. Wright (eds.) *Child Behaviour and Development*, New York, McGraw Hill, 1943.

Perret-Clermont, A-N, *Social Interaction and Cognitive Development in Children*, London, Academic Press, 1980.

Piaget, J., *Judgement and Reasoning in the Child*, New York, Harcourt Brace, 1928.

Piaget, J., *The Moral Judgement of the Child*, London, Routledge & Kegan Paul, 1932.

Piaget, J., *The Psychology of Intelligence*, London, Routledge & Kegan Paul, 1950.

Piaget, J., *Etudes Sociologiques*, Geneva, Librarie Droz, 1965.

Piaget, J., 'Piaget's theory', in P. Mussen (ed.) *Carmichael's Manual of Child Psychology*, Vol. 1, New York, Wiley, 1970.

Piaget, J., and Inhelder, B., *The Psychology of the Child*, London, Routledge & Kegan Paul, 1969a.

Piaget, J., and Inhelder, B., 'Intellectual operations and their development', in P. Fraisse and J. Piaget (eds.) *Experimental Psychology: Its Scope and Method, VII, Intelligence*, London, Routledge & Kegan Paul, 1969b.

Rosenthal, T., and Zimmerman, B., 'Modelling by exemplification and instruction in training conservation', *Developmental Psychology*, 1972, *6*, 392-401.

Russell, J., 'Children deciding on the correct answer: social influence under the microscope', paper presented to the Annual Conference of the Developmental Section of the British Psychological Society, Southampton, September, 1979.

Ryan, J., 'Early language development: towards a communicational analysis', in M. Richards (ed.) *The Integration of a Child into a Social World*, Cambridge, Cambridge University Press, 1974.

Siegel, I., 'The Piagetian system and the world of education', in D. Elkind and J. Flavell (eds.) *Studies in Cognitive Development*, New York, Oxford University Press, 1969.

Silverman, W., and Stone, J., 'Modelling cognitive functioning through participation in a problem solving group', *Journal of Educational Psychology*, 1972, *63*, 603-8.

Silverman, I., and Geiringer, E., 'Dyadic interaction and conservation induction: a test of Piaget's equilibrium model', *Child Development*, 1973, *44*, 815-20.

Sinclair, H., *Language et Operations*, Paris, Dunod, 1967.

Smedslund, J., 'The acquisition of conservation of substance and weight. II', *Scandanavian Journal of Psychology*, 1961, *2*, 71-84.

Smedslund, J., 'Concrete reasoning: a study of intellectual development', *Monographs of the Society for Research in Child Development*, 1964, *27*, No. 2.

Smedslund, J., 'Microanalysis of concrete reasoning', *Scandanavian Journal of Psychology*, 1966a, *7*, 145-67.

Smedslund, J., 'Les origenes sociales de la decentration', in J. Grize and B. Inhelder (eds.) *Psychologie et Epistemologie Genetiques: Themes Piagetiens*, Paris, Dunod, 1966b.

Waghorn, L., and Sullivan, E., 'The exploration of transition rules in consideration of quantity (substance) using film mediated modelling', *Acta Psychologia*, 1970, *32*, 65-80.

West, H., 'Early preschool interaction and role-taking skills: an investigation in Israeli children', *Child Development,* 1974, *45,* 1118-21.

Zazzo, R., 'Comments on Professor Piaget's paper', in J. Tanner and B. Inhelder (eds.) *Discussions on Child Development,* Vol. 4, London, Tavistock, 1960.

Zimmerman, B., 'Modification of young children's grouping strategies. The effects of modelling, verbalisation, incentives and age', *Child Development,* 1974, *45,* 1032-41.

Index

264   *Social Cognition*

Ethology, 166
Evolution, 34, 63, 67, 79, 165, 181, 229
Eye movements, smooth pursuit, 128

Fear of strangers, 99, 167, 173, 174, 175
Frame, 142

Games, 98
Genetic epistemology, 24-9
Gesture, 112, 116
Glachan, M., xiv, 11, 238
Gibson, J. J., 32, 33, 34, 35, 38, 40, 42, 51, 131, 160

Hamlyn, D. W., xii, 17, 18, 25, 27, 29, 31, 35, 39, 40
Harris, P. L., xiii, 4, 188, 193, 194, 195, 196, 197, 208
Hermeneutics, 49, 50
Hologram, 41, 43

Imitation, 53-74, 94-100, 106, 138, 157, 159
phylogeny and ontogeny of, 67-70
Implicate order, 38, 41, 42, 43
Indices, 115
Individualism vs. collectivism, 18
Information processing, 78
Innate, 28
Intelligence, social, 69, 77
Intentionality, xi, 6, 81, 113, 138
Intersubjectivity, 68, 69, 85, 90, 91, 138, 152
primary, 104
secondary, 69, 91, 105

Joint action, 43-8

Language acquisition, 85, 92, 110
Lexical labelling, 142
Light, P. H., xiv, 11, 226, 235, 238, 241, 260
Logico-mathematical concepts, 88
Logical necessity, 224
Looking, 116, 128, 130

MacMurray, 3, 7, 8, 48, 82

Metacognition, 4, 188
Memory, 143, 175
Monotropism, 165-86
Motives, 55, 77-109
Moral order, 48, 83, 86, 102
Multiple attachment, 174

Natural selection, 82
Neonatal period, 93-7
Newson, J., xii, 4, 5, 32, 168, 184
Nielson, I., xiv, 11, 213, 224, 225, 226, 234, 236
Non-atomicity of knowledge, 23, 24, 35, 39
Norms, 14-31, 48

Object permanence, 148, 175
Object schema, 140, 141, 143, 144
Olthof, M. T., xiii, 4, 188, 197, 198 208
Operative intelligence, 60

Peer interaction, 238-62
Perception and representation, 141
Perspective taking, 239
Phatic communication, 69
Piaget, J., xiv, 5, 6, 7, 8, 9, 10, 15, 16, 18, 28, 29, 31, 38, 51, 53, 73, 110, 114, 115, 127, 128, 132, 136, 139, 140, 160, 162, 213-37, 238-45, 261
Piaget's theory of imitation, 57-63
Play, 64, 98, 101, 106
Pointing, 110-36
Pre-reading, 94, 95
Prespeech, 95
Problem solving, 64-7
Protoconcepts, 138, 144, 149, 156, 160

Reaching, 88, 92, 94, 98
Reciprocity, 7, 241
Reference, 110-36
precursors of, 112, 130
Representation, 118, 130, 131, 137, 138, 141, 142, 144, 151, 166
Reversibility, 239
Role taking, 245
Rules, 45

Scaife, M., xiii, 10, 110, 118, 135
Semantic memory, 143
Sensorimotor development, 127, 132,
    148
  intelligence, 110, 113
  scheme, 114, 115, 128
Separation protest, 170
Shotter, J., xii, 5, 32, 34, 38, 42, 45,
    49, 51
Signification, 110, 113, 132
Sinha, C., xiii, 10, 131, 136, 137, 143,
    159, 161, 162
Smith, P. K., xiii, 13, 165, 167, 179
    185
Social cognition, xi-xiv, 3-5, 12
Social interaction, xiv, 11, 239
Social learning theory, 5, 53-74
Social order, 48
Social origins of knowledge, 6, 17-31
Social vs. physical knowledge, 6-8

Social smiling, 95
Spatial understanding, 110, 116, 140,
    188
Structural description, 142
Synchrony, 56-93
Symbolic representation, 101
Systems theory, 12, 13

Tower of Hanoi, 250-7
Trevarthen, C., xii, 7, 62, 68, 73, 77,
    92, 98, 99, 100, 101, 108, 128,
    136, 138, 160
Tutoring, 70, 71

Verbal communication, 247
Vygotsky, L. S., 8, 9, 10, 16, 18, 32,
    51

Word meaning, 217